W9-ACD-994

Classrooms at the Crossroads

The Washington Post
Education Companion

The Washington Post Writers Group

Edited by Leonard Kaplan
Wayne State University

Allyn and Bacon
Boston • London • Toronto • Sydney • Tokyo • Singapore

Editorial Director: Bill Barke
Editor-in-Chief, Education: Nancy Forsyth
Series Editor: Virginia Lanigan
Editorial Assistant: Nicole DePalma
Cover Administrator: Linda Dickinson
Manufacturing Buyer: Louise Richardson
Cover Designer: Suzanne Harbison

ISBN 0-205-14872-7

This book is printed on recycled, acid-free paper.

Printed in the United States of America

10 9 8 7 6 5 4 3 2   97 96 95 94 93

Contents

1 At Risk Schools   1

When Cultures Clash: Probing the Causes of School Violence, *Judith Lynne Hanna*   1

School Spanking—It Hurts, *William Raspberry*   6

Schools Using Peers to Press for Amity: Trend Toward Mediation Teams Cuts Across Grade Levels in Effort to Curb Violence, *Lisa Leff*   8

New Groups 'Filling a Void' Left By PTAs: Minority Parents' Forums Put Basic Educational Concerns Back on the Front Burner, *Stephanie Griffith*   12

Before Riots, Youth Programs in Shambles, *Michael Wilbon and Dave Sheinin*   16

School Mentors Steer Younger Students Through Teenage Troubles, *Jane Seaberry*   21

Staying in School . . ., *Debbie Goldberg*   24

From Dropouts to Graduates, *William Raspberry*   29

Adding Gentle but Firm Persuasion: Mentors Hope to Steer Young Boys from Lure of the Streets, *Rene Sanchez*   32

A Fresh Start in Heading Off Family Crisis: Preschool Centers Revive Two-Generational Mission, *Paul Taylor*   37

Why Head Start Needs a Re-Start: Poverty, Violence Threaten the Gains, *Douglas J. Besharov*   42

2 Assessment   47

Expecting Too Much from National Tests: It's Like Hoping a New Thermometer Will Warm a Cold Room, *William Raspberry*   47

Subtracting Multiple Choice from Tests: Pioneering Program Requires Students to Analyze, Explain Answers, *Mary Jordan*   50

3 The Profession of Teaching   54

Letter to the Teacher of the Year, *Colman McCarthy*   54

Instilling Students with a Love for Teaching: New D.C. School Program Lays Foundation for Classroom Careers, *Rene Sanchez*   56

A Late Call to the Classroom: Area Schools See Surge of Second-Career Teachers, *Stephen Buckley*   59

You're in the Army, Uh, School Now: Soldiers Encouraged to Become Teachers, *John Lancaster*   63

4 America 2000   66

Bush Unveils Education Plan: Local Innovation, Parental Involvement Stressed in Setting Goals for '90s, *John E. Yang*   66

The Artless Education Compromise: Critics Say Plan for Schools Overlooks Creative Side, *Kim Masters*   70

No 'Radical Change' for Nation's Classrooms: In Fact, Little Improvement Seen a Year After Bush Unveiled Education Plan, Secretary Says, *Mary Jordan*   73

5 School Choice   76

Give Choice a Chance, *William Raspberry*   76

Good Choice Proposals, and Bad, *William Raspberry*   78

School Plan Questioned by Senators: Private Education Incentives at Issue, *Helen Dewar*   80

A Real Test for School Choice, *William Raspberry*   83

Milwaukee's Controversial Private School Choice Plan Off to Shaky Start, *Paul Taylor*   86

Private vs. Public Schools: What Education Gap? *Albert Shanker*   90

California Parents Look Inward for School Aid: Private Fund-Raising Part of National Trend, *Michael Abramowitz*   96

6 Home Schooling   100

Home Schooling on Rise: U.S. Total Up More Than 20-Fold in Decade, *Stephen Buckley*   100

Home Schooling Without Guilt: It's One Family's Attempt to Find a Way Out of the Two-Career Rat Race, *William Raspberry*   104

7 Model Schools/New Teaching Methods   107

Education: Rebuilding the Schoolhouse: Radical Reforms in Search of a New National Learning Experience, *Linda Chion-Kenney*   107

A Strategy for Overhauling the American High School: Theodore Sizer, a Man with a Mission, *Alice Digilio*   113

A Strategy for Overhauling the American High School: Radical
Plan on Trial in Baltimore, *Barbara Vobejda* 119
Students Yearn for a Few Jolts of Inspiration, *Sandra
Evans* 124
Fixing Schools One by One: New Ideas Tested on Scale Across
U.S., *Kenneth J. Cooper* 130
New Teaching Lets Children Learn Like Children, *Sari
Horwitz* 134
Innovations in Education: Turning Classmates into Teammates,
Stephen Buckley 138
A Radical Prescription for Schools: Researchers See Bureaucracy
as the Problem, Autonomy as the Cure, *Kenneth J.
Cooper* 142
Schools in Transition: Parents and Educators Try Three New
Approaches: Neighborhood Control, a University
Affiliation and Parental Choice, *Diego Ribadeneira* 145
Whittle's for-Profit Schools: Bold Claims and Criticism:
Maverick Marketer Pushes Controversial Education
Experiment with Burst of Publicity, *Mary Jordan* 151
Low Marks for Channel One: Study Casts Doubt on TV
Program's Effectiveness in Schools, *David Streitfeld* 155
The News on Channel One: Communications and its
Controversial Program, *David Streitfeld* 158

8 Multicultural Education 165
When School Becomes a Melting Pot: Annandale Seeks to Close
Language, Education Gaps, *Peter Baker* 165
More Immigrant Children Face Double Disadvantage: Many
Have Had Little or No Schooling, *Erin Marcus* 170
Court Cuts Federal Desegregation Role: Schools' Anti-Bias
Obligations Eased, *Ruth Marcus* 174
Kansas City's Costly Integration Strategy: Results Mixed in $1.2
Billion School Plan, *Mary Jordan* 177

9 Education of Students with Special Needs 182
Mainstreaming Disabled Students: Move in Loudoun Schools
Generates Debate, *Robert O'Harrow Jr.* 182
Gifted, Talented and Under Siege, *Lisa Leff* 186
Mixed Grouping Puts an English Class on the Right Track,
D'Vera Cohn 191
Fast-Track Trap—How "Ability Grouping" Hurts Our Schools,
Kids and Families: Separating "Gifted and Talented"

Students from Others Is Divisive in More Ways Than One,
Patrick Welsh   198
Classrooms of Their Own: Are Single-Sex Schools Better for
Girls? *Alice Digilio*   204
Wide Gender Gap Found in Schools: Girls Said to Face Bias in
Tests, Textbooks and Teaching Methods, *Mary
Jordan*   208
For Boys Only, *William Raspberry*   211

10 Religion in Schools   213
High Court Bans Graduation Prayer at Public Schools, *Ruth
Marcus*   213
California Proposal Could Alter Teaching of Evolution
Nationwide, *Jay Mathews*   218
Teacher Training Program to Introduce Religion Curriculum,
Laura Sessions Stepp   220

11 Sex Education in Schools   223
A Tough-Talking Teacher Tells Teens About AIDS: Educator's
Candor Gets Attention of Students and Critics, *Shaun
Sutner*   223
Schools Aim to Balance Sex Education: Protests Have Subsided,
but Virginia Programs Continue to Draw Criticism,
Stephanie Griffith   228
New York Schools May Liberalize Condom Policy: Disputed
Plan Would Allow Unlimited Distribution, *Laurie
Goodstein*   231
High School Clinic Case Study in Sexual Risk: In Rural Florida
Town, Impact of Offering Free Condoms to Teenagers
Remains Unclear, *Paul Taylor*   234

12 Business-Education Partnership   238
Students Test Below Average: In World, U.S. Fares Poorly in
Math, Science, *Mary Jordan*   238
Why Mary's Math Skills Don't Add Up, *Judy Mann*   241
U.S. Graduates Seen Ill-Prepared on Workplace Thinking Skills,
Frank Swoboda   243
Business Goes Back to the Three Rs, *Cindy Skrzycki*   246

13 Technology in Education   249

High Tech Just Keeps Rolling Along: Videodisc Usage Grows in Nation's Classrooms, *John Burgess*   249

A Glitch in the Classroom Computer Revolution: Decade after Acquiring Technology, Area Schools Struggling with Best Ways to Use It, *Molly Sinclair*   252

Computing Teacher Skills, *Kenneth J. Cooper*   256

Introduction

Everyone at one time or another has attended school. In our society this gives every taxpayer, or non-taxpayer for that matter, the opportunity to criticize, discuss, or offer an opinion on what's right and what's wrong with education in the United States. We may have some shortages in various places in our economy, but we have no shortages of solutions to the educational issues in this country. Politicians, especially during election years, have education on their agenda. Theologians, particularly in the last few years, have raised issues about the organization and substance of our schools. Parents have always had comments. Business and industry have put forth ideas on what type of educational system we need to compete in a global economy. The media, who claim not to influence policy but rather report news, offer insight into the business of education. On occasion, we even hear about educational policy from leaders in education who have not always been quick to be proactive but rather reactive.

Some viewers of education have criticized the seeming lack of commitment to the teaching of math, science, or geography. We hear about students who cannot find Chicago on a map or other students who have a hard time delivering acceptable scores on some standardized achievement test. Some criticism may be more than justified. However, it is too simplistic to point a finger of blame without examining other causes that may impact on these so-called problems. Anyone who has been around schools for any period of time recognizes that children ill-fed, abused, seemingly uncared for or unloved, raised in an atmosphere of violence, substance abuse and so many of the other cancers of society, just cannot give the type of attention required to serious learning. If the "Leave It To Beaver" family ever existed, it currently is in very, very small numbers today.

In an effort to heighten awareness of educational issues, articles that have appeared in the *Washington Post* over the last five years have been drawn together for this reader. These syndicated articles were written in an effort to draw attention to issues that affect how decisions are made regarding the future of our children. Those who wish to become teachers will find these articles of interest because they attempt to provide the novice with a view of education they currently may not possess.

Those who are experienced teachers will find these articles of interest because they too may need to better understand what affects learners outside the classroom.

This book should be of interest to the school administrator who would like to branch out from the role of instructional manager to instructional leader. Principals, superintendents, and others who attempt to provide leadership in schools may best facilitate their instructional staff by better recognizing those impediments that keep teachers from doing their jobs.

The teaching profession continues to receive major criticisms from all sectors of society, much of it justified. However, it must be said that there are some wonderful examples of teaching going on in this country, much of it in spite of the obstacles and unnecessary bureaucracy. This end of the educational spectrum rarely gets its due.

It is anticipated that parents, communities, leaders in business and industry, members of the educational societies (public, private and parochial), as well as members in our government, will find value in many of these articles. By raising awareness and initiating dialogue, possibly better understanding of the business of educating our children will take place. The incompatibility or lack of agreement of values that exists between many of these agencies creates an impediment to education. Unfortunately, many of the disagreements that exist on educational issues have little to do with students and more to do with power and politics. Some good, honest dialogue between and among "caring" individuals may help ease some of the tensions that exist.

This book is not a novel. The reader will not necessarily start at the beginning and finish at the end. As an instructor of both preservice and inservice teachers and administrators, it is my intent to select various articles to be read with the idea that they will stimulate conversation in my classes. This book might also be used in the same fashion at faculty meetings, PTA discussions, or any other forum where it is appropriate to discuss specific issues pertaining to education. Hopefully, books such as this will provide the stimulus for better understanding. Some of the articles are purely informational. Others are reported with bias. All will inform.

L. K.

At Risk Schools 1

When Cultures Clash
Probing the Causes of School Violence

JUDITH LYNNE HANNA

Though most American schools are peaceful enough, many schools continue to experience troubling incidents of racial and class hostility. At worst such tension, inter- but also intraracial, has exploded into violence. At the very least it can have a crippling effect on academic achievement.

What are the sources of this problem and what can be done about it?

Studies since the 1970s show that conflicts among youngsters, regardless of grade level, are about seven things: styles of expression; ways of making friends and attitudes toward aggression; game rules; responses to learning about black history; perceptions of teacher fairness; reactions to formal schooling; and classroom work patterns.

I first learned about the realities governing many American children's experience of school during a study of Pacesetter, a desegregated magnet elementary school located in a black, mostly low-income neighborhood in Dallas. Whites, mostly middle-income and from families supportive of integration, volunteered to be bused to the school, which had about 700 students. What children in grades 2, 4 and 6 told me about their experiences was generally confirmed by my systematic observations over the 1977-78 school year. I sat in on classes and observed children at play, in the halls, at lunch and on field trips. I also interviewed adults in the school and the community. Additional research I have done in the past decade indicates strongly that my findings at Pacesetter reflected then, and still reflect, the situation in many of the nation's 75,000 public schools.

Much of what took place at Pacesetter involved conflict between low-income blacks and middle-class blacks and whites. The racial element is troublesome for many, because there has been a taboo against

1

discussing aggressive and anti-school behavior found disproportionately among low-income blacks. But diverting focus from today's problems by charging "blaming the victim" or censoring information does nothing to promote change.

I want to stress that aspects of social class, culture and race often overlap in schools with diverse populations. Other studies—in Appalachia, Boston and in some English cities—have shown that the attitudes of many poor whites are similar to those of many poor blacks. Conversely middle-class blacks and whites often have much in common.

This complicates the first source of conflict among children—the clash between different styles of expression. Middle-class children, both black and white, tend to be uncomfortable with the more emotional or excitable styles of many low-income children, most of whom were black at Pacesetter. Such children speak too aggressively, move too close and touch too soon. The reserved children may in turn annoy others by their supposed passivity and unresponsiveness.

How youngsters make friends is a second form of discord. Middle-class children generally initiate friendships with talk and sharing. Although they may fight, make up, then resume the friendship, aggression is not the norm.

In contrast, both black and white students said (and I observed) that blacks fight more than whites. Some low-income youngsters learn to fight first to establish peer ranking and then to become friends. Often left alone to fend for themselves, these youngsters contend that their parents encourage aggression: "My momma let me fight when people mess with me," a black second-grader explained.

Different game rules among groups are a third source of contention at school. Youngsters show group identity through the rules they accept. Schools, in middle-class tradition, usually follow standard game rules; however, children from some low-income neighborhoods do not.

A black educator and former president of the Pacesetter PTA told me that her 6-year-old child (who had been playing with middle-class whites and blacks) said, "Mommy, I don't want to play with blacks. They don't play nice." At age 12, the same black child asked his mother, "Why am I not supposed to like whites?" During free play, white children were usually excluded from black-organized games; if they tried to join, no one would throw the ball to them.

Responses to learning about the plight of blacks is a fourth arena of tension. A black child would tell a white one, "I'll make you my slave," or push a record choice: "You in soul country now." When I asked what caused fights, a white youngster replied, "It's because, like, they blame it on you, sayin' it's your fault that they were slaves. And it's not my fault, I didn't do it."

When Pacesetter school counselors queried children, both blacks and whites said the school accorded different, unfair treatment to their own race, a fifth point of friction. Teachers' efforts to give special help to low-income blacks, who were as a group two or more grade levels academically behind middle-class whites, led whites to feel that teachers favored blacks; yet blacks felt the opposite. Some low-income youngsters' perception of not getting attention was partly due to the adults' unemotional communication style. Trying to respect cultural differences, teachers disciplined whites for verbal and physical acts they ignored in blacks.

Opposite reactions to the demands of formal schooling are yet a sixth, and the greatest, source of difficulty. Academically-oriented children approve of cooperating with a teacher's request. By contrast, youngsters in the "counterschool" culture think cooperative classmates act "like fags, like real sissies."

The counterschool culture is a response among many low-income whites and blacks that develops from the perception that education does not pay off for them. They seek out nonacademic arenas in which they can excel and dominate. Being bookish is a renegade act provoking peer chiding, harassment or ostracism. Yet despite their devaluation of formal schooling, these children react as if to an assault on their dignity when a teacher calls upon them during regular lessons and they perform poorly in front of their classmates. Calling a counterschool culture child "dummy" triggers a fight.

The seventh and final point of contention, the clash between different styles or habits of working, can also cause antagonism in the classroom. Low-income youngsters brought up to work cooperatively at home often share their answers with friends in class. Middle-class children taught to work independently consider this behavior cheating. Merely bringing children of different colors or cultures together to fulfill the promise of school desegregation does not ensure equal opportunity. From the Pacesetter school experience, as well as that of other schools nationwide, a number of approaches have been developed that appear to help schools resolve clashes among racial, cultural and socioeconomic groups and improve academic achievement for all.

Addressing communication problems among different groups at school is critical. Conflict is often simply a matter of misunderstood messages. Sometimes messages are understood but their content or their apparently aggressive expression are disliked and feared. One solution is to teach the dominant culture's styles of communication, work and play without denigrating those of minority children. Just as people recognize the appropriateness of Sunday dress or work clothes, children can learn the need for specific behavior in certain settings and at certain times. In well-managed classrooms, teachers can still accommodate different expressive styles; for example, some black children's verbally or physically exuberant behavior signifies approval of what is going on.

While it is possible to transform the excitement of fights and disruptive behavior into academic contests in which all youngsters play a constructive role, aggression—a sure way of getting attention—should be nipped in the bud at the elementary level in order to stem more dangerous violence in higher grades.

Alternative schools may be appropriate for bullies if teachers, principals, counselors and parents cannot help them alter their behavior.

We know that academic progress is linked to feelings about oneself and one's peers. Although controversial, ability grouping and regrouping as children master skills fosters learning and self-esteem among children who react fiercely when their inadequacy is exposed in front of classmates. More than anything, students fear looking stupid.

Rewards for leadership or for academic, athletic or artistic achievement at school can foster self-esteem, provided it is done in a way that will not invite peer attack. Youngsters in the counterschool culture can often be brought into the school culture by giving them leadership roles in the school. Similarly, when children learn skills and then tutor others or contribute to the development of the rules they will be asked to follow, they begin to feel they have a stake in the school.

Small classes in which teachers become well-acquainted with students and their parents (or guardians) permit the teacher to identify and meet a child's needs, to develop realistic expectations and to recognize developmental change. Teacher-assigned seating and work/play groupings based on interest and ability can allow children of different backgrounds to appreciate each other, become friends without using aggression and to overcome the tendency of black children to exclude whites and vice versa.

Yet however much teachers can do, it will not suffice. Educational success requires a cooperative effort on the part of the school, of the parents, the community, the government and the private sector.

The principal is a crucial figure, not just within the school but also as the key liaison with the local community and the mediator among parents, and between family and school; and it is government and private sector leaders that are responsible for the long-range planning and financing of programs like Head Start, preschool and afterschool child care, health services, summer job opportunities and individual tutoring that are critical to some minorities' success in school.

In the same way that it took complex social forces to produce a nation at risk, it will take a multi-pronged, holistic approach to better American education. Intrinsic to schooling, communication is the two-way sending and receiving of messages. Let the children's voices be heard and their activities recognized, as they have not been in the recent spate of task force reports on educational reform. A large poor population that goes ignored will ultimately sap the resources and strength of the entire society.

Judith Lynne Hanna is the author of the book "Disruptive School Behavior: Class, Race, and Culture," from which this article is adapted.

April 4, 1989

School Spanking—It Hurts

WILLIAM RASPBERRY

Ever since D.C. Mayor Sharon Pratt Dixon came out for school spankings, I've been having flashbacks to my own school days.

I've been thinking of classmates who got paddled for playground fights, for failing to produce homework assignments or even for being late to school. I've been thinking of the occasional spankings I received, although I can't recall what they were for—probably for clowning in class.

In each of these cases, I'm sure the teachers were acting out of concern for us. They wanted to instill the values of study, self-discipline, punctuality and what used to be called "deportment." The spankings did no harm that I can see, and probably did some good.

But I've also been thinking about some other children who got spanked for things like missing too many arithmetic problems or too many words on spelling tests; hungry kids who were paddled for stealing a classmate's lunch; nonreaders and slow learners who were punished for being what we inelegantly called "dumbo". And though we couldn't prove it, my classmates and I were certain that some children were more likely than others to get paddled, not because their deportment was significantly worse but because the teachers didn't like them.

These spankings, we knew even then, were harmful. They humiliated their victims, confused them in their belief that they were stupid (or bad) and made them hate school.

The kids knew the difference, and so did their parents. Some of us knew that if our parents found out we'd been spanked in school, we'd get another spanking at home. But others, even at that tender age, knew their punishment to be unfair. Several times a year, parents—mostly from "cross the tracks"—would show up at school to protest the humiliation of their children and to charge the teachers with having "picks" and "pets."

Mind you, this was small-town Mississippi in the 1940s, a place and time when parental spanking was universal.

How could it not be worse in a city like Washington, where some parents are likely to think of spanking—even by parents—as teaching children that might makes right and that violence is an acceptable way

6

of solving problems, while others who might spank their own children don't want them spanked by teachers whose fairness they doubt?

It's easy enough to see what's on Mayor Dixon's mind. She, like most of us, would like to see a return to the old values. Teachers, she said in an NBC-TV special on education scheduled to air next week, "need to have the authority to instill standards and values and discipline in young people, especially in a society where so many women are working and trying to rear children alone."

But to return to the old values is not necessarily to return to the old methods, which—though they might have done some limited good in communities that were, for all practical purposes, villages—would likely be a disaster in the bigger, more impersonal schools of the '90s.

Dixon's nostalgic views seem particularly anachronistic at a time when, on the one hand, we are having serious discussions about the advisability of installing metal detectors to keep weapons out of school buildings and, on the other, advocating student-directed dispute-resolution programs to teach children how to settle problems without resort to violence.

Her frustration—and mine—is that too many children come to school from homes where the old values, including discipline, are too little enforced. And her implied question needs to be taken seriously: How are children, undisciplined at home, to gain the self-control that makes learning possible?

But to acknowledge the importance of the question is not to reach her conclusion that children need "some kind of authoritative figure in their lives" and that corporal punishment is the way to achieve it.

An analogy to law enforcement might be helpful. There was less street crime in the days when cops cleared street corners by personal edict reinforced by the threat of a station house beating. Today, we have less summary punishment by law officers and more crime. Therefore . . .

A moment's reflection on the recent police brutality in Los Angeles reveals the fallacy of that reasoning.

Dixon is right: We need to teach our children the time-tested values, both at home and at school. We need to find ways to reward good behavior and to punish inappropriate behavior. But school spanking, apart, perhaps, from an emergency swat on the behind to keep a kindergartner from dashing into a busy street, isn't the way to do it.

April 12, 1991

Schools Using Peers to Press for Amity

Trend Toward Mediation Teams Cuts Across Grade Levels in Effort to Curb Violence

LISA LEFF

Frustrated in their attempts to keep fights and weapons from invading public schools, local education officials are increasingly looking to students to settle conflicts among their quarreling classmates.

Across the Washington area, schools are empowering students to mediate disputes between their peers. More than a dozen high schools in the District, Maryland and Virginia regularly deploy teams of trained students to smooth the sort of frictions that once landed classmates in the principal's office or got them suspended.

The move toward mediation has not been limited to high schools. Some middle and junior high schools in the District and Prince George's County offer lessons in conflict management as part of their regular curricula. At several elementary schools in Prince George's and Fairfax counties, pupils are appointed to patrol their playgrounds and bus stops as pint-sized peacekeepers.

"Peer pressure and what kids think about other kids is important. They listen to their peers and probably give them more of an ear than they would their parents or other authority figures," said Vanessa Collier, the coordinator of a two-year-old student mediation program at DuVal High School in Lanham.

"You are helping kids work out their own problems so they develop a skill for it, rather than having an adult always be the heavy," said Mary McNamara, principal of Princeton Elementary School in Suitland, where 30 third-, fourth-, fifth- and sixth-graders were recruited this year to mediate scuffles during recess.

Most of the schools follow programs similar to those used by courts as alternatives to litigation. Students in conflict may not be forced into mediation, but rather have to be willing participants. The mediators promise to hold everything they hear in confidence and to remain neutral. The goal is to get adversaries to come up with their own solutions and to sign an agreement stating what they will do to avoid future conflicts.

Sometimes, the cures can be simple. On the Friday before spring break, Michele Carter, 9, and John Dowdey, 8, were on duty as PALs—playground assistant leaders—at Princeton Elementary when they spotted two first-graders pushing each other by the jungle gym. It turned out that Winston "Reggie" Curtis, 6, had picked up a stick and poked it at one of Joey Nowlin's friends. Reggie was upset because the day before, Joey, also 6, allegedly had punched and kicked him.

After leading the first-graders to a quiet bench on the edge of the playground, the two assistants got the boys to sign statements in which they promised to tell a teacher the next time they had trouble. John, according to custom, then ordered them to shake hands.

Although 12 secondary schools in the District have offered peer mediation training since the late 1980s, only in the last two years have such programs found widespread acceptance in suburban schools. Facing ever more brazen acts of violence involving weapons on school campuses—such as the March 13 shooting in a chemistry class at Potomac High School in Oxon Hill—school systems have begun promoting student intervention with a new sense of urgency.

A local coalition of conflict resolution trainers estimates that about 50 schools in the District and Arlington, Fairfax, Montgomery and Prince George's counties have peer mediation teams. Nationwide, there are about 2,000 such programs, according to the National Association for Mediation in Education, an organization based in Amherst, Mass.

At Prince George's DuVal High School, student mediators find plenty of opportunities to put into practice the skills they have acquired during 20 hours of training. An average of four or five disputes are brought to the two-room mediation center every day, said Collier, the program coordinator.

One day earlier this month, two girls nervously sat in the center waiting for their mediators to arrive. One was a junior who had just had a baby. The other was a freshman whose 17-year-old boyfriend is the father of the junior's child. The girls had never spoken to each other before, but each thought the other wanted to fight and had assembled her friends to start something.

The girls were ushered into a tiny conference room and seated at a round table. A senior helping oversee the session asked each to give her side. In a rush of words, the junior said the problem started because the freshman "thinks I want her boyfriend." Other students had told her that the younger girl "was supposed to be jumping me."

"I'm not trying to get kicked out of school, but I can't stand people walking around talking about me," she said.

The freshman explained that another student had warned her that morning that the junior was waiting outside school with a relative and wanted "to know if anyone wants to fight her." She said she did not plan to start a fight, but was not sure how to interpret the other girl's message.

Collier, who helped mediate the session, asked the freshman what she wanted the junior to do. Without hesitation, she said she wanted the older girl to stop calling her boyfriend and "to leave him alone."

The junior looked startled and said she never calls her baby's father, then gave the younger girl a list of all the reasons why she wants nothing to do with him. By the end of the session, it became clear that the two girls had less of a problem with each other than with the young man.

The senior mediator helped them work out details of a contract that is supposed to guide their actions toward each other. They agreed to communicate directly instead of through intermediaries and refrain from gossiping about each other.

Afterward, the junior said she found the session helpful. "I looked at her angrily because I jumped to conclusions," she said of her former foe. "She seems like a nice person."

DuVal's student mediators said most of the arguments they help resolve begin as this one did—with rumors and ruffled feathers. "Ninety-nine percent of it is 'he said, she said,' or girlfriend-boyfriend problems," said Natasha Walker, a senior who has been a member of the mediation team since its inception.

Tremayne Cobb, a mediator who is in 11th grade, said that although many of the disputes may appear petty, some students hesitate to walk away from physical confrontations because they fear it will make them look "soft."

"People will get into a fight, even though they don't want to fight, because they don't want to back down," he said.

The advantage of mediation, according to Cobb, is getting the warring parties away from the encouraging taunts of their friends. Although some students initially are reticent about the process, few refuse to go through with it, he said. Once they leave the mediation room, they are advised to tell curious classmates who may be gearing up for a big showdown simply that the matter has been settled.

DuVal's principal, Frank Stetson, said peer mediation has improved the climate at his school. Since the program started, the number of fights at DuVal has been reduced by half, he said.

At the same time, he and other school officials readily acknowledge that they do not expect mediation to eliminate weapons and fights entirely. Unfortunately, the students who are most likely to resort to force probably will be the most resistant to finding peaceful alternatives to violence, they say. At some elementary and middle schools, students with a history of behavior problems have been recruited as mediators on the theory that they would benefit from both the training and the increased responsibility.

"It doesn't solve problems. It helps bring problems to the surface and helps you deal with them, but everyone understands the limitations," said Pam Latt, director of student services in Fairfax County, where about one-third of the elementary schools have peer mediation teams. "But if you get people to recognize conflict at a trivial stage when they are not so vested in the conflict, students feel very good about resolving things."

April 19, 1992

New Groups 'Filling a Void' Left By PTAs

Minority Parents' Forums Put Basic Educational Concerns Back on the Front Burner

STEPHANIE GRIFFITH

Ana Leticia Moran and friends meet every Wednesday in a classroom at Arlington's Barcroft Elementary School, all of them Hispanic immigrants trying to learn about the education their children are receiving.

At Page Elementary in North Arlington, where most of the students are white, Portia Clark and other black parents who want to make sure that African American culture has a presence at the school have formed a group that is pushing for the hiring of more black teachers.

The Arlington groups are among dozens of Washington area organizations recently formed by minority parents with a common belief: that traditional parent-teacher associations, with their formal meetings: and lengthy educational and political agendas, have become ineffective at addressing many issues that specifically concern minority students.

Operating outside the PTA structure, the newer groups are offering parents a more intimate relationship with school officials and, in the case of several Hispanic groups, a chance to discuss their children's education in their native language.

"I don't think [the traditional PTA] has been effective in adapting itself to the kind of forum where the new parents feel comfortable," said Ana Sol Gutierrez, a school board member in Montgomery County, where Hispanic parents recently began forming groups that hold discussions in Spanish. The smaller groups "are filling a void, and they are very effective" in reaching immigrant parents intimidated by the large crowds and parliamentary procedures that characterize many PTAs, Gutierrez said.

The emergence of such groups throughout the Washington area comes at a time when national PTA leaders acknowledge that PTA membership is declining—in large part, they say, because of a failure to attract the parents of a rising number of minority students. PTA membership across the nation declined to 7 million last year, down about 200,000 from the previous year.

The PTA's national office in Chicago has begun a campaign encouraging local organizations to provide interpreters for non-English-speaking parents and pushing other initiatives designed to attract minorities. But some local PTA leaders say the new groups have sprouted because the focus of many PTAs has drifted from parents' most basic concerns to areas such as fund-raising.

"The PTA unfortunately has gotten away from educational issues," said Martha Moore, PTA president at Arlington's Page Elementary. "We try to fund maps, globes and additional aides . . . [but] nobody questions the kind of books the library buys."

School-based groups of minority parents have been especially active in Arlington, where more than half the students are members of minority groups, but where most of the PTA leadership remains white, school officials said. Black and Hispanic parents also have formed countywide parent organizations.

Black and Hispanic parents said the groups are essential to their children's academic success and tackle controversial issues that many local PTAs have been reluctant to take on, such as gaps between minority and white students' scores on standardized tests and the hiring of minority teachers.

"A lot of the problems that black children have in school are not addressed at PTA meetings," Tru Raqib, the mother of a first-grader at Arlington's Drew Elementary, said during a recent meeting of Parents in Education, a countywide black parents group.

When Moran and the other members of the Latino Mothers of Barcroft School meet, the conversation is informal, in Spanish and often accompanied by needlepoint. Several of the mothers are still learning about the U.S. education system, and their questions to Principal Ellen Kahan are basic.

At a recent meeting, for example, Kahan showed Moran the ins and outs of long division so Moran could help her son, a fifth-grader, with his homework.

"It's a lot more fun here," said Moran, 38, who also has a daughter in kindergarten. "We don't have to keep the regimen that [the PTA) sets."

Kahan said she sees working with the group as an opportunity to reach out to parents who believe they don't fit in with the PTA.

"The difficulty I have with the whole discussion on parental involvement is that we always define it as being active in the PTA," Kahan said.

That sentiment is echoed at Page Elementary, where Clark says her group's efforts also are aimed at making sure that black students across the county have access to the school, one of Arlington's three alternative schools that stress particularly challenging curricula.

Parents in other jurisdictions have formed larger yet similar groups.

In Fairfax County, last year parents organized the Fairfax County Parent Coalition for Minority Student Achievement, bringing together about 20 smaller groups to call attention to issues particularly affecting minorities, according to Gene Thornton, director of the county chapter of the NAACP.

The Alexandria Hispanic Parents Association was organized last year after parents complained that they felt ill-informed about issues ranging from the American grading system to what to expect at a parent-teacher conference. The group draws to its meetings about 75 parents, most of whom speak little or no English.

"These parents were missing a lot of the information that was being given out by the school," said Claudia Fitzgerald, a social worker with the Alexandria school system, who said few parents attend PTA meetings because of language and cultural barriers.

Advocates of the parent groups point out that they attract parents who normally would not get involved in their children's education. Educators say parental involvement is key to a child's academic success.

But the new parent groups do have critics, many of whom say that because the groups tend to form along racial, language or ethnic lines, they divide ethnic groups.

"I don't think I would want them at my school," said Gloria Hoffman, principal at Randolph Elementary in Arlington. "I think they polarize themselves if you have those splinter groups going."

Most PTA presidents interviewed said they are eager to work with the groups, but some members shared the views of a mother at Arlington's Oakridge Elementary, where a black parents' group formed earlier this year.

"After all these years of trying to work together, it's a return" to working separately, said the mother, who didn't want to be identified. "Everyone may be interested in their own children, but I don't see any evidence of interest in the school at large."

Despite the growing popularity of independent parent groups, school administrators still prefer to work with PTAs, said Arlene Zielke, a vice president at the PTA's national office in Chicago.

"Any system does not want to deal with all kinds of rump groups of parents," said Zielke, who said the PTA hopes to draw some of the new groups under its umbrella eventually.

Moore, the PTA president at Page, rejected criticism by some minority parents that PTA groups consist mostly of white members who have political control of the organizations.

"It's always described as a clique; we've tried to fight that perception for years," Moore said. To be involved in PTAs, she said, "all you have to do is raise your hand and step forward."

May 28, 1992

Before Riots, Youth Programs in Shambles

MICHAEL WILBON AND DAVE SHEININ

In the comfort of the San Fernando Valley, about 800 children from riot-torn neighborhoods in Los Angeles are learning the fundamentals of basketball, Olympic team handball and gymnastics. They are third, fourth and fifth graders bused from their schools, a 30-minute ride to another world.

Most never have seen a balance beam before. Some have never played sports on grass because street gangs have turned their neighborhood parks into war zones. But on this particular day, because of the Learn and Play Olympic Sports Program, they play without fear of being caught in a crossfire and without the disconcerting noise of police helicopters searching for trouble.

As community leaders here and across the nation grope to understand the lessons of the Los Angeles riots, there is renewed discussion of what role sports can play in solving the crisis facing America's cities. Some think it may be too late. Urban playgrounds and schoolyards, once a spawning ground for some of the world's finest athletes, are no longer a safe and stable hub of community activity.

"The parks are not available to these kids because they've been taken over by gangs," said Patrick Escobar, who helps run the Learn and Play Olympics. "There's no money for coaching. At school they're given a ball and told, 'Go play.' "

Escobar walks a visitor through the field of dreams and says he is pleased that this grass-roots sports program will reach approximately 16,000 Los Angeles school kids during its 19-day run. He is fully aware, however, that the conditions that led to the recent riots and rage in Los Angeles also wreaked havoc with sports, particularly youth sports.

The system is already hurting. Money woes have forced the Los Angeles Unified School District to slash $850 million in the past three years. Sports programs have fared better than some departments, losing about $1 million last year, but the cutbacks are telling nonetheless. Some sports have been eliminated altogether; coaches have been laid off and not replaced; facilities are not being maintained. There's a lack of facilities and lack of supervision. Intramurals are being cut out.

"Ultimately, what I'm afraid we're going to see is these changes taking away your elite-level athlete, and that's where Southern California has always been the leader," Escobar said. Since the late 1950s, the area has produced more professional and Olympic athletes than any region in the country. "Will schools in the Valley or private schools be the only ones developing elite athletes?" Escobar said. "Are we encouraging that kind of stuff?"

From Games to War

Keith Peddler, a gang member who has been one of the leaders in forging a truce between his Bloods and the rival Crips, is one of the people encouraging the reinstitution of programs that might give kids in L.A.'s troubled areas an alternative. Traditionally, the black and Hispanic males who dominate this city's gang activity have found that the most visible, accessible and successful alternatives involved organized competition. "Some programs should be sports, some might not need to be," Peddler said. "Whatever, they better get to these kids by the third, fourth grade, while you can be successful instilling an anti-gang mentality. Because if you don't get the kids by then, the gangs will sure get 'em."

Those are sentiments echoed throughout the city, especially in the wake of the recent riots that claimed 54 lives. Sports, as a vehicle to facilitate upward mobility, has been a less-viable option in most major cities in recent years, but the situation in Los Angeles appears to be more distressing because of the prevalence of violent street gangs and the massive school budget cuts that have affected almost every sport.

During the riots, some attention was focused on the impact of the unrest on professional sports: the Los Angeles Lakers, Clippers and Dodgers had games postponed, but very quickly pro sports resumed normal operation. By the time the Raiders and Clippers resume play in the fall, the burned-out stores surrounding the Coliseum and Sports Arena may be operational or even replaced.

The sports landscape at the youth and high school levels, however, has been and will continue to be dramatically altered. Kye Courtney, who coached Hawthorne High to seven straight state championships, has already noticed the pool of track and field athletes shrink noticeably. "The best sprinters in California are either in prison or they're dead," he said. "Most of these guys, they've got one parent or no parents. They live with their Uncle Anthony or with their grandmother. I'd say 70 percent of my team comes from split families.

"These kids are products of the inner city. And the problems are being compounded by gangs. The gang thing is a matter of survival.

There's a lot of kids on probation on teams across the city. A lot of them have criminal records. You go to practice, one of your kids isn't there, you ask around to find out where he is. The kids say, 'Oh, he had to go to see his probation officer,' or 'He had to see his lawyer.' This is the first year I've started hearing that excuse."

One of Courtney's former pupils, who seven years ago set the California high school record in the 400 meters that still stands, is in his mid-twenties and might be contending for a spot on the U.S. Olympic team—except he's in jail.

Paul Knox, football and track coach at Dorsey High, said of his 60-member football team: "We don't cut anybody from the team because being with the team keeps kids away from trouble."

Dorsey High is now infamous because of at least two of its football games were the backdrop for gang shootings. A baseball player fatally shot himself on the team bus. And the team's coach, Derrell Thomas, was arrested for drug use a few weeks later. While 70 percent of Dorsey's graduates continue their education, sports is obviously no longer the dreamy escape it used to be.

During a track meet at Dorsey last week, senior Abram Toomes, who runs the 100, pointed to his uniform and said, "Our coaches paid for these." Asked if he worried about high school sports becoming extinct in Los Angeles, he said, "Yeah, but man, I worry about schools closing down in general."

Even teenagers in the Los Angeles Unified School District are acutely aware of budget strains. The state of California asked the LAUSD—the second-largest school district in the country—to cut $200 million from its budget in 1990, $250 million in 1991, and $400 million this year. of last year's quarter-billion dollar slash, $940,000 came from sports. Both boys gymnastics programs are gone. There's no more junior varsity football. Some sports lost playoff seasons.

Mark Slavkin, a member of the Los Angeles Board of Education, saw this as the bright side. "At least in the end we didn't eliminate high school sports," he said during a recent conference on the matter. Slavkin notes that nobody has said a word about laying off "thousands of librarians, school psychologists and [having an average of] 40 kids per class in elementary school."

Slavkin went to Hamilton High, the school that produced Houston Oilers quarterback Warren Moon. "I'm not anti-sports," he said, proudly ticking off names of other professional athletes who went to Hamilton, "but we have to confront this on the overall budget context. L.A. will have 10,000 to 15,000 new students [next year] and with no new net money. High school sports will be on the chopping block as an issue for debate again this year. There's just no doubt about it. It's how much do you cut and where do you cut it. For high school sports to continue to expect general fund support into the future is a mistake."

Life on the Run

Karen Fletcher Briggs has found out about the lack of funds the hard way, out of her own pocket. As the person in charge of security at the 24th Street School—elementary schools have security personnel in Los Angeles—Fletcher Briggs started a track club on her own because there was no money available for the school to have one. She was a track star at L.A. High, grew up in south-central Los Angeles and still lives there.

Because there were so many kids who needed attention, Fletcher Briggs thought she could help 40 or 50 of them through her track club. Right away, 75 showed up to join. She doesn't get paid for her time; in fact, she feeds them some days, pays the entry fees for many of them when parents don't have the money or the inclination. She's close to being in the position of having to turn kids away.

One afternoon last week, at the junior high school field in Woodland Hills where the AAF's Learn and Play program is being conducted, Fletcher Briggs was in the middle of describing herself as "the baby sitter" when a third-grade girl walked up and called her "Mama." Two girls, one black, the other Asian, were walking together, both wearing blue T-shirts that say 'Guilty,' apparently in reference to the Rodney King verdict.

Of the 800 kids on the field that day, probably 50 percent were black, the other 50 percent were Hispanic, Asian and white or some combination of races. At least five different languages were identifiable. Fletcher Briggs is something of a Pied Piper with the 24th Street schoolers, regardless or race or ethnicity. She is 30 years old, and some days it's difficult for her to be this up. "Sometimes," she said, "I think I'm going to give up."

For a day or so recently, she did. Her resources were being stretched unbelievably and she just quit. But the kids pleaded for her return and wrote her notes. Their sad faces were far too much for her to withstand. So Fletcher Briggs is back, but warned that the club absolutely can't exceed 100 members. At the moment, students whose schools don't have track and field are coming over to the 24th Street School.

"The Mount Vernon kids are coming over," she said, her face breaking into a smile/grimace. "L.A. Youth Services canceled the annual track meet. No money."

Fletcher Briggs ran the 100, 200 and threw the shot. She ran in some TAC meets the last two summers and had aspirations of her own. "I was blessed growing up," she said. "my coaches were really coaches.

Now we don't have coaches. There's no money. A teacher who's never competed or coached may be the 'coach.' There's so much they need, I mean bare necessities and values. We've got to start somewhere, so this is where I'm trying to start."

Not Much Choice

While the 24th Street kids may have no idea how fortunate they are, LAUSD's compliance adviser Steve Munoz does. "There's not much of a choice for these kids," he said. "There's nothing provided, there's nothing to get involved in. It's not just sports programs that are lacking in these neighborhoods, it's everything."

Willie West, legendary basketball coach at Crenshaw High whose pupils included Darryl Strawberry, Stevie Thompson and the Bullets' John Williams, was recently lamenting the downfall of high school sports, track and field particularly. "Kids have become so materialistic," he said. "The concept of selling drugs, which produces immediate money, seems to appeal to them more. A lot of kids who would be scholarship athletes need or want the money now. They see it as being easier, immediate."

In the days immediately following the riots, churches and sports might have been the most stabilizing factors in Los Angeles. One Saturday before 8 a.m., the only sounds you could hear in south L.A. were that of the omnipresent chopper hovering above, a basketball dribbling and the signature chatter of a pickup game. "Sports has always been the factor that pulled things back together after a crisis," West said. "It's always helped normalize and relax life after tension." West added that he was talking about the short term. The bigger picture disturbs almost everybody with broad vision. Most major cities are having budget problems and most are losing promising athletes to drugs and crime. But Los Angeles, if not unique, is obviously the leader in a disturbing trend that few would have predicted 10 years ago. In the 1988 Summer Olympics, 168 of the 611 U.S. athletes—27 percent— were from one state: California. It's estimated that two-thirds of that total had some connection to Southern California. These are the people the AAF's Patrick Escobar meant when he used the term "elite-level athlete."

Even if corporate sponsorship comes to the rescue financially, who will be there to spend the money on if the cemeteries, jail cells and gang rosters are occupied by kids who, if they'd only been born a generation earlier, might instead have been on the winning side in an increasingly lopsided tug-o-war?

May 24, 1992

School Mentors Steer Younger Students Through Teenage Troubles

JANE SEABERRY

Four times a week Vanessa Cardenas, 15, listens to the heartache and frustration of 11- and 12-year-old Spanish-speaking children like herself.

"They ask me how it is to be in a high school. They ask me if American students in my school are prejudiced," Cardenas said. "They get down, depressed. They said friends told them Spanish was a stupid language. I try to cheer them up, always go forward, try to do their best. In a way, I see myself in them."

Cardenas, who arrived here from Bolivia less than two years ago, said she wanted to build the children's self-confidence and show them that a Spanish-speaking person could succeed in the United States. So, the Washington-Lee High School student became their mentor, one of dozens of teenagers in the Washington area who have taken on the adult responsibility of being role models for troubled youths.

While mentor programs generally have engaged business people or other adults to demonstrate to youngsters that they, too, can succeed, several schools in the District, Fairfax, Arlington and Prince George's counties are involving students as mentors for other students.

The idea is a throwback to many anti-poverty programs in the 1960s, in which high school students were used to teach younger ones. The concept is back in favor as another way to help so-called at-risk students, some educators said.

The high school mentors are more than tutors, helping youngsters with personal and nonacademic problems, and sometimes planning activities outside of school. Often, the mentors are not the school's highest achievers, but they have decent grades, listen to the same music and wear the same kinds of clothes as the pupils they counsel.

"Obviously, someone closer to his age is more aware of what he's going through," Hayfield High School junior Razi Evans said about the 14-year-old student he helped. Evans, 17, a B student, sometimes wears a stylish black leather jacket and a popular fade haircut.

"It's good that Fairfax County sees the situation and is trying to do something about it," Evans said, adding that there are "not too many positive roles for black youth today, particularly by the black men in the city with all the crime and all the drugs and the teenage pregnancy and all the poverty."

Educators cautioned that student mentors by themselves are not a solution to helping students with academic or social problems, but they usually are part of a larger approach involving intensive tutoring and counseling by teachers or other adults. Some schools also have engaged students as counselors to their peers.

Sometimes the mentors are not mature enough to handle the responsibility. For example, two students at Hayfield Intermediate who had high school mentors said the older students mostly joked around and they got little out of it.

The mentoring also may have little follow-up at home, where some parents don't speak English, or little emphasis is placed on schoolwork. Penny Isenberg, who handles the students with mentors at Hayfield Intermediate, said some students arrive at school angry because other children have the benefit of more stable families. "Some kids are resentful because they didn't have the support at home," Isenberg said.

Still, some local educators said the program has shown results. For the nine students who had high school mentors this year at Hayfield Intermediate, their grades either improved or stabilized, Isenberg said. Contrary to previous semesters, none of the students had failing grades this term.

"There was improvement you could actually see," Isenberg said. "All these students did their homework." None of the students had discipline problems, and tardiness lessened, she said. "They started to care about how they looked." The high school mentors were part of a larger program at Hayfield Intermediate that included intensive tutoring and counseling.

Hayfield Intermediate eighth-grader Brian Smith said his mentor convinced him that he could go to college by counseling him about studying every time they met.

"I went to this club in Woodbridge and I saw [the mentor] and he was talking to me about school," Smith said. "I'd see him at the mall, anywhere. He'd call my house."

Saith said his mentor used large words when he spoke, which induced Smith to buy a dictionary. He said if his mentor could be that smart, so could he.

Student mentors interviewed said they felt duty-bound to help youngsters with problems similar to their own, particularly youths from similar ethnic backgrounds.

Tatiana Aguilar, who spoke no English when she came to this country from Bolivia six years ago, constantly fields questions about life in the United States from Salvadoran and other foreign-born students.

"They want to know everything about me," said Aguilar, 16. "They want to know how much work I have, is the work difficult." The boys "ask me everything about girls. I told them when I first came to this country what it was like. I tell them I know what they're going through."

One by-product of mentor programs is that the mentors' grades and self-esteem frequently have improved, school counselors said. Such programs also give less stellar students their moment in the limelight.

"Our focal point is the average student," said Kathy Gwynn, who helps administer the District's peer mentoring programs through a private firm called Mentors Inc. "We found that the students that were getting A's and B's were getting a lot of attention from the faculty, staff, colleges, etc. The students that weren't doing well—D's and F's—also were getting a lot of attention. The C students were sort of plodding along. We decided that would be the focus of our program." An important factor in the District program is students having mentors who are much like themselves, who live in the same neighborhood and are seen in familiar settings.

"Sometimes the adults are more like parents, they're a little bit far removed," Gwynn said. "This is an older person who dresses the way they want to dress and listens to [singer] Bobby Brown."

Hayfield's Evans said problems his student faced in junior high school were similar to those he encountered, such as "not taking my studies seriously, not looking to the future like high school and college, what will I do afterward; problems like letting your peers determine what you were trying to do."

"You're trying to run along with a particular group of friends. most of the time that particular group of friends is up to no good," Evans said. "I overcame the situation simply by listening to those with advice older than me, telling me that that was not the right way to go."

May 9, 1990

Staying in School . . .

DEBBIE GOLDBERG

In light of growing concern about the educational performance of minority students, scores of programs—some encompassing entire school district, some consisting of no more than a few tutors—have cropped up from coast to coast, as part of the search for a better formula for educating minority youngsters, keeping them in school and enrolling them in college.

The problems are myriad. While minority children make up a third of the U.S. school population, in some school districts almost half the minority students fail to graduate from high school. While nationwide high school graduation rates have increased for black and Hispanic students, the number of those students going on to college has decreased since 1976. In addition, nearly half of all black children and one-third of Hispanic children live in poverty, according to the Children's Defense Fund, a non-profit child advocacy organization based in Washington.

Not surprisingly, the regions with the greatest number of minorities have taken the lead in implementing programs to help minority students. San Antonio, for instance, has taken a novel approach to dealing with students who are not doing well in school—they get to tutor other students.

Under the Valued Youth Partnership program, junior high and high school students with low grades and test scores and high rates of absenteeism, and who may be discipline problems—in other words, those students most likely to drop out—are enlisted to tutor elementary school students.

Eight junior high and high schools, filled mostly with students who are Hispanic, poor and often with limited English proficiency, participate in the program.

"There have been substantial gains for the kids being tutored, but the big pay-off is for the tutors," Cardenas said noting that test scores, grades and attitudes towards school have all improved.

Ironically, this set-up is almost the opposite of what one might expect, which is that better students would be enlisted as tutors. But

Cardenas chalks the success up to the fact that even mediocre students get a sense of pride by being chosen to help others.

"The kids are valued in ways they've never been valued before, no matter how poorly they're performing," Cardenas explained. The tutors receive a minimum wage stipend to work about eight hours a week, and the program provides support services, field trips and other group activities not generally available in the schools.

Although many of the teenagers are reluctant at first to take on the tutoring task, Cardenas said not one has ever refused to join the program.

In light of its success, Cardenas has sent materials on the partnership to hundreds of other schools, and is soon expecting a grant that will allow about six other school districts to implement the program.

While the Valued Youth Partnership program has a unique twist, conventional tutoring is one of the most frequently used approaches in helping minority students.

For example, the Math, Engineering, Science Achievement (MESA) program was started 20 years ago at the University of California at Berkeley to encourage minority students to pursue scientific careers. It is now offered throughout the state, said MESA Executive Director Fred Easter, and many other areas, including the Pine Ridge Indian Reservation in South Dakota have adopted this approach.

At the high school level, a designated MESA teacher works with students in special classes, providing enrichment and tutoring programs. College students get help by way of tutoring, group study and support, and summer job placement services.

About 20,000 minority students have participated in MESA since its inception. Of those, 73 percent have enrolled at four-year colleges, compared to 13 percent for California's minority students generally, Easter said. Two-thirds of the MESA students have majored in math and the sciences, and 2,000 students have received four-year engineering degrees.

One of the those graduates is Hulan Barnett, who was a MESA student at Richmond High School, in the Bay Area, and later majored in math at Morehouse College in Atlanta. Now, he's teaching junior high school math in Berkeley and is the school's MESA teacher.

"I wanted to give something back to the community," he said of his decision to return home to teach. Four days a week, Barnett's 40 MESA students get help doing homework and preparing for tests, hear guest speakers and are counseled in such matters as what classes to take in high school and how to deal with teachers. Visitors, ranging from Berkeley football players to professors, often come to talk to students, providing minority role models.

MESA students don't necessarily need to be shining academic stars. "I look for parental support more than anything," Barnett said. "I think ultimately the students who make it are those who get a lot of support at home."

Such programs as MESA are a response to the growing realization that the educational system is failing many minority students, who now make up one-third of the nation's students.

Many inner-city schools that serve minority students are in shambles, employ the least experienced teachers and have little in the way of resources, said Shirley McBay, dean of student affairs at the Massachusetts Institute of Technology and director of the Quality Education for Minorities Project staff at MIT. QEM was a two-year study of minority education in the U.S. that was funded by the Carnegie Corp. Minority youngsters may get little support at home for education, she added, since their parents often haven't been successful themselves in school.

To combat some of these problems, governments, school districts, colleges, businesses, foundations, and private citizens already are spending many billions of dollars. The money will be needed. A new QEM report has called for nothing less than a crib-to-college commitment for helping minorities do better in school.

To start with, McBay said, "we have to make sure that every child comes to school fully prepared to learn, and that means prenatal care, Head Start, good nutrition, and a sense of values. It's not enough for a child to just show up."

And these days, the need for a decent education is greater than ever. In the past, high school dropouts and even those barely literate could manage to get union-wage jobs in factories. According to the report 'Workforce 2000,' published by the Hudson Institute, very few new jobs will be created over the next decade for those who can't read, follow directions and use mathematics.

"The economics are straightforward," said Ray Marshall, a professor of economics and public affairs at the University of Texas at Austin, who contributed to the QEM project. "If we want to be a high-income country, we need a well-educated work force. People are either going to be assets or liabilities."

With the nation's economic future on the line, Marshall, a former secretary of labor under President Carter, said he feels the country will respond to the educational needs of minority youngsters. "Now, we have a convergence of economic necessity and moral imperative, and I'm optimistic we'll do something about it," he said.

Although the drive to improve minority student education has resulted in a plethora of different programs, some common themes have emerged. Tutoring, role models, and parental involvement are tactics that have been shown to work. Another component generally agreed upon is the need to provide early information on college admissions requirements and financial aid options.

While college counseling traditionally has been provided to high school juniors and seniors, there is a growing consensus that this is too late to reach out to many disadvantaged youngsters. Consider that fully 75 percent of the nation's Hispanic high school seniors have not taken the appropriate courses to enroll in college, according to the National Council of La Raza, a Hispanic advocacy group.

The Higher Education Information Center in Boston was established mindful of the fact that a lack of information is just as limiting to families as a lack of money. Through its youth outreach programs, the center's counselors visit junior high schools, churches, libraries and community centers that serve low-income minority students throughout the state.

"We found there are very important decisions that need to be made in 7th and 8th grade that affect students options for the future," noted Ann Coles, executive director of the center, which is headquartered in the Boston Public Library. "Many parents feel there isn't money for college, and don't want to encourage their kids because they think it's out of reach. We tell them there's a lot of financial aid available, and all different kinds of colleges with all different kinds of price tags." Colleges and universities, anxious to provide a community service and also to increase the potential pool of minority college students, also are getting into the act. For instance, Georgetown University sponsors several programs to provide D.C. students with the academic, social and cultural awareness needed to make it to college. At Brown Junior High School, 53 7th-graders have been chosen for a special enrichment program covering all subjects. Another 25 students in grades 7 through 12 from throughout the city participate in Georgetown's Amateur Science Program, out of about 100 who applied this year, said Paulette Nowden, until recently coordinator of the university's educational community involvement programs.

Students in both programs attend full-time summer programs on Georgetown's campus, as well as Saturday academic programs approximately every other week during the school year. Students are taught by District teachers, but university faculty members participate as guest speakers and judge projects for science fairs. Campus laboratories and other facilities are made available to the students.

According to Nowden, just having the opportunity to be on campus is a big step for some of these minority students. "They now understand that Washington goes beyond whatever street they live on." William

Reid, director of the Georgetown Center for Minority Student Affairs, said the university sponsors the programs because of its "commitment to the community," adding, "the best contribution we can make is to promote education."

One of the biggest spenders in this educational effort is the federal government, through its programs, ranging from Head Start to college financial aid that are targeted to low-income families.

For example, the U.S. Education Department will spend about $242 million this year on six programs designed to help pave the way to college for poor students. About 65 percent of the half-million students served annually through the programs are members of minority groups, said Phillip Cauthen, a department spokesman.

Upward Bound provides tutoring, admissions counseling and career advice to promising high school students. Talent Search is designed to reach junior high and high school students at risk of dropping out.

And the Ronald McNair program, started two years ago in honor of the black astronaut killed in the Challenger explosion, provides funds for 14 colleges to offer programs that prepare minority undergraduates for graduate work in the sciences. Institutions such as Florida A&M, Colorado State and Coppin State, have used the money to provide research opportunities, tutorials and internships for eligible students, Cauthen said.

Although more and more programs and financial resources are available for minority students, some question whether this relative hodge-podge of efforts can pay off in the long run. Although some programs have impressive statistics to support their approaches, the jury is still out on the impact of many others. In addition, many of those involved cite the need for more coordination of programs and guarantees of long-term funding to help implement successful programs in other school districts.

"We found a lot of exemplary programs and schools," said Marshall, the economist who participated in the Quality Education for minorities Project. "The next stage is [deciding] how to cause a school system to incorporate all these examples of success. We've got a lot of experiments going on now."

April 8, 1990

From Dropouts to Graduates

WILLIAM RASPBERRY

Patrick F. Taylor, a Louisiana oil man here to attend a National Dropout Prevention Conference, thinks he knows why so many young people drop out of school. He also thinks he knows how to fix it.

"Kids perceive high school as a dead end, which it usually is for those who can't go beyond high school. But while they know they will need a college education in order to succeed, they also know that the odds are against their going to college. Their families just don't have the money."

The result, he says, is that the children—including many who remain in school through 12th grade—simply don't see high school as worth serious exertion on their part.

His solution is simple and, he insists, economical as well. He would guarantee college tuition and fees for any high school graduate who can meet college admission standards. And he wouldn't lower the standards. "The kids can meet the standards," he says. "Up to now, they just haven't seen any reason to try."

He believes so strongly in his idea that he has virtually abandoned his day-to-day involvement with Taylor Energy Co., one of the biggest independent producers of oil and gas in the country, to spread his gospel.

The Taylor Plan, as he calls it, was born during a visit speech to 7th- and 8th-graders at New Orleans' Livingston Middle School, "one of the worst-performing classes in one of the worst school systems in the country."

"I asked these children—poor, black, from single-parent families, all set back at least one grade, and with every indication that they would leave school—how many of them wanted to go to college. Every hand went up. I told them if they would make a B average on a pre-college curriculum, I'd see to it that they got to go to college. The enthusiasm was tremendous, both from the children and from their parents, who had given up any hope of college."

His original idea was like that of Eugene Lang of New York: to put up personal cash and beg scholarships for the children who met his standards. But then it occurred to him that even if every child in his

29

audience managed to get a college degree, the effect would be negligible in a state where 40 percent of high school students fail to graduate.

What was needed, he decided, was for the state to invest in its children's future—an investment, he is convinced, that will be returned many times over as the children become productive adults. He took his notion to the state legislature, which in 1989 agreed to pay tuition at state universities for any Louisiana student who completes 17 1/2 hours of college prep courses, maintains a C-plus average, scores at least 18 on the American College Test entrance exam and comes from a family with an annual income of $25,000 or less (the cap rises by $5,000 for each additional child).

Last year, versions of the Taylor Plan were enacted in Texas, Florida, New Mexico and Indiana; Arkansas, Maryland and Oklahoma joined the list this year.

In Louisiana, support came from practically every segment of the population, including, he adds pointedly, "nonlegislature blacks." What opposition there was, he says, was from people who thought it was a scheme to send white kids to college to the further disadvantage of minorities. "In fact, it's the other way around," he says. "On average, 11 percent of state tax revenues go to subsidize higher public education. In Louisiana, the subsidy comes from a sales tax. But with nearly half of poor children dropping out of high school, that means that poor people have been subsidizing rich people's kids." Every year the plan has been in effect, he says, the college-attendance gap between black and white youngsters has narrowed.

"The interesting thing is, not one parent I've talked to, black or white, has questioned whether their kids could make the grade. They know they can do it if they have a reason to do it, and now they have a reason. The kids are working harder, and the schools are getting better. Parents—the same parents we keep saying aren't interested in their children's education—will show up at school to complain that a certain teacher is no good or that too little math is being taught or there's too little homework. 'Remember, my child is going to college,' they'll say."

Taylor sneers at Pell Grants, guaranteed student loans and other federal programs designed to get low-income students into college. "In the first place, these programs never covered more than half of the cost of college; now its only about 29 percent. But worse, they have no admission standards. As a result, even when the kids get into college, most of them don't graduate because they come to college unprepared.

"The Taylor Plan fixes the admission standards so that the youngsters can prepare themselves for college success. Once they know they will have their tuition paid if they meet the standards, they'll meet them. They'll take the right courses, and they'll do the work." Taylor, who describes himself as a conservative Republican and populist, says his plan works because it stands the conventional wisdom on its head. "A lot of people think the way to deal with disadvantaged children is to make life easy for them. All that does is lower their self-esteem and lead them to failure. High standards are not a barrier to achievement; they are the gateway to success."

April 17, 1992

Adding Gentle but Firm Persuasion

Mentors Hope to Steer Young Boys from Lure of the Streets

RENE SANCHEZ

Ray Casey's crusade began last fall, at an old school in a poor place, where little boys sit in class all day struggling to beat great odds.

When Casey first walked into Stanton Elementary, set in a Southeast Washington neighborhood pounded by crime and grief, he saw the battle that teachers wage to win the respect and attention of 7-year-old male students enthralled with the fast-lane lives of drug dealers.

And Casey, 29, an Alexandria architect, has kept coming back. Twice, often three times a week, he charges like a lightning bolt into Stanton's classrooms.

He checks homework. He repeats teachers' orders. He drops to his knees and listens, eye-to-eye, as boys explain their troubles. He bounds from one desk to the next with a gentle smile and a blunt message: Do your work.

He has gained their confidence and collects the kind of smiles reserved for heroes. Boys mob him on arrival, watch his every move in class, cling to his hips when he leaves.

The admiration is mutual. "These children have so much stress," Casey said the other day during a break between classes. "There's not a thing wrong with them, but they live in neighborhoods without many rewards. That's why I'm here: to reward what they do."

Winning the hearts and minds of Stanton's boys is a difficult, delicate task, one that Casey isn't tackling alone. Several dozen black professionals from around the Washington region are working at the school. They are joined each week by Howard University students, who travel across town to volunteer.

It's an effort called Project 2000, led by a local service group known as the Concerned Black Men, and it is an investment of time and energy intended to last for the next decade. All for one reason: Too many black boys are miserable in classes and are growing up to be casualties of the streets.

Any school system statistic—attendance, dropouts, retentions—shows as much, and there is a consensus among educators here that the problems those boys face are getting worse.

That fact is evident at Stanton, at Alabama Avenue and Naylor Road, in the Naylor Gardens neighborhood of Southeast. More than 60 percent of the school's kindergartners, first- and second-graders live in public housing complexes riddled with the dangers of the drug trade.

About 80 percent of them also live with only their mothers or grandmothers, and the absence of adult males is reinforced in class. Few D.C. elementary schools have more than three male teachers. Stanton has two.

Hiring male elementary teachers is a critical need, school officials say, but they concede they won't attract an army of males soon. So schools across the city and in Prince George's County are scrambling to match elementary students with black men eager to return to classrooms, and, for some, to their own roots. The drive has spawned many mentoring programs, yet none is as intensive or long-range in its goals as Stanton's Project 2000.

"The Machismo Is Incredible"

"We know what we've been doing in elementary classrooms is not working for a large number of inner-city boys," said Spencer Holland, a school psychologist who belongs to the Concerned Black Men and created the project. "And we know exactly what's missing for them: positive male role models.

"These boys usually have all women teachers, and they begin very early to define learning as a very feminine thing to do," Holland said. "At the same time they're growing up in the inner city, where the machismo is incredible."

That's the message Holland hands Stanton's volunteers, who attend an all-day training session before starting. Teachers explain common behavior problems of restless boys. A counselor tells them that many children don't know their fathers. And Holland stresses that boys are most impressionable in first through fourth grades.

Once that's done, the men leap with exuberance into Stanton's classes, though it's unclear at this point if they are leaving imprints on the boys' character. The school has just begun to analyze the grades and attendance of the second-grade classes that are participating. And volunteers know that no matter how much enthusiasm they stir up, many boys must return each evening to homes and streets that distort—if not erase—the lessons found at school.

Holland recognizes those threats. But he believes Project 2000 has a better chance at success than other similar programs because men work in class every day. They don't just drop by with once-a-month motivation speeches. And they don't just plan weekend outings or tutoring sessions.

"We understand the limits of what we're doing," Holland said. "We can't change their home life, but we can change their attitudes about education. That's what this is about. Just for them to see it's all right to be a man and to like to read is a major objective."

"We can't save everyone, but we can have an impact," said Albert Pearsall, a volunteer who is a security manager at the Department of Justice. "It's so important that these boys be around intellectual black men."

Project 2000 began with Stanton's first graders at the end of 1988.

The plan is to work with the same group of boys through elementary grades, then follow them as they depart to junior and senior high, until they graduate in the year 2000.

About three dozen men participate—lawyers, businessmen, government workers—and more are being trained. The number of Howard students who volunteer is growing. Last fall, the group acquiesced to women students at Howard who had complained that it wasn't tending to the needs of little girls. So now a group of those young women drop in to help as well.

A Man in the Classroom

"This is like manna from heaven," said Yolanda Coleman, Stanton's only counselor for 530 students. "You can see the effect the men have. The students' faces light up. And when the men leave, you hear the boys ask the same question, 'Will you be back? Will you be back?' "

Volunteers, who are required to spend at least half the day at Stanton whenever they come, work as teachers' aides. Stanton's classes usually have about 25 children, and it's tough for teachers to help students individually, while keeping order and instructing the entire class.

That's where men like Ray Casey play a key role. They circle the classroom as a teacher gives a lesson, tutoring those in need and casting stern looks at those not paying attention. They don't yell. And they never step into a teacher's spotlight; she remains in charge.

A few weeks ago, Damon Byrd, 19, a college student, spent hours coaching second-grade boys on prefixes. He knelt down and softly placed his hand on boys' shoulders as he offered tips. He flashed grins at those working hard. And he held private huddles with those who had little on their mind except leaving their seat to sharpen, break, then resharpen their pencils.

Byrd, a District native who attends Central State University in Ohio and was working at Stanton during a semester break, was nearly out of breath by the time class finished. But he wasn't complaining.

"These are good guys, and with the proper guidance, they can go a long way," Byrd said. "I'm not criticizing females, but these guys need males to support them, too."

For all the lessons Byrd has dished out, he has learned a few in return. Like remembering that your every move is being studied by young minds hungry for someone to emulate. Now, Byrd recites the Pledge of Allegiance. And get this: He even stands and sings.

"I felt funny at first, but I'm starting to like it," he said. "It's important. If you don't stand, they don't stand. We do the song 'My Country Tis of Thee' a lot. I'm just remembering the words."

Stanton's teachers welcome his help. They concede it's not easy to keep students' minds on learning. And they know that the boys are often reluctant to confide in women their family troubles or fears of neighborhood violence.

Tenina Sutherland's second-grade class receives visits almost daily from volunteers. "Many of these boys lack family support and aren't being taught to respect each other," she said. "Their needs are tremendous."

Cheers for the Architect

Spend a few days at Stanton, and that point is clear. The school is neat and orderly. Classrooms are colorful; posters and maps cover the walls. Scores of students wear uniforms, which are optional. Some teachers have worked there for two decades. Yet fear abounds on nearby streets and seeps inside Stanton.

One morning last month, with the halls all quiet: A first-grade teacher struggles to continue a lesson; the night before, one of her students was struck in the ear by a stray bullet and hospitalized. Principal Elbie Davis offers a substitute, but she decides to stay and discuss the incident with her class.

Another student keeps returning to Yolanda Coleman's counseling office. She stands alone in the hall, then whispers that she wants to talk about a man she knew who was shot dead in an alley.

Parents walk in and out the building. Some arrive to pick up coupons that give discounts for children's shoes; others attend a weekly session on being parents.

Project 2000 volunteers have given books and supplies to Stanton and have taken boys on trips downtown, the first time many of them had crossed the Anacostia River. The men discuss their careers. They attend school banquets. They gave all the boys a chance to get a free haircut for Christmas.

One recent afternoon, Sutherland's second-graders were in class matching numbers with letters to spell words such as flower, cake and apple. Sutherland patrolled the room, helped by a Howard student. But some students were still goofing off. Then Ray Casey, the architect, arrived.

The boys erupted in a chorus of cheers. They left their desks and tugged at his arms and waist to show good grades on homework or ask for help with the word-and-number work.

Before Casey appeared, Max Tardy, 8, was sneaking peeks at pictures of planets in science magazines he had found in the corner of the room. His papers were on the floor. And he ignored Sutherland's pleas to return to his desk. But Casey changed his mood: Max turned from the pictures, scooped up his papers, and raced toward him. He smashed with delight into Casey's hip.

"I like him because he wants to see what I do," Kax said. "If I get it right, he says 'very good,' and then he comes back to my seat." In an hour, Casey, who grew up in an impoverished Boston neighborhood, had visited four classes. He huddled with a group of third-grade boys, asked what work they had done that day, then shook their hands. He coached second-graders preparing for a spelling quiz and had the class applaud a student who had spelled his job, a-r-c-h-i-t-e-c-t, correctly.

Soon a bell rang, and halls filled with students bound for Stanton's doors. Teachers thanked Casey for coming. He asked how he could help during his next visit. Meantime, boys bounced off each other to tell him goodbye.

"These kids, they're so intense, they want every last thought you have," Casey said with a weary smile. "But that's great. They really need this kind of help. It's crucial that I keep coming back."

February 8, 1990

A Fresh Start in Heading Off Family Crisis
Preschool Centers Revive Two-Generational Mission

PAUL TAYLOR

At the Head Start center in this blue-collar Boston suburb, it has been a very good year for Percilia, who has raised her language skills two levels, and Marianne, who has become a wizard on the computer keyboard.

Pretty hot stuff for a couple of 4-year-olds, right?

No doubt it would be, but Percilia de Paula is 25 and Marianne Tavares is 21. Both are Head Start parents, each is a high school dropout, one is on welfare—and increasingly, America's favorite program for poor preschoolers is aimed at the likes of them.

In theory, Head Start has always been a "two-generational" program, to use the buzzword now in vogue. In the 1960s, its architects understood that the best way they could give poor children a boost was to give their parents a boost. Local Head Start policy councils have been run by parents ever since, and more than one-third of today's Head Start staff members are parents of current or former Head Start students.

But over the years, Head Start's efforts to minister to the ever-growing needs of its families have been stretched thin by budget constraints. Many of the program's social workers, for example, have seen their caseloads swell to as many as 150—more than quadruple the recommended level.

Now that is beginning to change. In the past two years, the Bush administration has funded 41 pilot programs—including one here—that offer Head Start parents counseling and referral services in literacy, job training and substance abuse.

The rationale for these Family Service Centers is twofold: The social fabric of poor communities has eroded badly since Head Start was launched; and research has shown that Head Start's positive effects on preschoolers tend to disappear after a few years, absent intensive follow-up.

Critics say the only thing wrong with these pilot programs is that they belong in all 1,500 Head Start programs nationwide. "We don't need another demonstration that's funded for a few years in a few places and then disappears," said Sarah Greene, executive director of the National Head Start Association (NHSA), an advocacy group of staff and parents.

"Maybe it's that I'm getting older, but there seen to be so many more family pathologies out there than there used to be—more domestic violence, more child abuse, more substance abuse, more sex abuse, more health problems, more obesity," said Jack Hamilton, who directs the Community Action Agency of Somerville, which has a three-year, $177,310 federal grant to create a Family Service Center for parents of the 190 preschoolers in its Head Start program.

Somerville is a dense, gritty, working-class community north of Boston where generations of Irish and Italians are making room, not always graciously, for recent arrivals from Haiti, Brazil and El Salvador. Half the parents in its Head Start program are on welfare, at least one-third have substance abuse problems and at least one-fifth are illiterate.

In one way or another, all have felt the lash of this region's deep recession. "Until a couple of years ago, I considered the meals we served the kids a nice extra," said Hamilton. "Now, they're a necessity. When you see a four-year-old wolfing down three cereals at breakfast, you know he hasn't had a real meal since the lunch he had here yesterday."

The staff worries, too, about hungry parents. "We used to serve donuts and coffee at our parents meetings," said Director Donna Cabral. "Now we make sure to serve fruits or bagels or something else with more nutritional value."

With its federal grant, Somerville's Head Start program has ambitions for parents that go beyond filling stomachs. It has used a portion of the money to create a new family service room, where parents can get training on three computers, borrow books from a small library and meet for parenting seminars. It has also established links with other social service agencies in Somerville to steer parents into job training, substance abuse, adult education and English-as-a-second-language programs.

"Head Start is the perfect setting for a social worker to get to the parent," said Roberta McCluskey, a Head Start teacher who, like 26 of her 36 professional colleagues in the Somerville program, is a former Head Start parent. "When you have goals for your kids, you tend to develop goals for yourself, too."

Sometimes those goals need to be teased to the surface—and the staff uses all kinds of strategies. "When parents enroll their kids, they have to fill out a bunch of forms," said Sandra Ford, the family service coordinator, who directs a staff of six. "Often a parent will ask if she can take them home. Our caseworkers are trained to push the issue.

We'll ask if it's because they've left their glasses home, or if they're having trouble reading."

Percilia de Paul, who arrived here from Brazil three years ago with virtually no English ability, had her language problems screened that way. Her Head Start caseworker got her into adult education classes, and she now volunteers in Head Start's lending library five mornings a week.

Marianne Tavares says she was wary of enrolling her son, David, in Head Start because "you hear so many bad things about day care." But now she is 'thrilled' with what the program has done for him. As for herself, she has recently been awarded her general equivalency diploma and is about to enroll in a nursing program at a local community college. "The staff here is like family," she said. "They helped me figure out what I want from my life."

Not all stories are so neat and clean. Given the recession, it is not clear how many of the more than 40 Head Start parents who have been placed in literacy or job training programs will be able to land jobs. And it is also not clear, when it comes to substance abuse, how much headway the Head Start staff will be able to make.

"No matter how much we reassure them, a lot of parents are suspicious that if they talk to us about their drug or alcohol problems, we'll take their kids away from them," said Vilma Riquelme, a family service case manager. "Sometimes, I sort of get the feeling they try to avoid me."

Head Start director Cabral tells the story of one 4-year-old who, during playtime, arranged sand the way someone would to sniff a line of cocaine. The family service worker paid a visit to the child's home. "The mother said her child must have seen that somewhere else—and that was the end of it," Cabral said. "People with substance abuse problems tend to be in denial. There's just so much we can do."

"It's no surprise that substance abuse has been the most difficult piece to put in place, but in some ways, it has the most potential," said Wade Horn, the federal official at the Department of Health and Human Services who oversee Head Start. "It's precisely because Head Start workers have the trust of the parents that they are in a position to do so much."

Anyone who has spent time in a Head Start center knows the bond between parent and staff can border on the magical—and has everything to do with the third party in the relationship, the child.

"Kids don't come with an instruction manual," said Sharon Piwinski, 27, a recently divorced mother of three who is on welfare, has two children in Head Start and volunteers as a classroom aide. "Head Start has made me a much better parent. I don't scream at my kids as much. I let them feed themselves, clothe themselves, do all sorts of things I'd always insisted on doing for them. My son is a different person. He doesn't throw his little tantrums anymore; he doesn't hit his head on the refrigerator when he gets mad."

Parents have been delivering these kinds of testimonials for 27 years, and they explain why the program seems to grow in popularity with each passing year—even as expectations of how much lasting impact it can have on the lives of poor children have been adjusted steadily downward.

When President Lyndon B. Johnson launched Head Start in 1965, his rhetoric reflected the lofty optimism of a society that thought it could conquer poverty in the span of a generation: "This program means that 30 million man-years the combined life span of the youngsters—will be spent productively and rewardingly, rather than wasted in tax-supported institutions or in welfare-supported lethargy." Since then, the great bulk of Head Start research has shown that while the program does produce short-term gains for preschoolers in academic readiness and social skills, these gains wash away in a year or two unless there is intensive follow-up in elementary school.

"I don't know why anyone should be surprised by that—if Head Start really could inoculate kids against all of the ravages of poverty, then we could get rid of the rest of the domestic budget and put all our money into it," said Horn. "But these kids go back to families that are mired in multiple generations of welfare dependency, to schools that are run down, to neighborhoods that are riddled with violence. There's no magic potion."

The Bush administration does believe there are smart investments. Its proposed 1993 budget calls for a $600 million increase in Head Start funding—the largest annual boost ever—to $2.8 billion. After lagging inflation during the 1980s, Head Start's budget will have virtually doubled in real dollars between 1989 and 1992.

Democrats would like to do still more. Sen. Edward M. Kennedy (D-Mass.), Head Start's foremost champion in Congress, is sponsoring a bill that would increase Head Start spending to $8 billion a year by 1997 and would guarantee that the program cover all income-eligible 3-, 4- and 5-year-olds, rather than the roughly one-third now served. Arkansas Gov. Bill Clinton, the man presumed to become the Democratic Party's presidential nominee, supports increases on a similar scale.

But while partisan differences remain over the speed and trajectory of Head Start expansion, there's little debate about the wisdom of the approach. For all of its successes, Head Start has shown that no short-term intervention can undo the ravages of poverty. When poor kids grow up and have kids of their own, says Somerville's Hamilton, "it's a good time to get another shot at them."

May 18, 1992

Why Head Start Needs a Re-Start
Poverty, Violence Threaten the Gains

DOUGLAS J. BESHAROV

The Head Start manual does not say what to do when the staff finds a decapitated body in the playground, or when a group of 4-year-olds finds a pile of used hypodermic needles and starts sticking each other with them. But it should, because in any high-poverty area in the country you can hear similar stories from the staff of preschool programs.

Since its inception in 1965, Head Start has been on the front lines of America's fight against poverty. But it now faces challenges never imagined in the simpler '60s. As a result, a growing number of experts are concluding that the traditional Head Start model needs to be beefed-up so that it can respond to sharply deteriorating family and neighborhood conditions.

Head Start began as a six-week summer experiment in using child development services to help fight the original War on Poverty. It quickly became a year-round, though not full-year, program and now serves about 600,000 children at an annual cost of approximately $2.2 billion.

Head Start is one of the nation's most popular anti-poverty programs. In 1980, President Carter praised it as "a program that works"; President Reagan included Head Start in the "safety net"; and President Bush has almost doubled its funding. Last week, he proposed a further increase of $600 million—the largest one-year increase in its history. With that, the program could give almost all eligible children at least one year of Head Start.

Head Start's impact on the immediate well-being of disadvantaged children is unambiguously impressive. "Children's health is improved through the program; immunization rates are better; participants have a better diet, better dental health, better access to health and social services; their self-esteem and cognitive abilities are improved; parents are educated and become involved both as volunteers and employees," according to Milton Kotelchuck and Julius B. Richmond writing in Pediatrics, the Journal of the American Academy of Pediatrics.

These are important gains, but Head Start's popularity is based on the widespread impression that it lifts poor children out of poverty by improving their learning ability and school performance. Unfortunately, actual evidence on this score is disappointing.

Claims that Head Start "works" stem largely from widely—and systematically—publicized research conducted at the Perry Preschool Project of Ypsilanti, Mich. In the early 1960s, researchers began tracking 123 3- and 4-year-old children to determine whether a five-day-a-week, 2 1/2-hour-a-day program (for either one or two years), reinforced by teacher visits to the home, would make a difference in the lives of impoverished children.

They found that children who had this preschool experience fared much better than a control group without it. On a test of functional competency in adult education courses, those who went through the program were more than 50 percent more likely to score at or above the national average than those who did not. Employment and post-secondary education rates were almost double; the high school graduation rate was almost one-third higher; teenage pregnancy rates were almost half; and arrest rates were 40 percent lower. A small number of other research projects report similar, though not as spectacular, success.

Lost in the publicity, however, is the fact that it is based almost entirely on non-Head Start programs, which tend to be better funded and professionally staffed. More importantly, most of this research was conducted many years ago under very different conditions of poverty. Indeed, the final report of the Cornell Consortium for Longitudinal Studies, one of the other major research projects on the subject, specifically warned that "caution must be exercised in making generalizations (about its findings) to Head Start."

When researchers study actual Head Start programs, the findings are less impressive. The most complete assessment of past Head Start research was the "Head Start Evaluation, Synthesis and Utilization Project," conducted for the Department of Health and Human Services in 1985. After reviewing 1,600 documents, including the results of 210 Head Start research projects, the study found that the educational and social gains registered by Head Start children disappear within two years, at which time there are "no educationally meaningful differences" between Head Start and non-Head Start children.

The absence of long-term gains among children in Head Start programs should not be taken as an indication of failure. Even the much-touted Perry Preschool had what can only be described as mixed success in breaking deep-seated patterns of poverty and welfare dependency—the point being that social and academic advances do not come automatically with a child's enrollment in a preschool program, no matter how good the program.

Programs like Head Start can do only so much to combat the powerful family and community forces that combine to keep families in persistent poverty. (In 1990, the blue-ribbon Advisory Panel for the Head Start Evaluation Design Project warned that early education and intervention programs such as Head Start "should not be oversold," they are not a "panacea.") It is unrealistic to expect the Head Start experience—about four hours a day for about eight months for one year—to overcome such powerful negative experiences as poor prenatal experiences and low birth-weight, inadequate nutrition, parental drug abuse, domestic or neighborhood violence and a host of other systematic degradations.

Moreover, Head Start is serving an increasingly troubled part of the poverty population. Many Head Start programs have, in effect, become child-care ghettos for low-income mothers who collect AFDC (Aid to Families With Dependent Children) rather than work. About 68 percent of all Head Start children are on AFDC, a figure that has climbed steadily over the years.

Parental substance abuse has become a particularly serious problem. "One out of every five preschool children is affected in some way by substance abuse," according to a Head Start Bureau handbook for grantees. The Central Vermont Head Start/Family Foundations program reported, for example, that one-third to two-thirds of its families had substance abuse problems in the home, that 40 percent of its mothers had their first child as a teenager and that 32 percent of the parents had no high school diploma or GED. (Thankfully, those preschoolers who were playing with hypodermic needles still test negative for the HIV virus.)

Among 5,000 families in one demonstration preschool program, five, and perhaps six, mothers died violent deaths in less than a year—17 times the violent death rate for women 15-24 in the population as a whole. But the violence goes both ways: One mother shot the caseworker assigned to her preschooler's class because the mother thought the worker was dating her boyfriend.

"It's amazing that more people who are working with children coming from homes and neighborhoods with these kinds of problems don't throw up their hands in despair," says Jean Layzer, a senior analyst for Abt Associates in Boston who has been studying preschool programs for 16 years.

Many of those who work with disadvantaged children have now concluded that, to counteract the intergenerational transmission of poverty, they must focus their services on both the child and the parent. "In the old days, we used to say, 'Give us children for a few hours a day and we will save them,'" says Wade Horn, the commissioner of

HHS's Administration for Children, Youth and Families and the senior federal administrator for the Head Start program. "Now we know that we have to work within the entire family context, that, if we are going to save children, we have to save the family, and that means working with the parents."

Thus, a 1989 Department of Health and Human Services study reported that 84 percent of all Head Start programs had used staff time and other resources to address family problems unrelated to child care. There is even a name for the revised approach: "two-generation programming" and it has three interrelated elements:

Reaching disadvantaged children much earlier with more intensive developmental services: Head Start and other early childhood education programs tend to focus on 3- and 4-year-olds, but by then the damage to young minds may already have been done. Program innovators are now experimenting with ways to involve 2-year-olds, and even 1-year-olds, in a much richer and more diverse set of developmental activities. (For example, there are now 100 Parent and Child Centers that provide instruction on infant care and child development to parents of children under 3, and in 1988, Congress funded the Comprehensive Child Development Program, a five-year demonstration project for pregnant women and mothers with children under age 1.)

Helping low-income parents to nurture and teach their own children: There is only so much that a child development program can do in the few hours that it has with a child. Thus, many local Head Start programs now provide concrete instruction for parents in infant and child care, health care, and nutrition. (Washington's Wider Opportunities for Women program has a slogan: "Teach the mother and reach the child.") Some also provide a range of more general support services for disadvantaged young parents; to assist these efforts, in 1991, Head Start Bureau funded 32 substance-abuse projects in local centers and 11 Family Support Projects for such problems as teenage pregnancy, homelessness and family violence.

Encouraging unemployed parents to work or continue their education: Being a good parent requires a healthy degree of self-respect. And, these days, with so many middle-class mothers working, self-respect -even for single mothers—means being economically self-sufficient, or at least partially so.

To help single mothers who have poor job-related skills and little work experience, Head Start programs have started to provide (or arrange for the provision of) various self-sufficiency services, including literacy classes, employment counseling and job training. Some Head Start programs are encouraging mothers to obtain work and job training under the Job Opportunities and Basic Skills program (JOBS) by providing full-day care.

In Washington, Head Start staff members work informally with the D.C. Department of Employment Services to ensure that spaces are reserved in its JOBS training programs for Head Start parents. Children are eligible for extended day care only if their parent are working or in job training full-time.

Up to now, individual Head Start programs have used their own funds, and the Head Start Bureau has used time-limited research projects, to provide two-generational services, at least on a small scale. So the president's budget proposal, which almost doubles funding for two-generational services—to $120 million—is a welcome enrichment of the Head Start program.

The impetus for this two-generational programming comes from local service providers, child advocacy groups and federal administrators who see first-hand the inability of current Head Start services to break patterns of deep-seated poverty.

No one knows, however, whether these kinds of parent-oriented services will work any better than the basic Head Start model. To find out, we will need a long-term effort to develop and test alternate program designs—a nationwide demonstration whose scope and status is equal to the original Head Start project: a "Project New Start," if you will.

Such a demonstration would be expensive and difficult to mount, but ignoring Head Start's problems—and failing to pursue the promise of two-generational programs—would be unfair to the disadvantaged children and families Head Start is meant to serve. They deserve the best we can deliver.

Douglas Besharov is a resident scholar at the American Enterprise Institute for Public Policy Research. Amy Fowler and Karen Baehler, both of AEI, helped prepare this article, which is based on a longer version in the forthcoming issue of American Enterprise Magazine.

February 2, 1992

Expecting Too Much from National Tests

It's Like Hoping a New Thermometer Will Warm a Cold Room

WILLIAM RASPBERRY

Brace yourself for the next irrelevancy posing as a cure for what ails public education. Get ready for the Great Testing Debate.

The people who have been plumping for a national test of what our children are learning just got a big boost. The congressionally appointed National Council on Education Standards and Testing (NCEST) has recommended the establishment of national standards for each subject and tests to see how well those standards are met. Education Secretary Lamar Alexander predicts the tests will be in use, on a voluntary basis, within three years.

Is that, as Colorado Gov. Roy Romer, the council's co-chairman, believes, "a turning point in American education"? Or is it, as some educators fear, just another attempt to embarrass the public schools without giving them the means to do better?

The correct answer (and the one least likely to be given by the partisans on either side of the incipient controversy) is: Neither.

Anyone who believes that national standards and national testing will cure the schools must also believe that the problem with education is that we don't know what we want our children to learn. But anyone who doesn't want you to know how the students in your school stack up against their counterparts across the nation thinks you wouldn't like the answer.

What NCEST (who dreamed up that acronym?) is recommending is not the standardized tests already in place in most of the country—the academic achievement tests, SATs and the rest. These are tests of general knowledge and designed primarily to see how much test-takers know in relation to other test-takers. The tests being advocated would measure students not against one another but against specific standards for specific curricula.

And what's the problem with that? Two things. First, the standards and tests don't exist and may be harder than generally believed to devise. Second, it isn't all that clear that Americans want a uniform curriculum in all academic subjects.

"There would be no problem agreeing on certain basics within every curricular focus," says Michael H. Kean, an executive of a major publisher of tests. "Here's the problem. If you stop at these basic, minimum requirements, you haven't accomplished anything very valuable. But if you go on to set higher standards, you move inevitably toward a national plain-vanilla curriculum that may leave no one pleased." For instance, he said in a telephone interview from CTB Macmillan/McGraw-Hill, where he is vice president for public and governmental affairs, Philadelphia social studies classes may place a heavy emphasis on what went on in and around Philadelphia during the Revolutionary War. San Francisco schools, while also teaching the revolution, may put more stress on the westward movement or the Gold Rush. In history, in geography, in literature, says Kean, there would be little consensus—nor much need for it.

But there are points to be made on the other side. Parents are interested in knowing how their children compare with other children, whether within the school district or across the country. Employers would like to know that a diploma has some meaning no matter where it was issued. Voluntary national tests would be a way of making useful judgments about individual graduates from different parts of the country.

One of the reasons German employers have such confidence in the national apprenticeship program, for instance, is the fact that every apprentice in a particular field studies the same curriculum and is certified by the same test.

There may, in fact, be merit in pushing for similar national standards here and for tests to judge how well those standards are met. That's a debate we ought to have.

What we are likely to get is an argument suggesting that national tests are a way to fix underperforming schools, to bring them up to the standards established by, say, middle-class schools in the suburbs.

But poorly performing schools are hardly a state secret. Parents, teachers and the students themselves know where the bad schools are— even if they don't know how to improve them.

To believe that voluntary national standards and tests will improve poor schools is to believe that voluntary engine performance standards and fancy new digital speedometers will make cars run better, or that a new thermometer will take the chill off a cold room.

A test may tell you that something needs to be done, but it won't tell you what, or how or who is going to pay for it.

February 3, 1992

Subtracting Multiple Choice from Tests
Pioneering Program Requires Students to Analyze, Explain Answers

MARY JORDAN

Inside the yellow brick school at the corner of Chestnut and Dupont, Sandy Genett has mothballed the nationwide multiple choice tests that American schoolchildren have taken since World War II.

Instead, she is a pioneer, one of 450 teachers in 17 states administering the first large-scale pilot of a radically new testing program that requires students to analyze and explain their answers. If successful, these exams could mark the first fundamental shift in decades in the way American students are evaluated.

Backed by President Bush, Democratic front-runner Bill Clinton and many members of the business community, this type of test is also being counted on to improve classroom instruction. Millions of dollars, from private and government sources, have been used to develop these tests.

"This is probably the biggest, most important thing happening in education," said Diane S. Ravitch, assistant education secretary for educational research and improvement. "There has been a lot of criticism about multiple choice tests, but it is the first time the Department of Education has lent its prestige and support for the need for change."

The current standardized test, for instance, might ask if the average 10-year-old watches a) 2 b) 4 or c) 6 hours of television a day. But the new type of test would require students to analyze TV viewing data, graph the results and write an essay on the subject.

Unlike the current standardized tests, there is no fixed time limit for the exam and, for the first time, instead of being scored according to how well he or she fares against other students, the student would be measured against "national standards" or a baseline of knowledge.

"This is far more than a change in the testing process, this is a fundamental change in education," said Frank Newman, president of the Education Commission of the States, a group that will convene 700 educators next month to discuss the new system.

"The fallout," Newman said, "is you can't run the classroom the same way anymore."

Christopher T. Cross, executive director of the education initiative at the Business Roundtable, a group of 214 chief business executives, said the Roundtable threw its weight behind the new performance exams because most students, in the view of industry, are graduating from high school without the skills required for jobs.

"The feeling is we need to make assessments more related to authentic uses of how knowledge is applied," Cross said.

But even though many states—including Delaware, Maryland, California, Connecticut and Kentucky—are moving fast toward completely changing over to the new tests, there still are many obstacles to eliminating the No. 2 pencil from testing nationwide.

High cost is one of them.

Because multiple choice tests can be scored by a computer scanning pencil marks, they are relatively inexpensive—costing from $3 to $7 per student. While price estimates for the still-developing new system vary wildly, they run from four times to 60 times the current cost.

Maryland, which last year scrapped multiple choice exams and has tested about 170,000 students on exams that required teachers to evaluate written responses, said its cost went from an estimated $5 per student to about $20 per student.

Although international comparisons are difficult to make, educators have testified before Congress that in Ireland a five-subject essay-style exam costs $135 per student. Costs would be even higher when teacher training time and classroom instruction time demanded by the new tests are added, some experts said.

"So what if the old tests only cost $5?" said Robert Gabrys, Maryland's assistant state superintendent for school performance. "Who wants to pay for something that isn't working? We got into these new systems because we want students to learn."

But Michael H. Kean, vice president in charge of public and governmental affairs for the CTB MacMillan/McGraw-Hill, the largest publisher of the current standardized tests, said he believes the country is unwisely latching onto a testing system as a panacea to fix bad schooling. He contends that it is unwise to "throw the baby out with the bath water," and that there is some place for multiple choice tests that cover a lot of ground cheaply.

In addition to cost, others warn that if "high stakes" are attached to the tests, such as a national ranking of students or schools, or a pegging of student graduation to passing test scores, it could place minority students and those in bad schools at a disadvantage.

"I think the new tests are first-rate," said Theodore R. Sizer, professor of education at Brown University and chairman of the group Coalition of Essential Schools. "But I think it is exceedingly unwise to tie them into a national set of standards. Who sets the standards and by what right do they do it?"

He said, "It's very hard for some kids to compete against a national standard if some kids are in good schools and some kids are in poor schools."

Sizer was one of 50 prominent educators who this year signed a statement of concern about the proposed national standards and testing system. They said they fear some students would be unfairly penalized by the exams and that the hallmark of the American education system—that it is locally controlled—would be abandoned.

The congressional Office of Technology Assessment, in a February report, also advised applying brakes to the momentum "building rapidly" for the new national tests. Among the questions raised: Will grading standards be clear? What happens to students who don't test well? Is this the best use of money for education?

Lauren Resnick and Marc Tucker, directors of the New Standards Project, which developed the pilot test administered in Gennet's Delaware classroom last week and in 16 other states and which is funded by a $2.5 million grant from the Pew Charitable Trusts and the MacArthur Foundation, contend that national standards and a new examination system can be devised that will satisfy all the concerns.

"What we are proposing is a system in which assessing kids' performance will be indistinguishable from the method we use to teach them," said Tucker, who is also the president of the National Center on Education and the Economy.

The National Council of Teachers of Mathematics had already reached a consensus on standards for math, which were incorporated in the pilot in Genett's class.

By summer, Ravitch said similar standards projects will have been launched in six additional subjects: history, science, geography, civics, the arts and English.

She expects that it will take two to three years before the standards in all these subjects will be agreed upon. More time would then be needed to develop new tests to measure how well students meet those standards.

But no matter how long it takes to put the new national standards in place for every subject, or even if the standards are never adopted, the movement toward the new task-oriented tests is clear. Almost half of all American schoolchildren live in states that have signed on as partners to the New Standards Project. That spells a probable end to the reign of the multiple choice tests that began after World War II but which became more widespread after the 1960s when computer scoring of them became available.

Sandy Genett, the instructor in room 2A at Bayard Intermediate, said she believes the time has come to admit that teachers teach what students are tested on.

"We have got to spend less time drilling basic skills," she said, "and teach them higher levels of thinking."

Robert Bies, an "A" student in Genett's class, is a veteran of both the old and new tests.

'You get a little bored sometimes with the old ones," the 10-year-old Bies acknowledged last week. "It's basically a review of things you learn, like how much is 4 x 8. The new ones make you do more with your brain."

Classmate Kurt Seibel said he was "feeling pretty much bad lately" because of all the news about how poor American students are doing. "If they expect us to pass harder tests," he reasoned, "I bet we will."

May 18, 1992

3 The Profession of Teaching

Letter to the Teacher of the Year

COLMAN MCCARTHY

Is success, plus $2,000 speaking fees, about to cause Rae Ellen McKee to lose her head, and possibly her students? She is the 1991 National Teacher of the Year, an award that brought a congratulating President Bush to Slanesville, W. Va., where McKee, 33, has been a reading teacher for 11 years. Most of that time, she's earned well below $20,000. Now, her income is $24,000, equal to what she can earn for 12 half-hour speeches on the lecture circuit and less than a fourth of the $100,000-a-year salary some corporations have been offering.

After her award, McKee took a year off from her classroom to travel the country meeting politicians, educators and being interviewed—and now she tells of being tempted to leave permanently. She said last week: "Now I have a platform and a voice. I feel I have to stand up and help bring about the changes teachers need. And if I were back teaching, I'm not sure I could do that."

Before it's too late, write to Rae Ellen McKee and tell this valued and gifted teacher not to become a former teacher. Here's the letter I'm sending, C/O Slanesville Elementary School, Slanesville, W. Va. 25444.

Dear Ms. McKee:

Please, stay put. You're more needed by your children at Slanesville Elementary than in front of a microphone or behind a corporate desk. Dime-a-dozen $2,000 speeches won't reform American education. If lecture hall windbaggery was effective, our school problems would have been solved long ago. Leave the big talk to such big mouths as William Bennett, the former secretary of education and acclaimed know-it-all. He has all the answers to every question from how to pad on more homework to denying college kids their stereos. But he is irrelevant compared with you. He talks, you act.

When we spoke on the phone the other morning—you were just back from speaking in Las Vegas—you mentioned having enough invitations to be booked for the next three years. School districts, teachers' conferences, state education groups and businesses want you. I can't imagine, though, that your students won't want you more. That you have been taking care of their wants, and needs, so remarkably well is why you were voted national teacher of the year.

Your choice is between shaping minds or shaping policy. You've had students in the past 11 years. Would their lives have been fuller or lesser if you had been elsewhere? Will the next 800 students in the coming decade be intellectually and spiritually richer or poorer if you aren't there for them? I say poorer. If you leave, you'll be richer financially. But how about emotionally or spiritually?

On the lecture circuit, you'll be battling for your kids, of course, at least in theory. You'll adorn advisory boards, national education commissions and be on task forces with Theodore Hesburgh and assorted heavyweights. You'll have access to the mighty and pseudo-mighty, and be able to broker your views, which, as you told me, is your goal: "Somehow I've been invited in on agendas at state and national levels. I have a platform now. I really hate to break off that network when I know that I'm the only teacher invited to forums where some real policy and business kind of decisions are being made on education. I hate to break that."

Here's a suggestion: Tell the big shots to come to you. George Bush did. Stage an annual summer education conference at Slanesville Elementary. It might be the first time in years the educational experts have been inside a schoolhouse without a camera crew in tow.

My fear is that you'll leave the classroom and within a few years sound like all the other talkers who have run out of ideas but not self-importance. They gab about reform, but does it have substance if they aren't in the classrooms with children and drawing their ideas from there and them? You need to keep teaching for your own benefit, otherwise you may end up dependent only on the past: "Back in the days when I taught at Slanesville Elementary" is how your speeches will begin. You'll get yawns, not applause.

Last summer in USA Weekend, you were asked how you motivate yourself. Your memorable answer: "I don't motivate myself. My kids motivate me. I get such a high out of seeing my kids learn to read. Apathetic kids usually are apathetic because the teacher is teaching them something that they see no relevance for in their life."

If you aren't in the classroom replacing apathy with relevance, who will do it? On the platform, you'll be just another expert describing the problems facing American education. In the classroom, you're the solution. Your kids know this, and I think you do too.

July 4, 1992

Instilling Students with a Love for Teaching

New D.C. School Program Lays Foundation for Classroom Careers

RENE SANCHEZ

Have a seat and watch Meta Jones teach. From atop a creaky stool inside a Coolidge High classroom, Jones is batting questions and fielding answers, pointing, prodding, shouting, smiling and moving in lightning-bolt bursts that have three effects: Heads are up, hands are high, and she's out of breath.

Jones, a 15-year-old Coolidge sophomore, is leading a spirited discussion about the history of education in the United States. As she conducts class, her teacher, Judith Shipley, offers friendly advice from the sidelines of the room.

"Remember," Shipley says, "a good teacher always gets to the main point."

Jones nods, agrees, yet still can't slow down. "I know you're probably going to hate me after this," she announces in a shy laugh to the class of her peers, all of whom are also aspiring teachers. "But I promise, I'll still be your friend."

Welcome to the first month of an ambitious new teacher-training project the D.C. school system has launched at Coolidge Senior High in Northwest Washington.

At least seven years before they can begin classroom careers, Jones and 29 other Coolidge freshmen and sophomores have begun an academic adventure that will make most of their high school days a dress rehearsal for teaching.

The program starts amid a flurry of national studies revealing a critical need for minority hiring in the teaching field during the next decade.

Coolidge's Teaching Professions Program, one of only a few of its kind in the country, is a school within a school: The aspiring young teachers, selected from around the city, supplement standard high school classes with a special string of education, speech, computer and humanities courses.

As high school seniors, in the final part of the four-year grooming plan, each student will be required to visit a city public school regularly and assist a full-time teacher. And if upon graduation the Coolidge students agree to teach at least three years in D.C. public schools, they will be guaranteed financial aid for college.

"Our goal is to prepare future teachers to understand that teaching is not just a vocation, it's a devotion," said Josie Paige, director of the program.

"If we're going to improve our efforts in the classroom, we have got to have teachers who feel that way every day."

Paige said she expects 200 other students, across four grade levels, to be participating by the time this year's ground-breaking class graduates from Coolidge, at Fifth and Tuckerman streets NW.

And along with other advocates of the project, she said she hopes it becomes a strong step in what soon will be an extraordinary struggle to attract and retain quality teachers in the city's public schools.

District school officials predict that nearly half of the city's public school teachers will reach retirement age by 1993.

Replacing them will not be easy: Suburban schools offer more money, and are striving to hire more minority teachers.

"In the next decade, we expect to see a vast change in the teaching profession in our city," said Elizabeth Smith, director of corporate involvement for D.C. schools, who helped start the Coolidge program. "Somehow, we're going to have to find teachers willing to get involved with the social problems we have here."

Coolidge's effort resembles efforts that have begun in only a few other large cities, such as Houston and Los Angeles. All have the same mission: to convince teen-agers that teaching in inner-city schools is heroic work.

"Many teachers just don't see the inner-city as attractive," Paige said. "Where the need is greatest, that's where many of the best teachers are avoiding. With these students, our hope is to eliminate that fear."

The Coolidge class of future teachers already is receiving a daily dose of instruction on how important classroom work with city children is. This fall, the 30 students—27 girls and three boys—are enrolled in a course called "Orientation to the Teaching Profession," tracing the evolution of education from the Pilgrims to present-day situations.

"We do a lot of thinking," said Larnella Cartwright, a Coolidge freshman. "And we learn to teach kids how to do a lot of thinking." During one recent class, the aspiring teachers examined several historical questions: What were the colonial New England town schools like? Why is Noah Webster called "the Schoolmaster of the Republic"? How does the Supreme Court decision *Brown v. Board of Education of Topeka* affect minority students today?

Front and center in the old classroom, surrounded by their peers, and still seeming reticent, the students take turns leading the discussion.

"What were schools like in the southern colonies and who was educated?" Meta Jones asks.

"Blacks were never educated then," a classmate replies. "They had to sneak around if they wanted to learn."

"Even though Thomas Jefferson's 'Bill for the More General Diffusion of Knowledge' was never enacted," asks Said Chestnut, a sophomore, "what was its influence in American education?"

"Jefferson thought the government should help pay for schools," another student replies.

Amid the clamor, Shipley shouts teaching tips to those momentarily in charge: A good teacher waits until everyone is paying attention. A good teacher calls on shy students. A good teacher gets to the point.

"A lot of them don't have a strong perception yet of all that a teacher is, or can be," Shipley said after the students left for the day. "What we need to show is that teaching is a wonderful thing to do."

It was with that thought that former D.C. schools superintendent Floretta D. McKenzie suggested a teacher-training school a few years ago, and found financial support from the Eugene and Agnes E. Meyer Foundation and the Edna McConnell Clark Foundation.

Paige has spent the past year shaping the teaching curriculum, rounding up support from local universities and recruiting students. The Coolidge project was the ninth magnet school for careers to be placed in a D.C. public high school.

To be accepted as teacher trainees, students must have 2.5 grade point averages and submit an essay about teaching, and be interviewed. Paige is also creating two councils to help direct the program, one composed of the students' parents, the other of local business leaders.

Meanwhile, students such as Shalana Millard already speak with pride about their budding classroom careers. With but one month of practice, Millard said she believes she's just about figured out how to keep a class in order. And awake. And excited.

"What I would do is calm them down, tell them they just have to listen, and have to learn, because nothing is so important as this," Millard said, her eyes lit with confidence. "As a black person, I know I have to work extra hard to get ahead, and I want to make sure the next generations have the chances I have now."

October 17, 1988

A Late Call to the Classroom

Area Schools See Surge of Second-Career Teachers

STEPHEN BUCKLEY

Bricklayer Robert Simpson, homemaker Susan Berrington and lawyer Susan Okun labored for years before responding to the tug of the classroom. All three are now among the rush of "late deciders" who have chosen to become teachers.

"I became a teacher because I felt it was closer to my values," said Simpson, 42, a special education teacher at Columbia's Atholton High School who spent 13 years as a bricklayer. "At the end of the day, I feel invigorated. I like to think that what I'm doing has some constructive effect on humanity."

Okun, 28, was an environmental issues lawyer with the District firm Beveridge & Diamond before turning to teaching, a choice that will mean taking a $50,000 pay cut. "I wasn't interacting with people. . . . I always wanted to be a teacher. I felt if I didn't do it now, I would always wonder if I would like it," she said.

This spring Okun is a student teacher in Columbia in the seventh-grade classroom of Berrington, 47, who became a social studies teacher in 1987 because she "wanted some new challenges" after 15 years as a homemaker.

The number of "late deciders" receiving teaching certificates has exploded in recent years. From 1985 to 1989—the latest years for which figures are available—12,000 teachers were certified through programs designed for career-switching college graduates, according to the National Center for Education Information in Washington. Almost half were certified in the last two years of that five-year period. "There's an overwhelming interest in teaching today," said Emily Feistritzer, director of the information center and a specialist on second-career teachers. "People are concerned about America's education system, and they want to help. . . . They realize that money isn't all there is to life."

Principals say late deciders bring a wealth of knowledge and experience that is difficult to find in fresh-out-of-college instructors.

"That maturity works tremendously in their favor," said Scott Pfeifer, principal of Atholton High, which has several second-career teachers. "Anyone who's been a brand-new, 22-year-old teacher knows it's hard. Second-career teachers might be more thoughtful about wanting to be here. They've made a very conscious choice to be in the classroom. And that means a lot."

Late deciders have forsaken a bevy of career paths for teaching. They are former lawyers and computer analysts, musicians and military officers.

Some, like Okun, are taking tremendous pay cuts; others find teaching more rewarding financially than their old jobs. But for most, money apparently was not the deciding factor.

"I had a fairly interesting job, and I was making good money. But I wasn't making much direct impact on individuals. I just began to think that there might be a better way to affect people," said David Weisz, a former program analyst with the Department of Labor whose income plunged $30,000 when he became a third-grade teacher at Fairland Elementary School in Silver Spring two years ago.

Some second-career teachers encountered skepticism or discouragement when they told friends and family of their desire to change fields.

Grace Wai Wissman, 27, was an engineer at the Goddard Space Flight Center for three years before becoming an elementary school teacher in 1989. As a child, she harbored dreams of teaching, she said, but her family pushed her into engineering and tried to dissuade her from leaving it.

"My family was not happy," said Wissman, who teaches fourth-graders at Glenridge Elementary in Landover Hills. "They thought I was really nuts. Now, they see how happy I am, and they're glad."

Wissman is a graduate of the University of Maryland's late decider program, which began in 1985 with about 10 applicants. There are a record 203 applications for 25 slots for the 1991-92 school year.

A similar program at Marymount University in Arlington has grown from 25 students in the fall of 1987 to 179 last fall. The number of applicants for George Washington University's program rose from 45 in 1986 to about 140 last fall.

The number of Marylanders receiving teaching certificates through the alternate route program has risen rapidly in recent years, from eight in 1985 to 57 in 1989. Virginia does not keep comparable statistics.

"It's the wave of the future," said Clark Dobson, assistant dean of education at George Mason University. "Otherwise, we're missing out on the best pools of teachers we can have."

Feistritzer cites several reasons for the growing popularity of teaching as a second career. First, she said, many people reassessed their futures in light of the Department of Education prediction that there soon will be a national shortage of teachers.

Second, she said, "Not everyone can be a lawyer or an engineer. People are realizing that not everybody with a college degree can get big-money jobs."

Those factors have combined with a sense among many adults that the American educational system aches for dedicated teachers, Feistritzer said.

Teacher salaries, which once kept many people out of the profession, are now high enough to be alluring to some late deciders.

In 1979, salaries averaged $15,970, compared with $31,304 today. Adjusting for inflation, teachers' pay has climbed by about $4,400 during that time.

Salary was a significant factor for Vicki Ellison, 27, a fifth-grade teacher at Lemon Road Elementary in Falls Church. Ellison, who has a college degree in textiles, takes home about twice what she did as manager of a clothing store.

"When I was in retail, the pay was very poor," she said, "and the hours were really tough."

She decided to change direction in 1988, after getting her first taste of teaching during a trip to China. "It kind of hit me," she said, "that that's what I want to do."

She returned to the Washington area, enrolled in Marymount's program and began at Lemon Road Elementary last fall. She enjoys teaching immensely, she said, but the career change has required adjustments.

"These kids come to the classroom with so many problems. And that affects how they behave," Ellison said. "Some days, when someone is having a tough time, I'm not always sure what to do. You deal with it the best way you can."

Okun identifies with Ellison's struggle. "It's a very draining day," said Okun, who lives in Silver Spring. "Just learning about kids, how they behave, how they think, how they interact with each other. . . . But the toughest thing is being really creative with lessons. I find that to be an endless challenge."

Okun has learned lessons in creativity by watching Berrington. During a recent class at Owen Brown Middle School, Berrington held up a can of chocolate syrup, a bottle of tonic water with quinine, a bag of shredded coconut and a can of tapioca. Her students quickly figured out the connection: products of the rain forest.

Throughout the 42-minute period, Berrington juggled instruction with discipline: "What's quinine used for?. . . . If you want to say something, please raise your hand. . . . Where's Washington state on the map?. . . I'll wait until everyone's paying attention . . ."

She never raised her voice.

Berrington said she entered teaching out of a yearning to serve. "I had a lot of idealism instilled in me during the '60s when there was such an emphasis on contributing something to society," said the teacher, who was an insurance underwriter before rearing three children. "With teaching, it's always challenging, there's always something new. I feel like I'm in the middle of an experiment."

At Atholton High, Simpson's challenge is to build students' skills the way he once built walls. Standing in a restroom with a 16-year-old named Eric, Simpson slowly walked him through the 20-step process of face-washing. A sheet on the wall spells it out: 1. gets washcloth, 2. goes to sink, 3. turns on water, and so on.

Simpson has nine students, ages 14 to 19. They are mildly to profoundly retarded.

Simpson, who is in his fifth year of teaching after receiving a college degree through night school, said he became a special education instructor because "I thought it would be more interesting, more challenging, more meaningful to me to work with people with disadvantages.

"They say the median burnout for special ed teachers is as few as three years, but I don't feel at all burned out."

April 14, 1991

You're in the Army, Uh, School Now

Soldiers Encouraged to Become Teachers

JOHN LANCASTER

Before his retirement from the Army last year, Col. Albert Laferte thought he knew a thing or two about giving orders. But after a year teaching math to ninth graders, Laferte is a humbled man.

"It is a bit of a shock," said Laferte, who flew air transports in Vietnam and finished his 24-year Army career supervising 1,000 civilian employees as director of logistics at Fort Bragg, N.C. "In teaching, you've got to apply a lot of patience. You've got to moderate your voice."

The leap from soldier to teacher might seem improbable, but as the Cold War fades into history, it is one the Pentagon is trying hard to encourage.

Over the next four years, the U.S. military will shrink by 500,000 people, and the Defense Department wants to make the transition as painless as possible. From courses in resume writing to financial incentives, the military is pursuing a range of strategies to nudge soldiers, sailors and airmen into new lives as civilians.

Pentagon officials say the nation's public schools could be among the first to benefit. Borrowing a chapter from the education-reform movement, which has promoted the idea of recruiting teachers from nontraditional backgrounds, the departments of Defense and Education are attempting to steer college-educated military personnel toward new careers in the classroom.

States are increasingly "open to diverse types of academic backgrounds. . . . They want to inject competition into the teaching profession," said John Roddy, a senior policy analyst at the Education Department detailed to the Pentagon. "It just so happens that with the downsizing [of the military], we want to take advantage of this reservoir of potential."

Although the program dates to 1986, it has greatly expanded in the past few months, with the installation of toll-free "hot lines" to provide information on teaching careers to U.S. military personnel in the

United States, Germany and South Korea. Another information line is planned for Panama.

Pentagon officials say it is too early to judge the success of the teacher recruiting drive, which so far seems noteworthy chiefly for its symbolism. But officials said they were encouraged by the initial response to the stepped-up effort, which has included advertisements on the Armed Forces Network featuring Gen. Crosbie E. Saint, the Army's top commander in Europe.

"'When I asked them to set up the lines, I said, 'I don't know if the interest will be there,'" said Patricia Hines, deputy assistant secretary of defense for training and education. "The first month there were complaints that, 'We couldn't get through on the lines.'"

Since June 18, hot-line operators have logged more than 7,500 calls from U.S. military personnel ranging in rank "from major general to Pfc.," according to Roddy. The pool of prospective pedagogues is about evenly divided between officers and enlisted personnel, with the "vast majority" possessing college degrees, one official said.

"We've just had some amazing calls," Roddy said, recalling one from a sergeant with a music degree. "He'd been working in an Army band at Fort Hood, 20 years in the Army, and he wants to go back and be a high-school band director. . . . We've had several generals call."

Callers who inquire about teaching careers are provided with information on state "alternative certification" programs, which typically combine streamlined training in education techniques with closely supervised, hands-on schoolroom experience.

Some education professionals have expressed doubts whether skills learned on the parade ground will translate to the classroom, but officials say the transition is a natural one. "We recognize the unique skills that members of the military have with regard to teaching," said Roddy. "Being a former Army officer myself, I can tell you that every officer and noncom [noncommissioned officer] is taught to prepare a lesson plan and how to give instruction."

Today's Army also likes to boast of its academic credentials. Of nearly 86,000 Army officers, 99.2 percent have college degrees, although the figure is much lower—about 2.6 percent—for enlisted personnel. Many acquire their degrees while serving in the military, using various tuition grants offered by the armed forces.

Laferte, the ninth-grade math teacher, was one of them. A New Hampshire native trained as an Army pilot, Laferte spent two tours of Vietnam flying air transports and Chinook helicopters, sometimes into dangerous combat zones. Later, he served in a variety of supervisory positions, generally involving logistics and maintenance.

Along the way, he picked up "a course here and a course there" before earning a bachelor's degree in aeronautical science—"a cheap engineering degree," as he called it—at Embry-Riddle Aeronautical University in Daytona Beach, Fla.

Laferte said he always had been interested in teaching, and that the idea became more attractive as he contemplated his retirement while serving at Fort Bragg. He learned of the alternative-certification route through a promotional video at the officer's club, and soon afterward began taking education courses at nearby Fayetteville State University.

Laferte said he found the adjustment a difficult one, but feels comfortable after a year on the job at Pine Forest Junior High School in Fayetteville, N.C. "The teaching business is not all imparting knowledge," he said. "A lot of it is managing people, and I know how to manage people."

September 5, 1991

4 America 2000

Bush Unveils Education Plan
Local Innovation, Parental Involvement
Stressed in Setting Goals for '90s

JOHN E. YANG

Calling for "a true renaissance in American education," President Bush yesterday unveiled a strategy for improving U.S. public schools that would leave most of the details to states and local communities.

"If we want America to remain a leader, a force for good in the world, we must lead the way in educational innovation," Bush told a group of congressional, business and education leaders in the East Room of the White House. "Think about every problem, every challenge we face. The solution to each starts with education."

By the end of the century, Bush said, he wants educators to ensure that all children have adequate preschool programs and that U.S. students meet basic competency requirements in core subjects, rank first in the world in mathematics and science achievement, attend drug-free schools and have a high school graduation rate of 90 percent. He also wants to end illiteracy.

To accomplish these goals, the president proposed revamping performance standards for schools, creating different kinds of schools for future students, encouraging those now in the work force to continue their educations and urging parents to become more involved in their childrens' education than they are now.

The federal government's role would be small. "People who want Washington to solve their educational problems are missing the point," Bush said. "What happens here in Washington won't matter half as much as what happens in each school, each local community and, yes, in each home."

Bush noted that school districts across the nation already have begun implementing innovations on their own. "They know the time for talk is over," he said. "Their slogan is: Don't dither. Just do it."

The federal price tag would be small, too—only about $820 million of the Education Department's $27.1 billion budget for the fiscal year that begins Oct. 1. Most of the money, $550 million, would go to help establish more than 535 special schools to demonstrate innovative educational techniques, at least one in each congressional district.

Another $230 million would fund locally devised programs that would allow parents to choose the schools their children attend—whether public, private or parochial—and $40 million would fund a grant program to reward student achievement.

"It's not a program, it is a crusade," Education Secretary Lanar Alexander told reporters later.

Bush's proposal, intended to make good on his 1988 campaign vow "to be the education president," comes more than 18 months after he and the nation's governors agreed on a set of goals for public schools at a much-heralded education summit at the University of Virginia and sore than a year since the governors adopted the goals that Bush embraced yesterday.

Perhaps more importantly, it comes less than a year before Bush is expected to formally launch his campaign for reelection. Indeed, the day had a campaign flavor to it, with a series of high-profile meetings and events.

Administration officials acknowledge that they hope the initiative will insulate Bush from charges that he has no domestic agenda. Because the goals are long-range, there will not be any yardstick by which to measure Bush's accomplishments in next year's campaign.

"Will the education issue decide the next presidential election? The answer is, of course it won't," said Alexander, who developed the proposals in his first month on the job. "There's going to be no great transformation of American education between now and next year."

But education is a major concern to Americans. According to the most recent *Washington Post*–ABC News poll, conducted earlier this month, seven out of 10 of those questioned said the nation is not "making enough progress" on public schools and education.

Increasingly the public is counting on Republicans to guide that progress, according to the same survey. Asked which party they trust "to do a better job improving education," the answers were evenly split between Democrats and Republicans. Asked the same question in January, more people picked the Democrats.

Eager to assert their own claim to primacy in education, congressional Democrats welcomed Bush's proposals but characterized them for the most part as thinly disguised imitations of Democratic initiatives that Republican administrations and lawmakers have been blocking for years.

House Majority Leader Richard A. Gephardt (D-Mo.) said the president's plan "falls short" of the "radical reform" necessary to improve U.S. education and economic productivity. "Had the Founding Fathers adopted this definition of revolutionary change, America would still be part of England," he said. Sen. Edward M. Kennedy (D-Mass.), chairman of the Labor and Human Resources Committee, which beat the administration to the punch Wednesday by approving a Democratic education bill, said the proposals were "too little, too late."

In recent weeks, Bush's focus on education has been highlighted by visits to schools. Yesterday he pledged to do more. To encourage workers to go back to school, he said, "Starting next week, I'll begin studying, and I want to know how to operate a computer. . . . I want to be computer-literate, and I'm not."

Called America 2000, and described as a "long-term strategy . . . not a federal program," for achieving national education goals.

The Goals:

1. All children start school ready to learn.
2. At least 90% graduate from high school.
3. Students demonstrate competency in "challenging subject matter" including English, math, science, history and geography.
4. U.S. students lead the world in math and science achievement.
5. Every adult American is literate.
6. Every school is free of drugs and violence.

Key Parts of the Plan:

National standards will be developed for five core subjects: English, math, science, history and geography.

A new, voluntary nationwide examination system called the American Achievement Tests will be developed. Colleges will be urged to use the exam results in admissions; employers will be urged to pay attention to them in hiring.

Report cards will be encouraged as a way to keep parents abreast of students' progress and monitor the nation's progress toward education goals.

Increased salaries will be encouraged for those who teach well, who teach core subjects, who teach in dangerous or challenging settings, or who serve as mentors for new teachers.

American business leaders will be encouraged to establish and solicit support for a new nonprofit organization that will award contracts to research and development teams. The teams will develop nontraditional approaches to education in communities.

Each community may develop a plan to create one of the first "New American Schools" with limited federal support for start-up costs. Governors will review these plans, with the assistance of an advisory panel, and will determine which community in each state will receive federal help.

Business and labor will be asked to establish job-related skill standards and "skill certificates" The secretaries of Labor and Education will spearhead a public-private partnership to help develop voluntary standards for all industries.

April 19, 1991

The Artless Education Compromise
Critics Say Plan for Schools Overlooks Creative Side

KIM MASTERS

George Bush may claim to be the Education President, but he never said anything about being the Arts President. Maybe that's why the arts are ignored in the administration's "America 2000" education strategy—despite repeated appeals from leaders of the arts community.

Those heavyweights—including Kennedy Center Chairman James Wolfensohn, National Gallery of Art Director J. Carter Brown, National Endowment for the Humanities Chairman Lynne Cheney and the rest of the President's Committee on the Arts and the Humanities—scored only minor success in their campaign.

Through some strenuous lobbying, they managed recently to squeeze the words "artistic expression" into a document describing key ingredients that should be incorporated into designs for model schools. The description was formulated by the New American Schools Development Corp. (NASDC)—a nonprofit organization that is supposed to commission model-school designs as part of the president's program.

Two words? So much for Leonardo, Beethoven, Shakespeare and all three Bronte sisters? That's hardly what the President's Committee had hoped for when it suggested an allusion to "the visual arts, the performing arts, literature, the history and aesthetics of the arts, and the media and design arts."

"I can safely say that we're all very, very disappointed in the results, and somewhat mystified," says Diane Paton, executive director of the committee.

The administration responds, via Etta Fielek, spokeswoman for Education Secretary Lamar Alexander, that no one means to exclude the arts (or foreign languages—the other most-protested omission). Instead, the education program is meant to be flexible. "Lanar has told people if it was his school district, he would include the arts and foreign languages," Fielek says.

America 2000 is an ambitious plan to cut the dropout rate, enhance education and eliminate drugs and violence from schools by the turn of the century. Students are expected to become competent in "English, mathematics, science, history and geography," according to the administration. Materials describing America 2000 emphasize science and mathematics, not the humanities.

The program is not long on federal funding. It relies in part on the development of "break-the-mold" school programs under the auspices of NASDC. But the organization's plan to come up with $90 million from corporate sources by 1992 has faltered in recent months. It has $36 million so far but most of that was raised last spring.

NASDC plans to select teams to design new schools and help communities use those designs. As a first step, the organization is seeking proposals from prospective design teams.

Kennedy Center Chairman Wolfensohn noticed that the arts were omitted when America 2000 was unveiled in April. He then wrote to Bush, urging a role for the arts in the program. And when NASDC started devising criteria for prospective design teams, he again urged that all applicants include the arts in their proposals.

In August, NASDC issued a draft of its criteria but made no mention of the arts. Wolfensohn fired off another letter. This time, he proposed language stating that designs for model schools should "take into consideration the role of nontraditional approaches, including but not limited to the role of performing and visual arts."

Wolfensohn also wanted language stating that inclusion of the arts would "strengthen the student's sense of worth and the likelihood of sustained academic achievement in a society that is increasingly multicultural."

A few weeks later, the President's Committee on the Arts and the Humanities got into the act. The committee met Oct. 3—the day before NASDC was to finalize its criteria for model-school designs—and hammered out its own suggested language. The committee urged that designs "take into consideration the vital role of the arts in education, including but not limited to such subjects as the visual arts, the performing arts, literature, the history and aesthetics of the arts, and the media and design arts."

Their language was faxed in haste to Camp David, where the NASDC board was mulling over its mission. The net result: The official 60-page request for proposals mentions in one section that they should "embody a strategy for integrating all facets of a school's life," including "artistic expression"—as well as "extracurricular activities, staff development and administration."

"I wouldn't declare it to be the greatest victory for the arts ever accomplished," concedes National Endowment for the Arts Chairman John Frohnmayer. "But it is a small victory."

Frohnmayer said he is surprised that merely gaining acknowledgment of "artistic expression" has proved such a struggle so far. "There are dozens of arts schools that perform far above standards," he says. "If we're going to crack the nut as far as education is concerned, we've got to use all the gifts of learning that human beings have."

The limited success of the President's Committee on the Arts and the Humanities is somewhat surprising because Barbara Bush is the honorary chairwoman, and close Bush friend Donald Hall, founder of Hallmark Card Inc., is chairman. (Hall did not respond to a request for comment.) The committee's Paton says she too doesn't understand why NASDC has been so resistant. "The arts and humanities have become so politicized in recent years. I guess this has to be the reason," she says. ". . . I think we're all mighty frustrated."

But NASDC Chairman Tom Kean says there's no mystery. "The problem is there are a tremendous number of people who have an interest in arts education, environmental education and several other areas," he says. "The feeling of the board as a whole was there were about six of those that people had legitimate reasons for [promoting]."

Instead of "driving" the applications in one direction, he says, "we wanted to be as unspecific as possible." The board stuck with the subjects that were outlined in the original America 2000 proposal (which in turn were based on a governors' education summit in 1989).

Kean says the arts may appear spontaneously despite their scanty mention. "My hope is that arts education will be an integral part of a number of these proposals," he says.

At the Education Department, Fielek says a letter will be sent to proponents of the arts and foreign languages explaining that the administration is not excluding those areas. She also points out that those subjects were mentioned in a September progress report by the National Education Goals Panel—a group of governors, administration members and three ex-officio congressmen. While America 2000 mentions other subjects, the report said, "A full appreciation of the fine arts and mastery of one or more foreign languages are examples of additional competencies that our schools must foster if we are to produce fully educated and well-rounded citizens of tomorrow."

If the arts are to get more recognition, the various factions of that world must unite to plot their next move, says Gerri Otremba, the Kennedy Center's director of government liaison. "The arts [community] has a tendency to factionalize and get involved in its own minutiae. We can squabble endlessly about whether a kid should be taught to play the violin or to draw. For this to succeed, people have to look at the big picture."

November 18, 1991

No "Radical Change" for Nation's Classrooms

In Fact, Little Improvement Seen a Year After Bush Unveiled Education Plan, Secretary Says

MARY JORDAN

One year after President Bush called for a "true renaissance in American education," little has changed in America's classrooms, Education Secretary Lamar Alexander acknowledged yesterday.

Alexander blamed the lack of improvement on public apathy and Congress's rejection of the administration's plan for "radical change." "All we heard from Congress is, "If we can put missiles down smokestacks, why can't we have better schools?" Alexander said at a news conference. "Well, we are ready to do it. They are sitting on it. . . . They seem stuck in the mud."

Congressional leaders responded yesterday by saying Alexander is playing election-year politics and unfairly trying to redirect blame, more accurately laid on the administration.

"In fact, Congress is acting, and acting effectively on education reform," said Sen. Edward M. Kennedy (D-Mass.), chairman of the Labor and Human Resources Committee. "Secretary Alexander's problem is that Congress has done too well."

Both the Senate and the House have watered down or rejected the four key components of the administration's "America 2000" strategy unveiled last April. They are: approving $545 million for "break-the-mold" schools; establishing new national tests and standards in math, history and other subjects; allowing parents to use tax money for public or private schools of their choice; and giving new power to the education secretary to waive certain federal education regulations.

Kennedy has been a key opponent of the "choice" program, which would allow federal money to be spent on private schools, a practice its critics say would destroy already hurting public schools.

"We have rejected the administration's proposals because we found them inadequate, and we are about to send two major reform bills to the president with broad bipartisan support," the senator said.

A key component of one of those bills would give $852 million to existing local schools instead of the $545 million for "break-the-mold" schools.

An education bill approved by the Senate rejects the "choice" provision for private schools, but accepts the national standards and tests and includes—in limited form—the two other components of the administration's plan. A pending House bill, however, rejects all of them. one House amendment goes as far as seeking a prohibition on national exams and standards. Congress last year approved $100 million for the America 2000 plan but has not yet determined how to spend it.

As the November election nears, Bush is expected to be pressed harder on precisely what he has accomplished to deserve his self-imposed title of "education president.' So far, many education officials say, there has been far more rhetoric than results.

"Everybody knows this administration is going to blame everything on Congress," said Keith Geiger, president of the National Education Association, the nation's largest teachers union. "But the fact is, the administration was wrong a year ago [in its reform strategy] and it is wrong now."

Geiger said real classroom progress will come when the administration pays more attention to the "real problems of our children, such as health care."

C. Peter Magrath, president of the National Association of State Universities and Land-Grant Colleges, said that "though nothing has changed very much" the administration has raised the level of discussion about education and its crucial importance.

"This is a political season, so we can expect blame lobbed back and forth," Magrath said, adding that it is too early to despair, because "fundamental change does not happen overnight."

Deputy Education Secretary David T. Kearns, former chairman of Xerox Corp., agreed that "at the school level itself, there probably has not been a lot of change." He warned that if Congress continues to make a [mishmash] of the administration's proposals, progress will be stymied, students will lose and the "'90s will look like the '80s."

Alexander, appearing frustrated at the lack of concrete results to report one year after the America 2000 unveiling, said a major "disappointment" has been the public's resistance to "revolutionary change." Many parents, he said, have the attitude: "What was good enough for me is good enough for my children."

On the positive side, Alexander noted that 43 states—including Arkansas, "Governor Bill Clinton's state"—have signed on to the six national education goals. The goals, devised by Bush and the nations' governors, include making American schoolchildren first in the world in math and science by the year 2000 and ensuring that all children arrive at school in a condition so that they are ready to learn.

The goal of raising $150 million to $200 million in private money for the administration's cornerstone "break-the-mold" schools also has fallen short, with only $45 million collected to date. But Kearns said yesterday that "there isn't any question in my mind' the goal will be met.

Alexander said he was buoyed by the movement toward voluntary national examinations and standards, and said proof of the administration's commitment to schools is in its budget. Bush's budget proposal for a 10 percent increase for the Education Department is higher than the rise for any other federal agency.

"We have a clearer focus, a more radical agenda, and more people are taking education seriously," Alexander said, summing up the progress of the year.

But asked if students were learning any more this year as a result of America 2000, he said, "I don't think it's right for us to say that."

April 2, 1992

5 *School Choice*

Give Choice a Chance

WILLIAM RASPBERRY

You don't have to be much of a psychic to make this New Year's prediction: Before the year is out, your community will be arguing about—maybe even implementing—some version of school choice.

Choice is the hot new issue in education. Long an item on the conservative agenda (remember vouchers and tuition tax credits?) choice has finally become a legitimate issue for political liberals as well. The two key reasons, apart from general dissatisfaction with the pace and direction of school reform, are the Bush administration's commitment to it and the recent Brookings Institution book, "Politics, Markets and America's Schools," by John E. Chubb and Terry M. Moe.

Its most fervent advocates are so enamored of the idea that they have abandoned the once-obligatory phrase for any new proposal: "It's no panacea, but . . ." For Chubb and Moe, it is a panacea, the ultimate in school reform, academic improvement and parental control.

The older arguments—chiefly that parents of modest economic means deserve the same options as the rich as to where their children will attend school—have given way to a newer, more compelling one: It works.

And it does. In some jurisdictions, choice has attracted both private school students and drop-outs back into public school classrooms. In others, it has prompted the institution of specialized and college-prep courses. In still others, it has increased the amount of racial integration.

But not always. In Norfolk, for instance, where an early version of choice allowed any child to attend—with transportation provided—any school in which his race was a minority, attendance patterns scarcely changed. Neither integration nor test scores showed much improvement.

Still, there is enough evidence that choice does more good than harm that most school districts are likely to be debating some form of the option during the coming year.

Should your schools try it? Yes, but start with the public schools only. I know this goes against one of the key principles of Chubb and Moe, who argue that the key to choice success is that parents be allowed to choose among both public and private schools, with the school district picking up the tab in the form of "scholarships" based on current per-pupil outlays.

If, as they argue, public school reform can't work because government itself is the problem, why not expand choice to include non-public schools?

Listen to Albert Shanker, president of the American Federation of Teachers, who gingerly supports public school choice.

"In principle, choice is a fine thing. Americans cherish their freedom to choose where they will live, what church they will worship in, what stores they will patronize. And public school choice . . . has worked well in some places. But schemes that allow public funds to pay for education in private schools are a different beast altogether; they give the real choice to the schools, not to the parents or kids." For Shanker, the mistake is in thinking of the Chubb-Moe "scholarships" as the equivalent of "shopping at Macy's with a big, fat gift certificate." If you've got the cash, Macy's will sell you the goods, in your choice of size, brand, color and price. In truth, he argues, choice that incorporates private schools is more nearly analogous to applying for membership in a private country club than shopping at a department store.

"Private country clubs don't accept you merely because you have filled out an application form and can pay the fees. A club that needs more warm bodies might be happy to get money on the barrel. But in an exclusive club, the membership committee will ask itself how you'll fit in with the crowd that already belongs. And if they have any doubts, they'll probably decide that it's not worth the risk of losing a bunch of old members to get one new member. You can choose a country club, but the real choice is the club's."

In short, thoroughgoing choice is more likely to segregate along lines of race and class than to provide real alternatives for children languishing in the worst of the public schools. Indeed, it could leave the principal victims of the present system worse off than they are now.

The advice here is to give choice a chance, starting with the public schools, while keeping alert for pitfalls, unrealistic expectations and unintended consequences.

December 31, 1990

Good Choice Proposals, and Bad

WILLIAM RASPBERRY

Under ordinary circumstances, the word that public school teachers are opposed to whatever happens to be the newest educational "choice" proposal would strike me as about as interesting as the news that the National Rifle Association doesn't think much of the latest gun-control proposal.

The opposition is automatic, frequently unthinking, occasionally paranoid.

But this time the reaction of the leaders of the California Teachers Association, here for a conference on school equity, is measured, thoughtful—and right.

The initiative the Excellence Through Choice in Education League is trying to petition to next November's ballot really would amount to an assault on public education, a raid on the budget and state support of private and church-sponsored education.

Sponsors of the proposition won't call it a "voucher" proposal, though that's what it comes close to being. The measure would provide state "scholarships" of $2,500 and up for every school-age child, to be used to pay for public, private or parochial schools.

The opposition among the teachers here is not merely over the constitutionality of using public funds for parochial education. It is the direct budgetary impact of the proposal on the ability of the public schools to do their work. Without providing any new funding, the Parental Choice in Education measure would not only hand over money (or its equivalent) to any child leaving the public schools but also to those who left years earlier—or who were never in the public schools to begin with.

That's always the problem with the voucher idea. It may not seem unreasonable to think of each student as proprietor of his pro rata share of the education budget, and to argue that any child who (by transferring to a nonpublic school) relieves the state of his portion of that portion of the budget ought to be able to use the money to buy education elsewhere.

The problem is that in every major city, thousands of children already are in nonpublic schools, even though their parents, as taxpayers,

78

support the public ones. Equity would require that these children be given the same pro rata share of the school budget that would go to those who leave the schools pursuant to the new initiative.

In other words: Even if no child transferred out of public schools as a result of the proposal, the immediate cost to the public schools would run into the millions—with nothing whatever to show for it.

It doesn't follow from my opposition to this particular measure that I oppose "choice' in general. Some "choice" proposals make a lot of sense, and a lot of them make some sense. This is one of the few that make no sense at all.

And yet it will find support as surely as the most sensible proposal will find opposition. If I wonder about the honesty of those who automatically see "choice" as the death knell for public education, I also question the sanity of those who believe "choice" will cure everything that ails the public schools.

To the first group, I offer the reminder that members of the middle class—including the nearly one-third of California's public school teachers who have their own children in nonpublic schools—have exercised choice for a long time. It's hard to see how they, in fairness, could deny the same options to others.

But I have a couple of reminders for the other side as well—those magic-of-the-marketplace true believers who argue that vouchers will create an excellent new school for every inadequate old one they finish off.

The first reminder is that it ain't necessarily so that terrific new schools will crop up in response to vouchers. Every top-rated private school in the Washington area has a long waiting list—comprising children whose parents have tuition money in hand—and yet where are the new schools that have sprung up to meet that demand?

And here's the second reminder: Virtually every election gives us, first, a choice among a variety of contenders for party nominations and then a choice between the party nominees. The system is open, the qualifications for running not particularly onerous, and every election is contested.

If the magic-market folk are right, America should be brimming over with stunningly excellent public officials.

The point is simple. Choice brings neither in death nor automatic salvation—for schools or for anything else. Too bad we can't learn to think rationally about it.

March 25, 1992

School Plan Questioned by Senators

Private Education Incentives at Issue

HELEN DEWAR

A provision in President Bush's new education program to encourage parents to choose among private as well as public schools drew fire from Democrats—and questions from some Republicans—as the program made its Capitol Hill debut yesterday before the Senate Labor and Human Resources Committee.

The proposal includes $230 million in incentives to help state and local school officials develop ways to offer parents more choice in selecting schools. Bush's plan anticipates that federal aid to schools with disadvantaged children, totaling about $6 billion, would follow children to the school they attend, including parochial and other private schools in states that enact "parental choice" programs.

In an otherwise cordial hearing on the administration's education plan, committee Chairman Edward M. Kennedy (D-Mass.) charged that the choice proposal could revive old bitterness over aid to private schools. Other Democrats said it was likely to intensify educational inequality.

"I fear there won't be much money available, and precisely those students you want to respond to will be left out," said Sen. Paul Wellstone (D-Minn.). "I'm very wary of this. . . . I think this could very well widen inequalities."

On the Republican side of the committee table, Sen. Nancy Landon Kassebaum (Kan.) said she was concerned that costs of the program could skyrocket, and Sen. Dan Coats (Ind.) questioned whether government-imposed standards might impede private schools from pursuing a "values-oriented" curriculum.

But Education Secretary Lamar Alexander defended the proposal both as a fundamental extension of America's belief in freedom of choice and as a way to expand opportunities for disadvantaged students and force improvements in all schools through competition.

By allowing parents to choose schools, they not only would get better education for their children but also put pressure on poor schools to

80

improve, creating a "competitive environment that would increase opportunities for all students," Alexander said.

Several committee Republicans commended the move toward parental choice. Sen. Dave Durenberger (Minn.) noted that 28,000 students in Minnesota are participating in choice programs, a success story, he said, that "shouldn't scare a whole heck of a lot of people."

Parental choice, which Bush has advocated for some time, was overshadowed in the education package by other proposals, such as goals for school improvement, national testing of pupil achievement and creation of nontraditional schools. Democrats have focused on the parental choice provision as a church-state problem and an illustration of what they regard as the program's insufficient focus on needs of poor children, who, they contend, may not be able to take advantage of choice programs.

Despite their differences, Democrats and Alexander vowed to cooperate in enacting new education legislation, which has been claimed as a political priority by both parties.

In opening remarks, Kennedy said Majority Leader George J. Mitchell (D-Maine) will hold up Senate action on the Democrats' education bill until the administration submits a formal legislative proposal to carry out its program, which Alexander said would be ready by next month.

"The administration is eager to work with you," Alexander responded.

"We're off to a very constructive and positive start," Kennedy said at the end of the hearing.

The Democratic bill stakes out many of the same goals as the administration bill but anticipates more federal funding for some programs, such as Head Start and other efforts to ready children for school. Its provisions for parental choice are nowhere near as far-reaching as those of the administration.

Kennedy yesterday introduced another education bill, which would turn Head Start into an entitlement under which the program, which serves 488,500 pre-schoolers, would be available to the 1.9 million who are eligible under existing criteria. The current $2 billion cost would rise to $7.6 billion by fiscal 1994.

In his criticism of Bush's education plan, which was announced last Thursday, Kennedy said it does not do enough to prepare children for school and pays for new programs by scrimping on old ones, which he called "nothing more than education strip-mining."

Kennedy did not criticize parental choice itself, noting that the Senate has endorsed it. But he said the administration's proposal "goes overboard" and added, "By offering public dollars to private schools, including religious schools, the administration is reopening the bitter and divisive policy and constitutional debates of the past about public aid to private schools."

April 24, 1991

A Real Test for School Choice

WILLIAM RASPBERRY

It doesn't matter what the educational question is these days, the Bush administration has the same one-word answer: Choice.

Is academic underperformance the problem? Private and parochial students—that is, children whose parents choose their schools—do better. Is it racial and social integration? The nonpublic schools in Washington (to take one example) are more integrated—by choice—than their public counterparts. Is the problem school completion, college attendance rates, excellence in math and science? Choice, says the administration, will fix it.

The "education president" and his people have even got an answer for the question of money for those parents who can't afford "choice." He has proposed what he calls a "GI bill for children"—a $500 million program of $1,000 stipends. (If parents chose private school, the money would go to the school to supplement tuition; if they chose public school, half would go to the school and half to the parents to cover additional educational costs.)

I suppose the proposal—which White House officials acknowledge has no chance of passage this year—is Bush's response to the criticism that he hasn't put his federal-funding money where his philosophical mouth is.

Well, I'm not such a fan of marketplace magic that I believe choice can solve all our problems. (Look at what political choice has given us in this year's presidential election!) But if Bush is so hot for choice, I've got a proposal for him.

Half a billion dollars is both a lot of money and not very much. It is roughly the size of the annual budget for the D.C. schools—a lot by that measure. But suppose the pilot project proved successful. Would Bush spend the money to take it nationwide?

Here's my idea. Let him ask medium-sized cities across America to volunteer for an all-out voucher program, the ultimate in "choice." The administration could pick (by lottery or otherwise) one city for the experiment: preferably a city with a fairly typical academic and socioeconomic mix.

Then, have that city issue vouchers to the parents of all school-age children, each voucher representing a pro-rata share of the cost of the public schools. Parents would then use the vouchers to purchase their children's education, at the school—private, public or parochial—of their choice.

Well, what's to keep any school district from undertaking the experiment on its own? In a word, fear: fear that the thing might not work and that they'd wind up with neither public school fish nor private school fowl.

My proposal—and the only reason for involving the federal government—is that the feds underwrite the risk of converting to vouchers. After a reasonable period of time—five years or whatever—the experimental city would be free to declare the experiment a failure. The federal government would then be obliged to pay the cost of restoring the status quo ante.

Bush should love the idea. If it worked as he imagines choice would work, the best public and nonpublic schools would continue pretty much as before, and the worst ones would either improve or else go out of business for want of customers. Parents, their freedom to choose guaranteed and their cash-equivalent vouchers in hand, could finally demand the education they want for their children. And the federal government could stand aside while cities across the nation rushed to voucherize their own systems. Wouldn't cost Washington a dime.

But suppose it didn't work. Suppose the experiment managed to kill off the public schools without creating enough new private schools willing to take the displaced youngsters. The school system would have two choices: It could offer a premium to schools willing to take the hard-to-place youngsters (the market, you know) or it could fold its hand and ask the federal government to underwrite the reinstitution of the public schools.

But wouldn't a lot be lost—perhaps irrevocably—in the meantime? Perhaps not. It seems reasonable to assume that only cities desperately unhappy with things as they are would volunteer for so radical an experiment. In addition, there's no reason to believe that the best schools, public or otherwise, would suffer unduly. Some poor and uneducated parents might be tricked into sending their children to worthless private schools (perhaps created just for that purpose). But again, what would be the appeal of such upstart schools to parents already happy with their children's education?

All right, but where (assuming the worst) would the money to reinstitute the public schools come from? Why from the same place as that

$500 million Bush is proposing to spend for his "GI bill for children"—with this difference: If the school-choice advocates are right, the feds wouldn't have to spend the money at all.

July 3, 1992

Milwaukee's Controversial Private School Choice Plan Off to Shaky Start

PAUL TAYLOR

The nation's first private school choice program, designed to shake up public education by subjecting it to the bracing effects of marketplace competition, has itself been shaken by unexpected shortages of both supply and demand.

"The whole thing hasn't amounted to a good-sized flea on the tail of a dog," Steven Dold, assistant state superintendent of public instruction, said of a pilot program that allows inner-city students here to attend non-sectarian private schools with taxpayer-financed vouchers of $2,500.

The Bush administration says it remains enthusiastic about the Milwaukee experiment, and the president this week sent Congress a legislative package that includes $200 million in federal seed money to encourage the development of private and public school choice programs around the country.

But the first-year experience here, while far from conclusive, raises questions about how deep a dent vouchers can make in the most intractable problem in education—the low academic achievement and high dropout rates in poor, inner-city schools.

When the Wisconsin legislature created a private school choice program last year, it capped participation at 1,000 Milwaukee students, fearing that, without such a ceiling, there might be an exodus from the troubled Milwaukee public school system. It turns out that the lawmakers needn't have worried.

Even though nearly 60,000 of Milwaukee's 98,000 public school students meet the program's low-income eligibility requirements, a mere 600 applied for the vouchers.

At the same time, only seven of the 21 non-sectarian private schools in the city chose to accept voucher students from the public schools, meaning that the light demand was still too great for the small supply. A lottery had to be held to apportion the 400 available voucher slots.

Then at mid-year, one of the participating private schools folded, leaving 65 voucher students no choice but to return to public school.

With attrition from the six others, the program nears the end of its first year serving just 252 students.

"We have been monitoring the Milwaukee program, we know there have been good days and bad days, and we attribute that to a normal start-up and transition," said a spokeswoman for Education Secretary Lamar Alexander.

Voucher advocates attribute the wobbly start to the opposition of public school teachers and administrators and civil rights groups, who are parties to a lawsuit—pending before the state Supreme Court—that seeks to have the program declared illegal for failing to meet the "public purpose" standard of the state constitution.

"The foxes guarding the henhouse have had ulterior motives," said Clint Bolick, director of Landmark Legal Foundation's Center for Civil Rights, a Washington, D.C.-based conservative group that is defending the program against the suit. "You wish they would have applied the energy they've spent fighting this program into fixing the schools."

But others, including an independent evaluator selected by the state, say the voucher program here has been undersubscribed for a more complex mix of reasons—including parental allegiance to neighborhood public schools.

"The idea of bringing marketplace competition into education may sound like a wonderful theory, especially for a nation that has its ears tuned to the bottom line, but I think we're in the process of discovering that it doesn't have much to do with the reality of urban education," said Diane Neicheril, principal of Clarke Street School, an inner-city public elementary school.

It's not difficult to understand why educators such as Neicheril feel threatened by vouchers: For every $2,500 voucher that follows a Milwaukee public school student into a private school, the city public school system loses that much in state aid.

Public school educators fear that the most motivated students will take the money and run, leaving behind a "dumping ground for the poorest and neediest students, all concentrated in one place," said Neicheril. "And meantime, we also lose financial resources and political support." Voucher advocates say that it's precisely this dire prospect they're after—because only then, they argue, will a top-heavy, calcified public education bureaucracy be forced to improve its product. "The goal of this program isn't just to give vouchers to a few students—it's to be a tail that wags the dog, the whole Milwaukee public school system," said Larry Harwell, chief aide to state Rep. Annette "Polly" Williams, a Milwaukee Democrat who is the political godmother of the voucher program.

Few here deny that the Milwaukee Public Schools (MPS) could stand some shaking up. High school dropout rates are nearly 50 percent; for black males, the rate approaches 75 percent. Standardized achievement test scores are well below the national average. The system has been under a desegregation order for the past 14 years that has led to widespread busing that has fallen disproportionately on blacks, who make up nearly 60 percent of the student population. Whites account for about 30 percent, while Hispanics and other minorities make up the rest.

The dissatisfaction in the black community with a combination of long bus rides and low achievement scores led Williams to propose five years ago that an independent black school district be carved out of the Milwaukee Public Schools.

When that idea went nowhere, Williams, a onetime welfare mother who twice ran Jesse L. Jackson's presidential campaign in Wisconsin, forged an unlikely alliance with Republican Gov. Tommy G. Thompson, an activist conservative. Together, they overcame opposition from the public education lobby to create the pilot program.

Many of the 21 non-sectarian private schools in the inner city are former church schools whose dwindling congregations could no longer support them. It costs them $2,000 to $3,500 a year to educate a child— about half what it costs Milwaukee Public Schools. The bulk of the difference is salaries: MPS teachers average $34,000 a year, private school teachers average half that.

But there are disincentives for private schools to participate in the voucher program. Under the rules created by the legislature, they have to give up their traditional control over which students they accept. They also cannot offer a religious curriculum.

The private school that folded in mid-year, Juanita Virgil, ran into trouble when parents of its non-voucher students objected to the discontinuation of the Bible studies class. The school also suffered from a host of woes with transportation services and food: Students were arriving anywhere from 7 a.m. to 10 a.m., and lunches were an unvarying diet of hot dogs.

By contrast, Urban Day School—the largest and most successful of the private schools that takes voucher students—seems like an oasis in the urban desert. Students wear uniforms, walk hand in hand down the hallways, get individualized attention and test above national averages. The student body is almost entirely black, and the curriculum has a heavy emphasis on African history and culture. About half of the staff of 55 has a child or grandchild attending the school, which helps to account for their willingness to work for low pay.

The rest of the parents at Urban Day sign contracts to donate at least 20 hours a year of their time to the school, on activities from classroom aide to hall monitor to fund-raising. "We insist that the parents be involved, and if they don't know how, we teach them," said Zakiya Courtney, the school's executive director.

"These parental contracts seem to work very well, and they are something the public schools might consider replicating," said John Witte, a University of Wisconsin political science professor who is evaluating the voucher program for the state.

Despite the positive features he sees in several of the private schools, Witte said he doubts there will be much of an expansion of the program. 'I'm not sure that the prospect of a $2,500 voucher program can create a new supply of schools in the inner city," he said.

And there are the parents who are satisfied with the public schools. "I wouldn't dream of applying for the vouchers," said Lynda Holloway, who has four children in inner-city public schools. "My kids go to a school where there are prostitutes on the streets outside, and you can see the needles discarded by the drug pushers. But I an very pleased with what goes on inside." Her children attend a magnet school for the arts—one of several dozen magnet schools created here to make busing for desegregation more palatable.

Between these magnet schools and the voluntary city-suburban busing program (which takes 5,000 MPS students to the suburbs and brings 1,000 suburban students into the city), Milwaukee school officials say there are already plenty of choices—within the public system.

Proponents of vouchers say that, despite its shaky first year, the program has had a substantial impact on the public school system. They note that the Milwaukee school board may replace outgoing superintendent Robert Peterkin, who opposes private school vouchers, with Howard Fuller, a longtime ally of Rep. Williams.

In addition, they note the board recently approved the creation of two "African-American immersion" schools in the inner city.

School officials said neither move is related to the voucher controversy. "I'd say we're getting our message across, loud and clear," countered Harwell.

May 25, 1991

Private vs. Public Schools:
What Education Gap?

ALBERT SHANKER

The notion of having the public pay for children to attend parochial and other private schools just won't go away. Ronald Reagan and George Bush have pushed such plans for years without success, and less than two weeks ago the Senate rejected the latest incarnation. But another version is still alive in the House, and Bush in his State of the Union address again called on Congress to "give parents more choice" in schools.

The risks involved in public aid to private education are substantial and familiar—would it, for example, destroy neighborhood schools and transform public education into a system for the have-nots? But the other side of the question is whether the risks are balanced by any educational benefit. Supporters say private schools—Catholic schools in particular—educate the same kinds of students as public schools and do a much better job. The reasons are clear, they say: Private schools don't have bureaucracies, teacher unions, tenure, desegregation orders, affirmative action, bans on school prayer or due process in student expulsion cases to contend with.

Is there anything to these claims? Do private schools outperform public schools? Are they really working with the same kids? Fresh empirical evidence—recent analyses of the 1990 National Assessment of Educational Progress (NAEP) math examinations—demonstrate that the answer is no on all counts.

Most news stories about the NAEP exams concentrated on the state-by-state comparisons of achievement among eighth-graders. But everyone ignored the simultaneous release of NAEP's national study of math achievement among fourth-, eighth- and 12th-graders—and the fact that it allows us to compare public and private schools. What these results tell us is that there is virtually no difference in the performance of students in public and parochial and other private schools; all are achieving at disastrously low levels.

The most logical place to start is with the 12th grade, the end of the elementary-secondary school road. There we find a 6- or 7-point difference in average scores among seniors in public, Catholic and other private schools—not much of a gap and certainly not convincing evidence of the superiority of private over public education.

We also see that about half of private-school seniors achieve at the 300 level, which means they can handle content that NAEP says is typically introduced by the seventh grade: decimals, fractions, percents, elementary geometry and simple algebra. This is a few percentage points better than the public school figure. But the relevant and disturbing fact is that both school sectors performed miserably: Approximately half of our graduating seniors, from both public and private schools, cannot handle math operations they should have mastered before they even entered high school.

Now, look at the proportion of graduating seniors who achieved at or above the 350 level (readiness to do college-level math): 5 percent in the public schools and 4 percent in both the Catholic and other private schools. Public schools therefore managed to get a higher proportion of their seniors prepared for college math. But, again, it's nothing to cheer about. Private-school supporters may argue, with justification, that public schools have a higher dropout rate and that more kids who would score poorly are gone. So let's adjust for that; the results now are identical for public and private schools: 4 percent of their graduates are prepared to do college math. But that's terrible—and even more shocking when you consider that in our competitor nations, 20 to 30 percent of students meet standards that are at least as high as NAEP's 350 level.

"Okay," you say, "so there's not such difference between the performance of public and private schools in the 12th grade. But look at the fourth- and eighth-grade average scores: a 10-to-17 spread in points and a clear case of private school superiority at those levels."

Well, what those results really say is that the longer students stay in private schools, the worse they do, and the longer students stay in public schools, the better they do. This conclusion becomes even more compelling when you look at the dramatic difference between public school students and those in Catholic and other private schools—especially differences in socioeconomic status and in the courses they take.

The critical factor is that public schools are obliged to take all comers while private schools select their students, turn away applicants who do not meet their standards and are free to get rid of students who do not work out (and who generally end up in public schools). For example, entrance exams are required by 71 percent of Catholic high schools, 43 percent of other religious schools and 66 percent of independent schools. Moreover, 71 percent of Catholic high schools cite student discipline as their chief admissions criterion and 80 percent require that entering students have successfully completed their previous year of school.

In theory, the selectivity of private schools should give them an enormous edge over public schools in performance. Consider some of their students' advantages: In the sample tested by NAEP, about 50 percent more private school youngsters than public school youngsters had parents who were college graduates. According to the latest national figures, about three times as many public school students as private and parochial school students had family incomes under $15,000, while twice as many parochial school students and more than three times as many other private school students had family incomes of $50,000 and more. And 81 percent of the private school seniors and only 56 percent of the public school seniors in the NAEP sample were in an academic track.

Because of such differences, the average scores of private school students are indeed somewhat better (though well below what you would expect). But when you compare the NAEP scores of public and private school students who have similar family backgrounds and who have taken similar courses—if you compare apples with apples—their achievement is almost identical. Among 8th-graders who have had pre-algebra, public school students score 274 and private school students 273. Among eighth-graders who have taken algebra, public school kids score four points better than kids from private schools—298 to 294. Among seniors who have gotten only as far as Algebra 1, private school students score slightly better; and among kids who have taken more advanced courses, public school students score slightly better.

The point is that among private and public school kids who have done the same coursework, there are no big differences in their achievement; there is no 'private school advantage." And when you consider that these comparisons did not factor in students' backgrounds, the result is additional confirmation that public schools add more value to their students than do private schools.

Some supporters of private schools discount the NAEP results and argue that Catholic and other private schools do such better on two other measures: SAT scores and the dropout rate. John Chubb and Terry Moe, authors of "Politics, Markets and America's Schools," raised that issue in a Wall Street Journal article last July. They point out that private school kids average 12 percentiles higher than public school kids in SAT scores. But they fail to mention important factors: that vastly more public than private school kids take the SAT (which depresses the average public school score); that there has been a dramatic increase in the proportion of public school kids from the bottom half of their class taking the SAT; and—most importantly—that the SAT scores of comparable public school kids match or exceed those of private school students.

As for dropout rates, the 24-percent figure Chubb and Moe cite for public school is certainly shameful (if inflated) and the 12-percent figure for private schools is obviously better. But, again, remember that private schools pick their students while public schools accept all comers. Wouldn't hospitals that refused terminally ill patients or physicians who rejected smokers have lower patient death rates than ones who didn't screen out the bad risks?

The 1990 NAEP math assessment is not the first evidence that the supposed superiority of private schools is a lot of smoke. Nor an I the first person to point it out. In 1988, Chester E. Finn Jr., now an adviser to Secretary of Education Lamar Alexander and then assistant secretary of education, presented unpublished public-private school comparisons from the 1986 NAEP assessments of reading, history and literature achievement to the annual meeting of the National Association of Independent Schools. According to Finn, private school students averaged only about four points higher on reading and six points higher on history and literature.

This "very small differential," he said, was probably explained by the fact that twice as many private school students as public school students taking the tests had parents who were college graduates. "With differences that large in parent education," he said, "it is conceivable that there's no school effect showing up here at all." His advice to the private-school audience: "You need to improve faster than the public schools if you expect to continue to have people paying an average of $6,200 a year for day schools . . . in order to get a presumably better educational product."

Even James Coleman, whose 1981 analysis is cited as the premier source of scientific evidence of private school superiority, warned in that study that "one should not make a mistake: Our estimates for the size of the private-sector effects show them not to be large." A small army of other researchers proved that the small private-school edge found by Coleman disappeared when differences in students' family background and course taking were examined.

The latest piece of evidence to debunk the private school superiority myth comes from Milwaukee's Catholic school diocese, which made its students' test scores available to the Milwaukee Journal's Marie Rohde. On Aug. 1 she reported: "Minority students enrolled in milwaukee's Catholic elementary schools suffer the same lag in achievement test scores as their counterparts in the public schools, according to test results made public for the first time." The test was the same one used by the Milwaukee public schools, the Iowa Test of Basic Skills. The scores,

Rohde continued, "run counter to longstanding claims by most Catholic educators that they are doing a superior job of teaching disadvantaged children." In fact, while the scores of public school minority students have been stable, those of minority children in the Milwaukee Catholic schools have declined.

All of this, however, does not mean private schools have nothing to teach public schools. For instance, public schools could stop giving students a choice of curriculums—they choose easier ones—and insist that they take more academically challenging courses as they do in Catholic and other private schools. And the public school system could start heeding the message many parents, especially poor minority parents, have been trying to convey when they remove their children to Catholic and other private schools: Teachers can't teach and students can't learn when a handful of violent or disruptive kids are allowed to terrorize the school community. Private schools do not tolerate that, and neither should public schools.

The dismal NAEP math results challenge the orthodoxy of both private and public school partisans. For private schools, the scores mean that those who have charged that bureaucracy or teacher unions or desegregation orders or democratic control is chiefly responsible for our crisis in education had better look elsewhere because private schools are not constrained by any of these. But the scores also mean that public schools cannot blame their dismal performance chiefly on the deterioration of families and communities. What, then, is the explanation?

There are a number of factors, but one stands out: Unlike kids in other countries, our young people have no reason to work hard in school because it doesn't make much of a difference in getting them what they want: a job or admission to college. The one exception is students who hope to attend elite colleges—they have to work very hard indeed.

Kids who plan to get jobs after high school know that working hard to do well in school doesn't make a difference, at least not in the short run. Employers don't ask for transcripts, and most top companies don't hire high school graduates until they have been broken in by someone else. So a student who took four years of math competes for the same poor job at the same low pay as a student who filled his schedule with soft courses and barely passed them. This is a bad lesson for our young people. Parents won't succeed in pressuring them to work harder when the kids can tell them, "I've already done what I need to do to get what I want." And teachers, who have a hard enough time persuading kids that history or physics or even regular attendance is "relevant" to their future lives, find it hard to respond when the kids can say, "I don't need that to get into college or to get a job; it doesn't count."

If we want to change things in education, we have to take some tough positions. One is for American businesses to link getting jobs with high school achievement; another is for colleges to do the same thing in setting admission standards. Elementary and secondary schools would then have support for upholding standards. Parents and teachers would have support when they say, "Unless you turn off the television set and work harder, you're not going to make it." And our students— whether in public or private schools—would have evidence that working hard and learning something are essential to getting what they want.

Albert Shanker is president of the American Federation of Teachers.

February 2, 1992

California Parents Look Inward for School Aid

Private Fund-Raising Part of National Trend

MICHAEL ABRAMOWITZ

It is called the "Main Event," the biggest social engagement of the season on the Palos Verdes peninsula, a tony seaside community of bankers, lawyers and other professionals south of Los Angeles. Every May, 1,000 residents pay as such as $175 a ticket to don tuxedos and evening gowns and mingle under a huge tent overlooking the ocean.

Guests eat, dance and bid on auction items, ranging from rounds of golf at fancy country clubs to autographed jerseys from sports stars. Organizers say they usually raise about $200,000.

This considerable sum is not for charity or special philanthropy but for the general budget of the Palos Verdes Peninsula Unified School District. It is part of $1 million in donations that parents and other private sources are expected to raise here for the school year.

Palos Verdes is on the cusp of one of the most interesting and, to some critics, disturbing trends in state government: privatization of public education. Frustrated by what they consider inadequate government spending on schools, groups of parents in several states are looking beyond the proverbial bake sale to increasingly sophisticated efforts to supplement tax dollars.

The numbers are relatively small compared with overall education budgets. At Palos Verdes, for instance, private fund-raising through booster clubs and a special foundation totals about 3 percent of the school system's budget.

But the principle at stake alarms many educators and public officials, who contend that increased private fund-raising, no matter how well-intentioned, helps to subvert a sense of public "community" that surmounts geographic and ethnic boundaries. Earmarking donations for particular school districts, they say, undermines support for general tax increases that could benefit education everywhere.

"You're going to further create a disparity between the haves and the have-nots," said Jackie B. Goldberg, a teacher and past president of the Los Angeles Board of Education. "The threat is that it lets the public

96

off the hook from feeling that they have to support public education. That's the biggest problem. You shouldn't have to have a bake sale to have a field trip for a kid."

That privatization should become part of education is hardly unusual. Robert Reich, a Harvard University economist, has written about how increasing numbers of upper-income Americans have turned to private security forces, mail collection and other services once purely associated with the public sector.

Moreover, as Goldberg readily acknowledged, parents rushing to raise money for their children's schools are responding to a genuine dilemma. "People want to keep their kids in public schools, and the schools can't provide the necessary resources," she said.

Increased private funding for public schools has been reported in states as diverse as Massachusetts, Arizona and Florida. But nowhere is the trend wore evident than in California, where parents in nearly 200 school districts, about one-fifth of the total, have created private fundraising foundations in the last decade, according to the California Consortium on Education Foundations.

This grass-roots movement is largely a response to Proposition 13, the initiative that slashed property taxes and was approved by California voters in 1978. Proposition 13, which for unrelated reasons is being reviewed by the Supreme Court, essentially undermined local funding of education and turned it over to the state government. Unlike counterparts in other states, districts here have very little power to raise funds for education, instead relying on uncertain annual appropriations by the Legislature.

In response to a lawsuit in the early 1970s, California also was one of the first states to try to eliminate spending disparities between rich and poor districts. In a move that was to be studied closely by New Jersey, Texas and other states that have tried to equalize spending, California slowed funding for rich districts such as Palos Verdes while accelerating spending for less affluent areas.

The result is that California is among the most 'equalized' states in the country, with spending differences among most districts of no more than a few hundred dollars per pupil. But the combined impact of Proposition 13 and the equalization effort has retarded overall school spending, according to school-finance experts.

California spends about $4,000 a year per student, nearly $1,000 less than the national average and far less than other industrial states such as New York ($8,165) or Pennsylvania ($5,728), according to Policy Analysis for California Education, a think tank. Class sizes in California—about one teacher for every 30 students—are the nation's second largest.

Ironically, the funding squeeze has been especially severe for some rich districts. Here, student enrollment was about 17,000 in the mid-1970s but has been halved over the last two decades, in part because of development restrictions that curbed influx of new residents.

Because state education dollars flow on a per-pupil basis, administrators here have been forced to trim operations considerably. After much political wrangling, the school district recently closed two of its three high schools, consolidating 3,000 students in one. Last year, the district laid off 108 employees, including 55 teachers and one-third of its 35 central administrators, according to Superintendent Michael W. Caston.

Despite the cutbacks, Palos Verdes has maintained an academic reputation. Students consistently score well on standardized tests, and almost 95 percent move on to some form of college. Part of the credit, Caston and other officials said, is due a devoted cadre of parents who have become a quasi-official development arm for the district.

Inviting a visitor into his office, Peninsula High School Principal Kelly Johnson, a 23-year resident of Palos Verdes, pointed to assorted pieces of furniture and quipped, "donated, donated, donated."

He was joking but just barely. Booster clubs and parent-teacher associations raise about $500,000 annually, providing a major part of the budget for sports, drama, the band and drill team. A Korean Booster Club helps to provide for growing numbers of Asian-American students. Items as diverse as the basketball scoreboard, band uniforms and a support group for special-education students have been funded through such targeted campaigns, Johnson said.

About 10 years ago, parent volunteers began holding small coffee klatches to vent dismay about education financing.

They created the Palos Verdes Peninsula Education Foundation, which raises almost $500,000 annually through such vehicles as the "Main Event" and direct-mail solicitation. The school district retains spending discretion and, among other things, has used the money to establish a drug-education program and hire middle school teachers' aides and high school writing instructors.

"They keep us going," Caston said of the parents' initiative. "Without them, we would have a tremendously bigger problem" with financing.

Attractive to many parents here is that contributing even a few thousand tax-deductible dollars is minimal compared with what they would pay to send their children to private school.

"If you want to get the very highest caliber of education, you need the money, and we enhance that," said Steven T. Kuykendall, a mortgage banker and past president of the foundation.

The problem, he said, is that parents cannot count on additional tax dollars for services. Under Proposition 13, districts need a two-thirds vote to pass a parcel tax to raise more education funds. A few years ago, such an initiative failed by a few percentage points here.

Citing the 75 percent of Palos Verdes residents with no children in the public schools, Kuykendall said, "It's a tough sell to tell them that they should give more to supplement public education. Their feeling is that my kids have been through, so why should I give more?"

Administrators and parents alike admit to misgivings about the current system. "I do feel badly for areas like Los Angeles or Long Beach" that do not have the means to raise such private funds, said Paula Del Vicario, an activist parent. "We want the government to help, but they're not helping. This is the only way to go until we get someone who thinks education is important."

March 1, 1992

6 Home Schooling

Home Schooling on Rise
U.S. Total Up More Than 20-Fold in Decade

STEPHEN BUCKLEY

Home schooling, once seen as an option only for conservative Christians, has become increasingly popular among Washington area parents who don't believe that public schools can effectively educate their children or who fear for their children's safety.

In Maryland and Virginia, an estimated 5,600 children are being home schooled, state Board of Education officials say. Only 90 children were being taught at home in Maryland in 1985, a state education spokeswoman said, compared with more than 1,600 today. Virginia officials say they've seen a leap from slightly more than 1,000 home schooled children in the 1985-86 school year to about 4,000 students today. District officials say just 17 children are taught at home.

The U.S. Department of Education estimates that 350,000 children nationwide are being educated by their parents today, compared with 15,000 during the early 1980s.

The three daughters of Maurice and Ivy Wilkins, of Forestville, now 6, 8 and 10 years old, once attended the elementary school down the street. Then the youngsters began to complain about bullies. And the academics bored them. So last spring, the Wilkinses pulled them out.

"They just seemed to be less and less excited about going. They would get these phantom illnesses," Ivy Wilkins said. "We couldn't afford a private school, so we decided to try it on our own."

Now, the Wilkinses say, Evy, Olivia and Charlene are prodigious readers who are constantly writing letters and stories and are generally more excited about learning. The daughters say they love all the one-on-one attention.

"The best thing about it is that you have the ability to decide and monitor what your child learns," Maurice Wilkins said. "You have total say-so. And you don't have to worry about them getting beat up."

Although home schooling is legal in all 50 states and the District, the laws vary widely. In the District and some states, parents must be certified teachers, a practice that tends to discourage home schooling. Other states mandate home visits by school officials.

The standards in Maryland and Virginia are less strict, requiring only that parents notify school officials of their plan to teach their children at home and that they have their curricula approved by school authorities. Virginia requires that home-taught students take standardized tests; Maryland does not.

As diversity has come to the home teaching movement, stereotypes have begun to crumble. The movement, long believed to be the domain of poverty-stricken social outsiders who "don't need no education," now includes middle- and upper-middle-class moms and dads, many of them with advanced degrees and teaching experience.

"We're real normal," said Cathy Williford, a Rockville resident who teaches her two children at home. "We ride the Metro. We have a TV and a VCR. We have a dog."

However, conservative Christians still make up a large portion of home-schoolers, experts say, and most have turned to that option because they want greater control over the values their children are taught.

Lynn Estalote said she and her husband removed their son, now 13, from Fairfax County public schools three years ago. She said the system's health and sexual education curriculum "crossed lines I felt were the parents' responsibility."

"The state has no authority within the home," said Estalote, whose husband, Ed, is a physicist. "The state believes they should have the last word, and we don't believe that's true."

Proponents of home schooling cite various advantages. They say they develop a closer bond with their children. They point out that youngsters aren't as vulnerable to negative peer pressure if they're not at school. And they say their children can learn at their own pace.

Although no comprehensive data is available, a survey by the Home School Legal Defense Association found that home-taught children typically score in the 80th percentile on standardized tests, about 30 percent higher than their peers in conventional schools.

Manfred Smith, a Columbia resident who is president of the Maryland Home Educators Association, said hose teaching allows "totally individualized learning."

"You don't have to push a child to do something he's not ready for," said Saith, who teaches social studies at Montgomery County's public Takoma Park Intermediate School. "He can focus on the things he's good at, the things he likes to do. Everything is done according to its time."

Smith has three children, 14, 10 and 5, who are taught at home by his wife. He said public-school students don't get enough intellectual stimulation and don't have enough teachers who act as mentors and friends.

Some critics, many of them professional educators, say they are concerned that many parents who instruct their children do not have teaching certificates, which are required for all public school teachers. They also express worry that home education can stunt the growth of children's social skills and stifle their ability to articulate and defend their ideas and beliefs.

Carol Seefeldt, a professor in the University of Maryland's College of Education, said home schooling is a disturbing trend. "The interchange of ideas and values is critical to the growth of democracy," she said.

Keith Geiger, president of the National Education Association, a teachers union, said he believes children "should learn and play together, and this is missing if they're being taught at home. There's just not enough interaction.

"You can't keep the kids at home forever," he said. "They eventually have to get out with others at some point."

Jonathan Rockett, 15, and his brother, Jeremy, 13, have never had to endure crummy cafeteria food or fend off schoolyard bullies or contend with inept classroom teachers. They've never stepped foot in a public-school classroom, and they probably never will.

On most mornings, after chores, Jonathan and Jeremy grab their books and their pencil cases and head for the dining room of their Upper Marlboro home, where, under the guidance of their mother, they may spend a few hours wrestling with geometry or working on analogies. They take breaks whenever they feel like it.

Jonathan, a wiry, gregarious youth who frequently performs as a clown at parties, said the best part of home schooling is that "if you're learning something hard, you can stop, take your time, learn it correctly. You don't have to move on, or learn it just so you can pass a test."

On a recent weekday afternoon, neighborhood boys came to their house after school, beckoning them to play outside. The boys said they play with the neighborhood children all the time.

Marilyn Rockett, their mother, said she didn't like the reputation of Prince George's public schools. Her sons are active youngsters who have played baseball and soccer, worked with volunteer groups, and developed friendships with other children who are home schooled, she said.

"They're well adjusted children," Marilyn Rockett said. "It's been a privilege to watch them grow and develop and learn."

The Rocketts are enrolled at Valley Brook Academy in Columbia, one of many schools and support groups that now cater to home-schoolers. At Valley Brook, students can pursue subjects their parents don't feel capable of teaching, such as foreign languages or biology and chemistry. More than 100 children take classes at the school.

Many home educators commit themselves to the task up through their children's high school years. Others evaluate whether to continue every year. Even those who are open to returning their children to regular schools don't relish the idea.

Larraine Falk, a Silver Spring resident who took her 7- and 9-year-old daughters out of school last December, says, "They're so happy now. I love spending the time with them. I don't know if I want to throw them back into the jungle of school."

May 26, 1992

Home Schooling Without Guilt

It's One Family's Attempt to Find a
Way Out of the Two-Career Rat Race

WILLIAM RASPBERRY

"We're not radicals, not earthy homesteading types. We're both public school all the way, then Johns Hopkins for Jeff, Goucher College for me. We're not Christian fundamentalists; in fact we're Jewish. Both of us were born in Pikesville..."

Michele Goldman is trying to explain how two "extremely conventional" people reached what even to them seems a radical decision: to forgo conventional education in favor of home schooling for their daughters, aged 4 and 2.

It was, says the Eldersburg, Md., homemaker, a conclusion reached through the process of elimination. And a tentative conclusion at that. It's a good bet they'll keep at it through the elementary grades, but high school? Who knows? The only commitment she makes is to do it as long as it works—and to let us know from time to time how it's going.

"I was not as bright a child as Betsy [the 4-year-old] seems to be, but even still I remember a haze of boredom in elementary school. If we could avoid this for our kids, why not?"

So they went looking for a school with some academic excitement. What they found, in the Calvert County exurbs, was crowding: trailers and open space being used even for the early grades. The county hopes to build a new school, maybe in five years.

Maybe they could move to someplace like Towson, where perhaps the schools would be less crowded. But the people at the Towson school board weren't particularly helpful.

"Oh, they were lovely," she says, "but their message was clear. You may have heard that some schools are less crowded or generally 'better' in some way, but we cannot divulge statistics. You could go to a lot of expense and effort to buy a house in the school district of your choice, but we will change the boundaries to suit the needs of all students."

Private school, then? They visited some lovely ones—state-of-the-art facilities, French classes for first graders—but with one annoying catch:

tuition averaged $10,000 a year, and the Goldmans are a one-earner household.

"I didn't want to have to work or assume a financial burden of such magnitude," Michele Goldman says. "I watch my neighbors, and I see the chaos in their lives caused by a chronic lack of time and money. Then I had one of those illuminating flashes, and suddenly I could see the future: Mornings spent in frantic preparation, evenings consumed by chores and homework, weekends for catching up. No one would have the time for real leisure—the productive kind where you read a book, or think or write letters."

So one day last May, when Jeff Goldman took the girls to an independent school fair at Johns Hopkins, he stopped at the Calvert School booth and, for the first time, heard the term "home schooling."

"You would never mistake Jeff as a demonstrative guy," his wife says, "but he was hopping when he got home. Apparently Calvert 'which also operates a conventional school' developed a correspondence program around the turn of the century for the children of missionaries and diplomats stationed abroad. It provides a quality education for a reasonable price—$400 to $600 per child per year. Teacher assistance is available for things like French and music. And since they seem to assume that you're living in the Mojave, they include absolutely everything you'll need, down to pencils and paper."

The fly in the ointment? Goldman loves her children, but didn't want to stay home all day to teach them. Nor did she want the girls to "get weird" from the lack of social interaction with their age peers.

Then she learned that home schooling needn't take more than three hours a day, five days a week, with no homework.

"That one fact outweighed all the arguments against home schooling I could think of," she said. "My kids will have time to pursue art or dance or music lessons, really anything they fancy. Friends can be culled from neighbors, Girl Scouts, home-schooling clubs. The girls can run their own businesses and expand their hobbies. We'll have time to volunteer in our community, visit elderly family members. The possibilities seem endless."

High among those possibilities, the Goldmans believe, is that they will have found a way out of the rat race that entraps so many two-career couples.

"My friends' lives are a mess, and they don't know why," Michele said. "They work hard pursuing their careers. Breakfast is a Pop Tart, then they come home to a house where there's dinner to be made, laundry to be done. Their husbands are modern and somewhat liberated—but not really. They don't have time to enjoy their children.

"You know what they tell me? 'I give you a lot of credit for doing this, but I couldn't stand all day with my kids. I'd go crazy." Well, I do enjoy spending time with my girls—and I do go crazy sometimes. But when that happens, I have no problem leaving them with a baby sitter or something.

"Home schooling won't take that much time. And since the kids will be involved in other stuff, I'll have time for myself. The way I look at it is, if I give them this, anything I,have left for me is mine, without guilt."

Stay tuned.

May 25, 1992

Model Schools/New Teaching Methods 7

Education: Rebuilding the Schoolhouse
Radical Reforms in Search of a
New National Learning Experience

LINDA CHION-KENNEY

In seventh grade, David Andrew Bloom was getting A's and B's. Three years later, he was a borderline dropout.

Today, as a college freshman, Bloom, 19, is a steadfast believer in the need for Americans to rethink the fundamental nature of schooling.

"I was bored and frustrated," Bloom says of the conventional school where the trouble started. "I was being force-fed everything that everybody else thought I should know. My thought was: 'Where does this apply? How is this going to help me when I'm out in the real world?' "

Instead of dropping out, Bloom, who says he failed Spanish, geometry and study hall, "primarily on the basis that I never went," was enrolled at the Jefferson County Open School in Lakewood, Colo., a last-ditch effort to make something of his secondary-school experience.

Through this unusual public school, he studied American history at Yellowstone National Park, presidential politics here in Washington, literature in New England and the life and culture of the Navajo people while living on their reservation in Arizona.

Jefferson's radical experiential approach to learning is out of reach for many of the nation's 83,000 public schools. But it illustrates the almost unlimited possibilities when a school is freed from its shackles of the status quo.

At Jefferson, Bloom was no longer restricted to narrowly focused studies, to set periods of class work, or to the confines of the school building. He found teachers who worked with him as coaches and mentors, not simply as lecturers. His progress no longer measured by a rigid grading system, he was held accountable by how well he evaluated his learning experiences in terms of personal and intellectual growth.

"I learned to work with and through others to accomplish objectives," Bloom wrote of his trip to Santa Fe to study the history of mountain men. "I learned to communicate effectively and I learned to organize and implement complex tasks. And, especially important for me, I learned to complete what I had begun."

These skills—the ability to find and analyze information, to pose problems and seek solutions, to persevere, to collaborate, to take responsibility for one's own learning—are in demand as America stumbles headfirst into the complex challenges of the Information Age.

The question is how best to provide students with "lifelong learning" skills. And therein lies the heart of the education reform debate: how to restructure (some say re-create or reinvent) an obsolete system of schooling that is not producing what America increasingly needs—citizens who can adapt to change, cope with ambiguity and, in short, think for a living.

Since 1983, when the highly publicized report "A Nation at Risk" revealed many of the failings of America's public schools, much of the reform has been regulatory in nature, with a focus on more course work, more homework, more time on task, higher salaries, more professionalism, more testing, and more sharing of power.

"The reform movement, while energetic and impressive by the tenacity of its interest, has been only marginally effective at best," says Ernest Boyer, president of the Carnegie Foundation for the Advancement of Teaching, and consultant to CBS-TV News for "America's Toughest Assignment: Solving the Education Crisis," which airs Thursday at 9 p.m. "On the one hand," he says, "we have an attempt to impose enormously traditional and generally inappropriate strategies that conjure up past models of schooling that most people have experienced.

"On the other hand, we have some creative and bold efforts. But to me, they're excellence by exception, isolated examples of creativity that in no way represent systemic change. And there just aren't enough years in the century to deal with 83,000 schools on a piecemeal basis. That's not the way we're going to improve public education in America."

The real reform, say Boyer and others, needs to occur in the minds of educators and citizens alike, who need to rethink what a school should be.

"We're still dealing with an institutional framework that was designed to meet the needs of the child 30, 40, 50 years ago," says John A. Murphy, superintendent of schools in Prince George's County. "And the children coming through the front door of the school are entirely different in terms of socioeconomic status, their preparation for schooling, the home conditions from which they come."

With the growing number of working mothers and single-parent homes, "children are alone more, and more vulnerable," Boyer says. One could argue "that the school would have to change its climate so that it's dealing with children on a more direct, humane basis, rather than through an impersonal, factory-like model of instruction."

And that, he adds, "raises serious questions about the school calendar and clock. We're still organized around the agrarian model, which assumes children get home at 2 in the afternoon to help with chores and stay home in the summer to harvest crops. What it really means is that children spend endless hours alone, drifting, isolated, unconnected either to family or school."

As it stands now, "you can't imagine why anyone would organize something the way a high school is organized. It's so inefficient and ineffective," says Rexford Brown, director of communications for the Education Commission of the States, a nonprofit compact formed in 1965 to help governors, state legislators, state education officials and others develop policies to improve the quality of education. "Suppose that your business were organized the way a school is organized. People would have eight or nine different bosses. Every 44 minutes a bell would ring and they'd go to a different boss with different standards; they'd have to stop what they were doing and do something else. People couldn't work together because that would be called cheating. And instead of dealing with problems as they arise in the real world, they'd have to deal with them one subject at a time."

Talk of reform begs a closer look at some of education's most common rules of operation—many of which are under fire. Chester E. Finn Jr., professor of education and public policy at Vanderbilt University, asks, "Do all kids learn at the same speed? Does everybody learn the same amount in 180 days? Should everybody be going from third grade to fourth grade at the same time? Why do we have grades anyway? Why do we write our compulsory attendance laws in terms of birthdays, so that you can leave school at (a certain) age, even if you haven't learned a thing?

"Why," he adds, "do we insist on treating all teachers alike, when we know perfectly well that some of them are good at it and some of them are not, that some of them are in shortage fields and some of them are in oversupplied fields, that some of them are in hardship conditions and some of them are in cushy situations? Why do we insist on treating them all alike and paying them all alike?

After writing "Horace's Compromise: The Dilemma of the American High School," Theodore R. Sizer, professor of education at Brown

University and former dean of the Graduate School of Education at Harvard University, founded the Coalition of Essential Schools, a restructuring project that is in place at more than 100 schools nationwide. Among other things, participating schools challenge traditional tracking, promotion and curriculum, with emphasis on the belief that less is more.

Students at Central Park East, a Coalition high school in Manhattan, study two subjects—humanities and science—by answering a series of "essential questions." For example, the question, "Whose country is this, anyway?" leads to an interdisciplinary study of history, politics and labor sociology that, in sum, explores "the peopling of America." Teachers determine what is studied, how time is spent and what materials and pedagogies are used.

Students, coached by teachers who work together in teams, are responsible for their own learning, working in integrated groups of gifted and slow learners, all of whom are held to equally high expectations. Getting the answer right isn't as important as how a student arrives at it. So testing, a demonstration of mastery, can take many forms: a skit, a speech, an essay, even a rap song performance. Students earn a diploma by exhibition, not credits earned.

Generally, Coalition principles provide guidelines for change, but not hard-and-fast rules. The point, Sizer says, is not to design a model for replication, but to force a rethinking of ideas and practices that shape schooling.

Sizer likes to work from the inside out. That conflicts with other education reformists, like Chester Finn, who like to work from the outside in, by setting national education goals as a matter of public policy. "We can reinvent schools until we're blue in the face and we won't necessarily like the product any better," Finn says. "It isn't going to work in very many schools because of the nature of the circumstances you have to have in the school . . . a human chemistry that is so scarce in American education."

Instead, Finn believes in setting "outcome goals" for schools, "encouraging many different approaches" to a prescribed end and holding schools accountable for results. Yet, the two approaches overlap. Sizer and Finn agree that Americans must decide what they want their children to learn from formal schooling.

Brown calls for Americans to take the home view, to think about the frustrations they confront at the store, on the street, in the workplace. "There's this feeling that kids just don't use their minds very well," he says. "It's what Ted Sizer calls 'docile minds.'"

"I don't think," Sizer says, "that most Americans have ever thought about what their kids should be able to do with their heads and hearts as a basis for high-school education. They say: 'Can the kid get into Stanford?' 'Can the kid get a diploma?' 'Can the kid get a job?' " The focus should be on: 'What kind of problems can the kid solve?' "

Answering that question has been the work of Brown, who, with a $1 million grant from the MacArthur Foundation, has been studying a "literacy of thoughtfulness."

"It includes a capacity to think critically, to think creatively, to work collaboratively, to be a problem solver, a good reasoner and to communicate effectively with a variety of different audiences," he says. "It's an ability to analyze, synthesize and interpret information, to know what good information is and what bad information is . . . ." And if that's the kind of literacy you want, Brown says, "then the question is: 'How do we change schools, how do we change policy, how do we change practice, so we get a far higher level of literacy from a much broader range of students than we've ever tried before?' "

Undertaking that is difficult because, Murphy and other educators say, it combines fear of the unknown with demand for quick results. "There's an inability to take people from where they are to a new level and keep them there consistently," Murphy says. This "backward slippage" makes it difficult to promote change, he adds, "because people have set feelings about what education should be and it's what it was when they went to school."

Compounding the difficulty are the subsets of the general population—adults with no children in school who don't feel connected to, or affected by, the work of schools; and students' parents who feel no need to rock the boat, so long as they believe their children and their schools are doing okay.

"We haven't paid attention to our schools," says Ann Lynch, president of the National Parent-Teacher Association, who believes education has been left too much to the educators. "We're so busy thinking about our jobs, our careers, our houses, raising our own children, and economically staying alive, we haven't turned around to see what's happening in the first grade and high school.

"I've never seen anybody drop a baby off at the emergency ward and come back in two weeks and say, 'How's my baby doing?' But I see thousands of parents drop their children off in kindergarten and pick them up years later in high school and say, 'How'd they do?' Education is not viewed as part of a child's life. It's viewed as an adjunct, and somebody else has the responsibility for how it works."

This national mind-set has to change both inside and outside the schoolhouse, reformers say. And while policy makers, politicians and educators seek systemic reform, lighthouses of excellence are shining throughout the country, lighting the way by example. Consider the work of Ron Fortunato, a teacher in Norfolk who turned his high-school classroom into a NASA laboratory.

"When the kids come into our classroom, they're in a NASA lab," says Fortunato, whose students won a grant from the space agency to design an experiment in gravity for a future space launch. "Instead of us telling the kids what to do, we let them run it, to be responsible for it," Fortunato says. "We had a student project scientist, a student chief engineer, a student electrical systems engineer and a student management specialist. We put a student in charge of each part of the organization, and we had a NASA mentor to offer each student guidance.

"The bottom line was that we didn't tell the kids what to do," Fortunato says. "They were free to make their own decisions and to learn from their mistakes, because that's the way it works in the real world."

September 4, 1990

A Strategy for Overhauling the American High School

Theodore Sizer, a Man with a Mission

ALICE DIGILIO

Theodore Sizer stands in his small orderly office at Brown University, talking on the telephone to a harried school principal. He's got to ring off soon, but he's not about to rush her, because she's got problems, and her problems are his problems. Shifting from one foot to the other, and occasionally tugging at his tie, he doles out a stream of sympathy, reassurance, suggestions and humor, telling her to let him know how things go, even to call him at home.

The principal, in an urban high school, is one of 46 around the country who are trying, with Sizer's guidance, to revolutionize American secondary education. As members of the Coalition of Essential Schools, an umbrella organization headed by Sizer at Brown, where Sizer is education department chairman, they are implementing radical changes in the organization of schools. And as all of them can tell you, it may be exciting to start a revolution, but it isn't easy to sustain one.

Sizer's approach to high school, laid out in his book "Horace's Compromise" (1984), is to strip education down to its essentials—literacy, numeracy, the ability to think and reason. The ideal Sizer high school would have students work in small classes of no more than about 20, with teachers who act as guides rather than as authority figures, making students do the work of learning by constant questioning, exploring ideas, and, importantly, writing, writing, writing. The ideal Sizer student will learn how to learn. He may not have memorized every element of zoological classification but if asked to define orthoptera, he will know how to go about the task.

Sizer has spent his lifetime teaching young people or guiding those who would teach them, first at Roxbury Latin School near Boston, later as the dean of the education faculty at Harvard (1964-72), and now as head of Brown's education department. But, he says, "Most of my theories and ideas about education came to me in the '70s, when I was headmaster of [Phillips Academy] Andover. All these studies started coming in. There was a lot of pessimism. There was an awful lot of attention paid to the Coleman Report and its offspring with their messages that 'schools don't make a difference—tell me your income and I'll tell you your SAT scores,' that kind of thing. There was another study about literacy in the Third World. And they all seemed to talk about cohorts of kids. The impersonality of it all nagged at me. They talked about 14-year-olds as if they were all alike."

While Coleman and others were saying schools didn't make a difference, Sizer said he was looking at Andover, which with its large endowment supports many scholarship students, and it was making a difference.

"About the same time I started having regular meetings with other school heads. We'd sit there and puzzle over public education. Why was everything going bad out there? What was happening?"

Sizer decided to find out for himself. With funding from the Commonwealth Fund and five other foundations, and joint sponsorship from the National Association of Secondary School Principals and the National Association of Independent Schools, he assembled a staff of observers and began the five-year project known as A Study of High Schools. The project turned into an odyssey that took him and others to more than 100 high schools around the country. *Horace's Compromise* was the result of the study.

The book is a scathing indictment of American secondary education. The average comprehensive American high school, Sizer argues, is like a shopping mall offering a vast array of wares. Too many students are left to drift through the diversity, and for lots of them the school is little more than an elaborate baby-sitting service.

Sizer's criticisms and his call for improved American education came on the heels of two other reports, "A Nation At Risk" (1983) and The Carnegie Endowment "Report on High Schools" (1983). Not since the Russians launched Sputnik in 1957 had there been such a hue and cry for improvements in American education.

However, the political response, which continues still, has not been to adopt Sizer's plan for smaller classes and fewer subjects but rather to impose more requirements, more regulations, more competency tests, in some cases more days in school.

Sizer acknowledges that he's been swimming against the current. "But the current is easing," he says. "Improvements [brought about by state regulations] have so far been so slight that they are virtually meaningless."

And according to Holly Houston, executive officer of the Coalition, more and more schools are inquiring about the Sizer reforms. Her office receives about 10 written inquiries each week, and countless others by phone.

Teachers are the Key

The key to any improvement in education, according to Sizer, is the teacher. In an Essential School, the teacher's role is drastically different. In addition to being responsible for about 80 students, instead of the standard 150 many public high school teachers face in a single day, teachers are expected to act as mentors and guides through academic material. The Coalition stresses a personal relationship between teacher and student.

Teachers work in teams. They, not administrative curriculum specialists, decide what they will teach, based on the needs of the class.

Michael Goldman, a teacher for 14 years in Manhattan, developed a social studies program for 7th and 8th graders at Central Park East Secondary School, which last year studied the American and French revolutions in tandem.

"At the beginning of the year, I told them, 'Here's what we want you to do: compare the French and American revolutions; debate the merits of both sides of each revolution; and finally, know the chronology and the geography of the American revolution.'

"You'd be surprised, some of the kids came to the conclusion that the Americans had been wrong," added Goldman.

Now Goldman is busy devising a curriculum on immigration, to be used next year.

At Paschal High School in Fort Worth, Texas, English teacher Jhani Williams had her 10th graders study *The Iliad* last fall. The conclusion of the project was a paper on the poem and, according to Williams, the students wrote and rewrote their compositions five times. In a conventional class, there would have been time to rewrite papers only once, she said.

As befits a champion of good teaching, Sizer himself has never lost touch with the art. Even as Andover's headmaster, he taught an American history course. And now, at Brown, he teaches an immensely popular course called, "Going to High School in America: 1930 to the Present." Three hundred students signed up for the course in 1985-86. Sizer, who believes firmly in class discussion and the Socratic method, found himself teaching with a microphone in an auditorium, the only place big enough to hold everyone. The course is now limited to 150 students—still too large in Sizer's view.

Sizer's own teaching talents have also been credited with doubling the number of Brown undergraduates majoring in education since he came there in 1984.

"Worth Every Penny"

The Coalition of Essential Schools is a loose organization. Being anti-bureaucratic, Sizer has insisted on keeping a small staff of six. They answer inquiries and oversee the Coalition's business from offices in the rear of Brown's campus police station.

At present the Coalition consists of 46 schools, both public and private, including 11 who signed on when the project began in 1984. More are being added gradually—six in the past year. In order to join, a school must make the first overture. Then follows a kind of courtship period when Sizer, Houston, or other staff members visit the school, talk with teachers and determine how serious the intention is. If there is enough enthusiasm on both sides, a formal agreement is signed with the local school board, pledging support for the program for at least four years.

This procedure is "more formal" than it once was, according to Houston, partly to ensure that even if principals and school boards change, the Coalition school will have some continuity in the community.

Sizer has his critics, who point to the absence of universal standards against which to measure how well Essential Schools are preparing their students. Also the schools are relatively expensive to operate, which can spell local political trouble for them. Sizer estimates that running one will cost 10 percent more per year than a conventional high school. Others disagree.

"It simply cannot be done with a 10 percent cost override," said Larry Barnes who administers the essential school program at Paschal High School in Fort Worth. "But you can do it with 15 percent more. It's an expensive program, but it's worth every penny." Barnes said Paschal manages because of a generous sustaining grant (he declined to say for how much) from the Tandy Foundation.

Sizer's staff came up with the 10 percent override figure after studying the $3 million budget of an actual high school.

"You can have smaller teacher/student ratios, but you can't do it and have all that a comprehensive school has," said Sue Follett, an economist who worked on budget projections. To finance a lower teacher/student ratio, trims must come off the top, Follett said.

Resources must be rearranged with the result that there are fewer administrators and guidance counselors and smaller athletic budgets (with parent boosters making up the cash difference).

Teacher Power

As his ideas gain favor, Sizer is finding himself more and more in the eye of political storms. Both liberals and conservatives claim him as an ally in various causes, and both teacher unions, the American Federation of Teachers and the National Education Association—known to disagree on occasion—support his views on the importance of teachers.

This clearly worries Sizer a bit.

"Empowering teachers is the new fashion," he says. And since one of the cornerstones of the Essential School is giving teachers more autonomy, Sizer is naturally thought to favor the movement.

"But," he demurs, "Empowering teachers doesn't interest me. What is important is helping kids learn better."

Another issue that Sizer supports, a favorite among educational conservatives, is that of parental choice. Sizer points to New York City's District 4, in East Harlem as a promising development. There parents may choose among schools with a variety of programs—a fine idea, according to Sizer. He would let the market determine which schools survive and which ones fail.

"Most of the private schools begun in the 19th century went under or were absorbed," he says. "The reason? They didn't serve their constituency. If they didn't, they died."

Now, says Sizer, hundreds of moribund schools are living on, supported by public funding. Better to let them die.

There are schools from all kinds of communities in the Coalition, but according to Sizer they are "probably disproportionately skewed to lower income groups."

"The program is particularly attractive to teachers who know they've got to do something radical to reach students," he says. "It's harder to change the status quo if the status quo is getting kids into Yale." The Coalition of Essential Schools, as it's currently structured, is due to conclude its business in 1994. By then, essential schools will have produced scores of graduates. (Since most began their programs with 9th graders, there have been none so far. The first graduates receive their diplomas next spring.) And the schools themselves will have been the subjects of study and scrutiny and perhaps even more books. Sizer looks a little wistful when he contemplates 1994.

What does he hope will have been accomplished?

"The first step is to show it works," he says slowly. "Then I predict that seven years from now, you will be able to demonstrate that essential school students will out perform a matched sample of students from ordinary schools—and by matched I mean matched by socio-economic grouping—on any rational test.

"Next, I think we'll see that our graduates are more thoughtful. They'll be better able to see the consequences of actions.

"And finally, I hope that the schools that produce these kids will be stable. For that I will be grateful."

Alice Digilio is the editor of The Education Review *and managing editor of* Book World.

August 8, 1987

A Strategy for Overhauling the American High School

Radical Plan on Trial in Baltimore

BARBARA VOBEJDA

For 150 students at Walbrook High School, the return to school Aug. 31 will be a risky educational experiment. They will enter a program with no grade levels and no 50-minute class periods. Progress won't be measured in grades or credits. They won't be tested with paper and pencil, but required to demonstrate their skills in "exhibitions." Teachers will studiously avoid lecturing.

This is Phase 2, an expansion of the experiment that was launched a year ago in Walbrook's "school within a school." Here, students and teachers are testing the theories of Theodore Sizer, chairman of the education department at Brown University and an advocate for revamping American schools by simplifying their structure and curriculum.

The change has been startling and, at times, difficult for 14-year-old Ulanda Pryor and 99 other students who experienced Phase 1 last year as ninth graders.

"At first, I didn't like it," said Pryor. She complained about the longer hours expected of students in her program and a teaching approach that forces students to "do it on their own."

But over the past year, she said, she changed her mind. "The teachers, they get more involved in you personally," said Pryor. "Usually, teachers don't care if you come to school or not."

Pryor was referring to two tenets in Sizer's "Coalition of Essential Schools' program: "Personalization," aimed at teaching for the needs of individual schools and students, and the "student as worker," an effort to teach students to make their own discoveries.

That means that in biology class, Pryor learned genetics by staining fruit-fly chromosomes, not by taking notes on a lecture. And in English class, she has learned to figure out on her own how to pronounce the unpronounceable words the teacher doesn't provide the answers.

Walbrook's program like all academic trends and experiments—is a gamble. There are no guarantees that it will mean success for these students, who volunteered or were chosen randomly from the Walbrook student body, a virtually all-black, lower-to-middle income enrollment.

Principal Samuel R. Billups is well aware that there can be pitfalls in trying to translate scholarly notions and educational research into classroom practice, especially in the hard realities of today's urban classrooms.

"Many times, we leap at something like the 'new math,' " said Billups, referring to the trend that changed math teaching briefly two decades ago. "I'm trying to nurture this more slowly, make it a means to an end, more than an end in itself."

As a result, Billups has introduced the Essential School concept gradually, beginning with 100 ninth graders last year. Youngsters in the program studied in classes of 22 at most, while class size elsewhere in Baltimore high schools and for the 1,900 other students at Walbrook often exceeds 35.

For these 100 students, the program meant coming to school at 8 a.m., a half-hour earlier than the rest of the school, and often leaving at 4:30 p.m., 90 minutes later than their counterparts.

They used better equipment, were taken on more field trips and given more sophisticated work than the other ninth graders—reading Shakespeare's Julius Caesar, for example, and conducting their own scientific experiments on heredity, working alone at microscopes instead of in groups.

By comparison with most high schools, the schedule is flexible and the curriculum relies heavily on college preparatory content. A block of time is set aside each morning for science, humanities and—almost unheard of as a mandatory course in modern high schools—Latin. If students want to take electives, like art, business or home economics, they do so during a 90-minute period around lunchtime.

The afternoon is a three-hour block for math or science, humanities and computer literacy.

While teachers used a traditional grading scheme last year, this year grades will be replaced by written evaluations and progress reports to measure how well students have learned the skills deemed "essential" by their teachers. School officials say this may puzzle colleges who want a more traditional grading system to assess prospective students, but they are confident that they can prove—through standardized tests and course work—that students will be prepared for college work.

Coalition schools also avoid traditional testing, the end-of-the-semester examination consisting of multiple-choice questions and a few essays. Instead, the program requires students to demonstrate that they have mastered the essential skills in an "exhibition." That could mean conducting a scientific experiment, reciting poetry, writing essays or answering a series of questions orally.

When students have mastered a specified group of skills, they can move up to a higher "level," rather than grade, without waiting for the next school year. In order to graduate, Sizer says, students must prove in a final demonstration that they have mastered the critical skills and knowledge.

Walbrook hasn't specified yet what it will require for its final demonstration, but Billups said he expected it would resemble a major project, with an oral presentation and a term paper on a subject chosen by the student.

While Billups will argue that the strength of Sizer's program is its flexibility—the specifics are always designed by the individual school—that may also be its limitation, said Ernest L. Boyer, who heads the Carnegie Foundation for the Advancement of Teaching.

"Choosing laboratories [to test] innovations within the context of their own staff and priorities is splendid," said Boyer, calling the Sizer theories "truly exciting." "But since each is unique, it will be more difficult to generalize school renewal beyond the case studies." The delicate move from theory to classroom is further complicated in this case because Sizer's model runs counter to much of the current thinking in education, which pushes for more standardization, tougher requirements and testing.

Sizer calls instead for "less is more:" a simplified school structure and curriculum in which students can concentrate on fewer, critical areas.

According to Sizer, students should not be forced to brush over extensive content, but instead concentrate on "essential" skills—how to speak coherently, read and comprehend, conduct research in libraries and compute basic math—allowing them to continue learning in any discipline, throughout their lifetimes.

Science teacher Pauline Edwards said the theories have dramatically changed her teaching approach. Instead of dominating the class, lecturing or demonstrating, she directs the students to work on their own.

Instead of forcing the students to memorize lists of scientific facts, she teaches basic scientific skills, with an emphasis on technique—using the microscope, making wet mounts, staining specimens.

"This is less," she said. "They're just learning the basics, but it's applicable to all sciences."

"Most people think the more content kids get, the more skills they get," said Marian R. Finney, who formerly headed the health education department at Walbrook and now coordinates the program. "That's not necessarily true."

Finney, who will eventually teach in addition to her administrative role, has found her biggest concern is not whether this experiment with instruction will work, but whether it will draw sufficient financial support. In its first year, the program ran on a $50,000 foundation grant and a $15,000 state grant. This year, the program will run on grants totalling $50,000, but Finney is already out looking for funds for later years.

Sizer has stipulated that program costs should not exceed by more than 10 percent the costs of the traditional school. At Walbrook, start-up costs have exceeded regular school costs by about 30 percent. But administrators said the per-pupil costs will decline in the future, after expenses for equipment, training and materials go down.

Because Sizer's guidelines are broad and individual schools design their own programs, the process of implementing the program at Walbrook has been one of constant revision.

"We try this, try that, scratch over," said Finney. "We're developing it year by year."

Not only must teachers and administrators identify which skills are essential for their students, they must also design curriculum, discuss teaching styles and otherwise incorporate Sizer's ideas according to their tastes.

"If it works, it will depend on what they do to make it work," Finney said of her teachers. "Had there been a whole lot of immovable guidelines . . . it probably would not have worked."

Walbrook teachers decided to put most emphasis during the first year of the program on the principle of "student as worker." That has placed much of the pressure for the success of the program on the students.

Finney said the students are told, bluntly: "Your failure is our failure. The program can only be proven by the kids . . . You have no right to fail."

Sizer's theory was introduced to Walbrook after Baltimore City School Superintendent Alice G. Pinderhughes and Maryland School Superintendent David W. Hornbeck became familiar with Sizer's ideas and agreed to implement then in one school.

Billups must fend off complaints from some other teachers and parents disturbed because they believe the Sizer program is draining resources from the regular classes. But he is a strong supporter.

He agrees the program can't be assessed yet, but if it succeeds, it may be expanded school-wide, with all students required to participate at least for the ninth and 10th grades. The program would not work, he said, for juniors and seniors who will not go on to college and must use their high school years to gain essential vocational skills, like typing or a craft.

But these students, said Billups, would still benefit by the learning skills they could acquire in two years in the program.

Eventually, Billups said, the concept could be expanded to other Baltimore high schools.

"As an experimental program," said Billups, "you're not going to see amazing results overnight . . . (But) if it works at Walbrook, it will work at all the [regular] high schools.

"What's in it is good for everybody," he said. "The more you deal with it, the more power it has."

August 9, 1987

Students Yearn for a Few Jolts of Inspiration

SANDRA EVANS

Room A214, 7th period: The Bolsheviks have taken over in James Biedron's Russian history class at Bethesda-Chevy Chase High School, and a comrade wants to know the names of all the nobles in the village.

Hands wave excitedly, as "peasants" and "workers" volunteer to turn informer. Up until now the nobles have enjoyed privileges: being late with homework and having serfs sharpen their pencils. Now they are called "scum" and soon they will be publicly convicted of crimes against the people. Their punishment: to perform a 10-minute play extolling the glories of socialism.

Eager students such as senior Lindsey Hauck actually rush to this class some days, though many say it is a tough course.

"I've never put forth this much effort in a history class. . . . I've never cared about history," said Hauck, who had just become a member of the Russian proletariat.

Because students at a large public high school are often left to learn as much or as little as they want to, teachers such as Biedron, who have the ability to excite and motivate, are a prime commodity.

In several weeks of classroom visits and interviews, *Washington Post* reporters tried to find out which kinds of classes and teachers at B-CC spark students, help them learn, and also which ones fail. Again and again, students told them to check out Russian history.

Biedron's methods combine role-playing and a crisp, easy-to-understand lecture style. He plays the part of tsar, comrade, and, of course, teacher—one able to answer almost any question put to him by a group of curious teenagers. His students act out the rise and fall of peasants, serfs, nobles and workers across the sweep of Russian history.

"I think you can't help but be inspired by someone who loves his subject as he clearly does," Hauck said. "If he were any more excited, he'd die."

Local and national political leaders, including President Bush, are calling for education reforms that include more rigid national standards in such subjects as math, science and history, and more testing to try to force learning on those that American education seems to be passing by.

But students at this large, relatively affluent public high school already take plenty of academic subjects. They are tested continually, in class, on statewide achievement tests and for college admissions and placement. And, according to *The Washington Post* Poll, most of them find only some of their course work interesting.

Biedron, for one, worries that more course requirements will squeeze out elective classes like his and says what students need is more classroom give and take, not more testing.

"When they keep throwing these hurdles and artificial hoops to jump through . . . then they stand in the way of real education," said Biedron, 49. "This is all in the name of making kids strong students. It does nothing but stultify."

Not all of B-CC's classrooms work as well as Biedron's. Although many students there get a marvelous education, students at all levels also know how to get through, even ace, an uninteresting course without learning much.

"I couldn't tell you anything that happened between the Civil War and the present" because of an easy and disorganized 10th-grade American history class, said Cecily Baskir, a straight-A senior.

According to students, the best teachers solicit their opinions, encourage active class discussions and make them think. The worst regard students as passive vessels to fill with facts.

In scores of interviews, students said they looked to their teachers for an intellectual jump-start. Those teachers who really know and care for their subjects, can and will answer any question, and those who care about students personally are best able to provide the spark.

"The teacher makes the entire difference," said Carrie Gaiser, a high-achieving senior.

A good teacher can even change a student's mind about a subject. Elise Morgan, one of the senior class's top students, became interested in math despite herself in Sydelle Silberman's classes.

Silberman, a trim and energetic woman who constantly paces around her classroom, nudging and cajoling as her calculus students work, is recognized by many as a challenging teacher.

"I went through a phase where I said [math] isn't practical; I'm not going to use it," said Morgan, 18, who is headed for Stanford in the fall. "I didn't really want to pay attention, but the teacher was really great . . . and so a lot of times she kept me interested—she cracked a lot of jokes, and she has this outrageous New York accent."

As many good teachers as there are at B-CC, there also are those who get scathing assessments from students who are not fooled by the unprepared, the unimaginative or the unenthusiastic.

"Most history teachers don't know what they're talking about," said senior Amber Frid. "When you ask then questions, they don't essentially know what to say. They assign these busy-work assignments."

Room D102, 5th period: About 20 foreign-born students are happily bending glass using a Bunsen burner in Lawrence Levin's lab science class. Delighted to be using the equipment, the students never stop talking as Levin goes from student to student.

Occasionally tubes shatter and a student braces for criticism, but the teacher shrugs off the breaks. "It's learning by doing," Levin says.

Students often point to firsthand experience as the best teacher.

Christina Fernandes, a vocational education student, said the mock trials in law, her favorite class, and a stock market game in economics got her interested in both subjects.

"I would wake up and run to the paper to see how my stock was doing," she recalled.

"I remember freshman year in lab science," said Hadley Carmichael, 17, a junior. The teacher demonstrated principles of condensation and evaporation using a bobbing glass duck.

"You had to figure out why he kept going up and down. We did a series of four or five experiments within two weeks, trying to figure this out. I will never forget that duck—Albert the Dunking Duck."

Specialists say there's plenty of research to support the students' view that they learn best by doing.

"There is a whole raft of scholarly and commission reports and without exception those . . . agree with the kids. . . . You have to do science to know science. You have to use mathematics to see it's interlocking," said Theodore R. Sizer, professor of education at Brown University and chairman of the Coalition of Essential Schools, an umbrella group overseeing scores of schools trying new teaching methods.

"To memorize and regurgitate formulae may get you a high grade on a test. . . . But if we want kids to learn serious mathematics, you have to get them to use it."

Room C316, 6th period: In a Spanish class, the teacher and students recite the same sentence in Spanish over and over with one word changed. One girl sits with her head on her desk, trying to doze.

The teacher gets up, walks over and waves a hand in front of her face.

"Go away," the student says. And again, "Go away."

In interviews, most students said that the majority of their teachers stress lectures and rote learning, two methods students say they despise.

They show their disdain. In many cases, students sleep or chat about the weekend as the teacher drones on. They appear to ignore efforts to get their attention.

While honors classes are usually more lively—possibly, say teachers, because the more motivated students excite their instructors—many students in regular classes say they get pretty dull fare.

"You just sit there. It's not fun having to sit there and read a book and get lectured to," said Matt Holland, 17, a junior. Only a third to a half of his classes are otherwise, he said.

Some teachers defend the use of more conventional methods, such as drill work, at least occasionally.

"It's impossible to duplicate in a classroom [how] a child learns a language," said Paul Anisman, head of the foreign language department at B-CC since 1979. "You very often have to present a new construction and do some drill work. We try not to make that the centerpiece."

When a class plays a game, he said, the energy level is higher, but "I personally don't think that learning only takes place in these high-energy conditions," he added.

Room C214, 3rd period: The topic is a comparison of Thomas Hardy's "Tess of the D'Urbervilles" and Toni Morrison's "Beloved." One student in Evanthia Lambrakopoulos's English class objects to the dialogue in "Tess."

"She's sitting there upset and passionate, but . . . it's almost like Shakespeare—people could have talked like that, but they didn't rhyme!"

Class members eagerly add their two cents as the discussion heats up.

Through it "Miss Lamb," as she is known, is like an orchestra conductor. She points at students to speak, she nods, she pulls it all together. She picks up on what each student says, giving background information throughout, and makes sure dissenters are heard.

Lambrakopoulos's students say her class, with its free-flowing discussion, sharpens their thinking and heightens their interest in what they're reading.

Few things rankle students as much as being told what to think.

Andrew Youdin, one of the senior class's top students, said that in one history class that bored him, "The best way to get along was to do it the way [the teacher] wanted."

The teacher "takes the exact same thing every single year, gives the exact same test," Youdin said.

Mike Carroll, who teaches both that European history course and the non-honors economics class that Fernandes recalls so fondly, said the idea that he wants his own opinions repeated back to him is "baloney." At the same time, Carroll says that the syllabus for European history is determined largely by the questions asked every year on the advanced placement examinations, which some of his students take.

"I have more leeway in my economics class to make it more fun in terms of the games we play, as opposed to the AP class where the curriculum is pretty much set. . . . I tell the kids, if I were as entertaining as Bill Cosby, I wouldn't be teaching history. Maybe that's what they're used to."

Room A208, 4th period: Four seniors on a panel are discussing the Federalist Era in Lester Olinger's honors American history class. They know what they are talking about. Jed Shugerman is so enthusiastic about John Marshall's Supreme Court he can barely yield the floor.

Then come questions: "Didn't anyone argue that the Supreme Court was too powerful?" "Were these issues really hot issues at the time?" The students on the panel field all of them.

Through the 47-minute period, Olinger speaks up only once, to arbitrate the pronunciation of "mandamus."

Olinger, a faculty star at B-CC, has raised behind-the-scenes teaching to an art form. He assigns groups of students to research each topic in the yearlong course. They in turn present the information to the class.

"Mr. Olinger, he was the one who really turned me on to history," Shugerman said. "He makes you learn on your own. . . . But even so, he still challenges you."

A political science and sociology major, Olinger found himself teaching history at B-CC in 1961 and cramming every night to stay ahead of his students. As he lectured his way through the book, he noticed his students seemed bored. Then one day a student asked to teach a class, and Olinger let him.

That one-day experiment stuck in his mind, and he eventually made student teaching a centerpiece of his course.

School library, end of 4th period: Olinger is approached by students who have been researching the antebellum period and are now on their way to lunch. They want to know what he thinks of the movie "JFK" and the Kennedy assassination; they want to talk about last week's basketball game; they want to tell him how they are doing on their college applications.

"I care about them as people," said Olinger, 56. He asks those in the school play to autograph his program, is unofficial scorekeeper for the football team, talks with students' mothers at soccer games and has given students his home phone number.

Whenever students and teachers talk about good classes and successful teaching, they frequently mention one essential element that no standard can require and no test can measure: that teachers be interested in students as individuals.

One senior, whose parents declined to allow his name to be used, recalled what a difference it made when Olinger, his teacher for a current events class, took a personal interest in him, came to B-CC's varsity baseball games to watch him play and offered him extra help, even though "I screwed around a lot in his class," the student said.

"He was really a friend. . . . We just clicked," he added. "It was a reason to come to school."

Staff writers Lisa Leff and Robert O'Harrow Jr. contributed to this report.

April 6, 1992

Fixing Schools One by One

New Ideas Tested on Scale Across U.S.

KENNETH J. COOPER

At South Pointe Elementary School, the desks are never aligned in neat rows. No classroom is completely walled off from another. Each has a television, computer, telephone and a rocking chair in the reading corner.

Each student at South Pointe will be assigned to one of four "communities," a school within the school, and spend all of his or her elementary years there. "We want to have an atmosphere like home," said Beth Rosenthal, a third-grade teacher.

South Pointe opens here today under joint management of the Dade County School Board and Education Alternatives Inc., a for-profit company based in Minnesota. But the partnership, believed to be a first in public education, is not the only radical experiment in the classroom as the 1991-92 school year begins.

Many of the reforms at work in U.S. schools are on a smaller scale than in the past: Educators have shifted from trying to change the system to changing schools one at a time.

"It's kind of a period of creative redesign, experimental redesign, at the local school," said Ernest L. Boyer, president of the Carnegie Foundation for the Advancement of Teaching.

"The highly standardized strategies that were mandated from the top—school districts and states—did not produce the results that were hoped for," said Sharon Robinson, director of the National Center for Innovation, part of the National Education Association. "Then how do you do it? You do it school by school," she said.

Denise Callaway, spokeswoman for the Milwaukee public school system, which is set to open an "African-American Immersion School," said: "We're becoming a system of schools, rather than a school system."

Detroit also has created three Afrocentric elementary schools which, like the one in Milwaukee, will be coeducational but originally were intended to serve only young black males.

President Bush has incorporated the school-by-school approach into his education plan, which seeks business support to design 15

130

model schools suitable for the next century. A separate component of the plan, announced in April, proposes more immediate federal funding of more than 535 existing schools that would become models.

In one recent sign of the growing popularity of experimental schools, more than 500 educators, consultants and business representatives attended a conference in Arlington last week for information on designing schools for the next century. Because of the interest, two more conferences are planned.

"You have to think about a learning environment in a whole new way, and that's exciting," said David Kearns, deputy secretary of education and a former Xerox executive.

Some educators have expressed concern about the limited impact of any model schools and possible abandonment of more sweeping approaches.

"One might call the current strategy 'excellence by exception,' " Boyer said. "The question is, how do we make it available to all? Or are we going to abandon the notion of the common school for all?"

Boyer, a former U.S. commissioner of education, said the school-by-school strategy lets government officials "off the hook" by allowing them to avoid more expensive and difficult solutions, such as providing quality preschools, reducing class sizes in early grades and finding ways to involve parents.

By design, no single type of experimental school has dominated, because each is intended to address the needs of that school's students. This theory is borrowed from a new business practice of decentralized decision-making.

In general, the school innovations have altered long-standing management or scheduling practices, introduced specialized studies and instruction methods or addressed emotional problems that hinder learning. Because the purpose often is to reshape an entire school, the innovations tend to have many dimensions.

That is the case with South Pointe, where nontraditional approaches are to be taken to instruction, classroom design and technology, in addition to management.

Education Alternatives, based in suburban Minneapolis, has helped to hire South Pointe's principal and faculty, revise blueprints for the new Spanish-style building and train teachers in "Tesseract," an instruction method used in its private schools. The for-profit company also is expected to raise about $1.2 million over five years from grants and donors interested in the experiment. That money will cover the firm's annual management fee of as much as $275,000.

South Pointe was built to relieve overcrowding at two Miami Beach schools whose enrollments have been predominantly Hispanic and poor. The educational experiment has attracted some higher-income parents whose children attended private schools, but South Pointe's expected enrollment of 550 will roughly resemble that of an urban school.

"This is where all the new immigrants come, and the rents are cheap," said Patricia Parham, the principal. "They come in and move right out." About 650 parents and students got a peek at the new school, which will enroll pupils from preschool to sixth grade, during an open house last week.

Besides the classroom innovations, the parents learned about Tesseract, an instructional method similar to Montessori and preschool techniques. Kathryn Thomas, vice president of Education Alternatives, described Tesseract's three principles as individualized learning, classroom flexibility and a change in the teacher's role "from being someone who knows it all and pours out knowledge to being a guide, counselor and manager."

One example of Tesseract's flexibility might astonish many public school veterans. "Our teachers don't have set lesson plans they work from," Thomas said.

The role of textbooks is reduced. "This is my [base] reading series—fine [children's] literature," Rosenthal said, opening the cabinet above her sink to rows of books such as "Charlotte's Web."

Rosenthal, 24, cited her bulletin board as an example of the Tesseract approach. There she has tacked keys of various types, with no further explanation. "I could do 100 different activities with these," she said. "I'm going to let the kids decide what we're going to do." The keys could be used to teach basic geometry [shapes], science [sorting and classifying], math [estimation of the number] or writing [an imaginative story about a key's use], Rosenthal said.

"The reason I decided to put Jorge in this school is the educational plan. . . . The way they're going to teach is wonderful," said Astrid Gamez, a Honduran immigrant and mother of a second-grader.

Around the country, much of the experimentation in public schools has been orchestrated by groups other than the local school board.

There are about 200 schools in the Coalition of Essential Schools, based at Brown University in Rhode Island; a similar number in the School Development Program, pioneered by James Comer in New Haven, Conn.; 29 schools in the Next Century Schools Program funded by the RJR Nabisco Foundation; and six in the Mastery in Learning Consortium, a program of the National Education Association. The schools are spread out nationwide.

Nearly all of those programs said inquiries or members have increased in the last year. In 1990, 1,000 schools applied for competitive

RJR Nabisco grants, while 1,600 did so this year, according to Roger Semerad, the foundation's president.

Among the nation's school districts, Dade County has been one of the most active experimenters. This fall, South Pointe and five other "Saturn schools," named for the Tennessee automobile plant that workers helped to design, will be open. One high school will emphasize maritime studies, another architecture and interior design. An elementary school will focus on aerospace.

In addition, Dade County has three "satellite learning centers" at workplaces, and 147 of its 283 schools have implemented various innovations under a program that gives teachers and parents a role in decision-making.

"South Pointe is certainly the most dramatic in terms of departures from traditional instructional techniques," said Andy Gollan, a spokesman for the Dade County schools.

Faculty excitement about the experiment was apparent to Betty Castor, Florida's education commissioner, when she attended the open house. "I think the enthusiasm and the approach is almost a guarantee that this is going to be successful," she told reporters.

Castor said that, even before South Pointe has opened, she talked to Education Alternatives about expanding Tesseract into other Florida schools. Minnesota, North Carolina and Washington state already have moved to create a small number of model schools for the next century.

September 3, 1991

New Teaching Lets Children Learn Like Children

SARI HORWITZ

Inside District elementary schools, the children are taking charge. To a visitor, it looks like chaos, but teachers say the noisy, playful classrooms that let children be children are where youngsters learn best.

Starting with pre-kindergarten, District schools during the last two years have been phasing in a new program for educating young children with the hope of converting all classes up to the third grade by 1995.

In classrooms throughout the city, young children no longer sit silently in rows of desks, facing forward to watch the teacher write on the blackboard. Instead, they've become more active participants in their education, choosing the type of learning they engage in each day. By playing math games, acting out readings and talking to each other, the children are learning in an environment better suited to their needs and abilities, early childhood specialists say.

At Horace Mann Elementary School in Wesley Heights, teachers plan the school day so that children can move freely around the room to a reading loft with an array of books, a music center with records and tapes, a sandbox, a water table, a painting table, an area to play house and dress up and a corner to stack blocks.

At Garrison Elementary School in Shaw, youngsters learn to count by adding up colored beads or rolling dice. At Shaed Elementary School in Edgewood, children learn fractions with a pie pan of plastic pizza.

This effort to let young children learn based on the way they think and behave is drawing praise from school systems in the Washington suburbs and from educators across the country, many of whom are moving ahead with similar revisions.

It's a major philosophical shift for the D.C. schools, probably the most dramatic change in elementary school teaching since the back-to-basics movement of the 1970s. And it is the latest effort to improve education over the long term in the troubled D.C. school system, which has been chronically afflicted with poor student performance and a high dropout rate.

134

In its first two years, the program has been commended by parents, teachers, education specialists and the Committee on Public Education, an advisory group that found few other bright spots in the school system.

At the same time, however, the new methods are viewed with skepticism by some parents who remain loyal to the back-to-basics program. Their concern is that the relaxed environment may imply a relaxation of educational standards that will leave students unprepared for the rigors of testing in higher grades.

The director of the early childhood program and its most impassioned advocate is Maurice Sykes, who says, "Most kids in school are bored out of their gourd. Why? Because nothing is happening. Children learn by doing, by having fun."

It's too early to know the full effects on District children. There are no test results yet; testing children before the third grade goes against the grain of this philosophy, and the students taught this way since kindergarten have not yet reached the third grade.

Changes in public education in the last decade have emphasized these "back-to-basics" rules: Tighten standards. Formalize instruction. Increase testing. Increase course requirements. Foster competition.

But, said Sharon Lynn Kagan, an early childhood specialist at Yale University, "The pendulum swings in education."

Many early childhood educators believe that although the 'back to basics' measures may improve the performance of high school students, they don't work as well with children ages 4 through 8.

They say that children in these critical early years are influenced by their relationships with people and their experience with materials. Children learn best, they believe, by exploring their environment and building on their curiosity. Youngsters also depend heavily on approval from parents, as well as other adults.

So, Sykes says, if children like to move around, why keep then seated at desks? If they don't think of the world in separate categories, why not integrate reading and mathematics into art, music and cooking? If children like to play and explore, why not teach through games and relevant hands-on experiences? If they develop at different paces, why force them all to learn the same skills at the same time?

Parental support is crucial to the success of the program, its proponents say. To allay parents' fears, Sykes has organized citywide panels explaining the new classrooms and the more complicated report cards that teachers use. He usually brings along District parents who swear by the new method they believe has worked with their children.

"I love what the system has done," said Loraine Wilson, mother of a second-grader at John Eaton in Cleveland Park. "Drop in any time and you will find engaged, interested children having a good time learning." Parts of the present theory of early childhood education have been around for decades, certainly as far back as child psychologist Jean Piaget's writings in the 1950s.

But it was not until a few years ago that the National Association for the Education of Young Children pulled all these principles together into one document that embodied the latest thinking. In 1988, these ideas were embraced in a highly regarded report by the National Association of State BOards of Education called "Right From the Start." Two years later, the District became one of the first cities to implement the recommendations. The school system was spurred on by Sykes, an engaging and energetic administrator, and the local group of civic leaders who formed the Committee on Public Education.

Although many educators have accepted the idea that these practices are good for pre-kindergartners and kindergartners, few have pushed the concepts for higher elementary grades, as Sykes has.

"Maurice Sykes is doing something that other school systems are doing or should be doing," said Muriel Farley, the Fairfax schools' director of early childhood programs.

"It's definitely the wave of the future. We're all moving in the same direction," Farley said. Fairfax elementary school teachers are being trained in the new methods, she said.

The Maryland State Department of Education released a report this year endorsing the same childhood teaching methods. The Montgomery County school board has decided to make a similar early childhood program a high priority.

"I wish everyone in the world was doing what the District is doing," said Sue Bredekamp, a leading authority on childhood education with the National Association for the Education of Young Children. "It is a model," she said. "I would put my kid in there."

Sykes said the research on early childhood education shows that children best learn the concepts of mathematics, for example, and put them in a meaningful context by playing with objects. So at Shaed, Jeanne Hunter uses play to teach her kindergartners how to count and measure.

In one corner of her colorful, bustling classroom, children punch their codes into a homemade automatic teller machine and withdraw play money to count up and use to buy doughnuts at the class store. Other students gather around tables to measure a plastic elephant with building blocks and then use crayons to chart its height on graphs.

Hunter also tries to teach the children to be independent, accept responsibility and make good choices by allowing them to choose from the activities around the room.

These methods also emphasize social skills. A District study two years ago concluded that traditional teaching tended to neglect social development and that an emphasis on competitiveness led many children to think they had fallen short by second grade. That led to bad grades, poor attendance and an increased likelihood that children eventually would quit school, the researchers said.

In each of these new classrooms, children are given the chance to take charge, get to know each other and receive a little positive feedback.

During "morning meeting" in Joyce Love's third-grade classroom at Garrison, each child introduces the youngster in the next seat and adds a kind comment. In Stephanie Abney's class there, the kindergartners gather in a circle during morning meeting, each hugging and greeting the one to the left.

For the "sharing" period in her class, Hunter's kindergartners take turns sitting behind a cardboard "television set" and conducting a talk show with their classmates.

"Good morning, children," said kindergartner Akilah McCoy, as she recounted a weekend picnic. "Any questions or comments?" she asked her classmates at the end.

Several hands shot up. "My brother and me went to get pizza," one boy said about his weekend.

"My brother and I," the classmates corrected him in unison.

Hunter laughed. She has been a traditional teacher for more than 30 years, but she's enthusiastic about the change. "They take charge," she said to a visitor. "I'm just a handyman now."

Confident and creative teachers such as Hunter are the key to the program's success. These methods, educators say, are not teacher-proof as is the traditional workbook, so a key element is retraining teachers. In some schools, teachers can sit in their colleagues' classrooms to watch how they've put the new methods into practice.

"We tell the teachers, 'Give those children a real childhood. Provide islands of excellence and create awe and wonderment,' " Sykes said. "You give those children six good hours and they can figure out the rest."

June 15, 1992

Innovations in Education
Turning Classmates into Teammates

Stephen Buckley

Years ago, teachers required students to sit stock-still and silent for 50 minutes. Instructors lectured for the entire period, every day. And social development took a back seat to academics.

But no longer. In recent years, a quiet, if incomplete, revolution has occurred in Washington area schools. Students now spend much of their time in groups, hashing out answers and coming to consensus. Teachers have become facilitators instead of lecturers. And educators are paying equal attention to social skills and academics.

The growing movement is called cooperative, or collaborative, learning, a strategy that in the last few years has moved from being regarded as yet another education fad to a mainstream classroom tool.

"Five years ago, there were isolated instances of teachers using cooperative learning," said Jean Hall, director of the Office of Staff Development and Training for Fairfax County schools. "Now, it has gained national attention, and it's become a very important part of a teacher's repertoire."

Cooperative learning can be used to teach subjects as diverse as art and algebra, as well as history, literature, music and English vocabulary. Teachers said they like it because, among other things, it involves all students and helps pupils gain a fuller understanding of the material. Instructors say pupils also genuinely enjoy themselves in class, so teachers don't have as many discipline problems.

"You spend less time disciplining kids because they're involved with what they're doing," said Jeanne Bohlin, a seventh-grade math teacher at Carl Sandburg Intermediate School in Alexandria. "They're too busy to get into trouble."

Students say they have the best of both worlds: They can be social while still doing their work.

"It gives you a break from the teacher," said Tom O'Connor, a senior at Yorktown High School in Arlington. "Fifty minutes a day, listening to a lecture, can get old. I like having a chance to talk."

Sandra Benson, a junior at Mount Hebron High School in Ellicott City, recalls that being in classes that employed cooperative learning helped her survive freshman year: "It helped me get to meet more people. I didn't feel so alone," she said.

Researchers have found that students who worked in teams tended to perform better. Students who rarely raised their hand in traditional classes now regularly shared their ideas. Youngsters who previously disliked a particular subject suddenly found it interesting.

English classes once bored Rinn Lawson, a junior at Mount Hebron High. But after one English teacher used cooperative learning, "I really got into it. I'd never really got to discuss a book before. When you discuss it, you get a whole bunch of different perspectives."

Students also say they interact with a broader range of their peers. "That's the cool thing about it," Lawson said. "You have to deal with jocks or other people you wouldn't normally deal with."

The technique is widely used in Washington's Maryland and Virginia suburbs and hardly at all in the District itself, local educators said. Franklin L. Smith, superintendent of schools in the District, said he plans to make greater use of cooperative learning because it "teaches students that complex problems can often be more easily solved in groups, and that cooperation has some very practical advantages."

In the past five years, the use of cooperative learning has become popular across the country. Many teachers resisted the strategy, in part because it required instructors to make a dramatic role change, according to Robert Slavin, of the Center for Research on Effective Schooling for Disadvantaged Students at Johns Hopkins University.

"I think teachers tend to teach the way they were taught," said Slavin, who developed a popular technique for cooperative learning using competitive teams. "Some teachers were afraid that 'cooperative learning' meant chaos, 'open classroom,' 'do your own thing.'"

Slavin reviewed 60 academic studies of cooperative learning. In three-quarters of the studies, students in cooperative learning classes did significantly better on achievement tests than children in control groups that did not use the technique.

Educators say no single factor has caused cooperative learning's increased popularity. But Neil Davidson, president of the International Association for the Study of Cooperation in Education, says it has to do at least in part with increasing ethnic diversity in many metropolitan areas.

Davidson, an instructor at the University of maryland's College of Education, said educators realized they had to create teaching designs that not only would cater to various learning styles, but also would help break down class and racial barriers.

At Eastern Intermediate School in Silver Spring, Betsy Brown's second-period English class consists of mostly blacks and Hispanics. Early in the year, when Brown allowed the seventh-graders to form their own learning groups, several were either all black or all Hispanic. But when Brown, who uses collaborative learning extensively, picked the teams, they were all integrated.

Brown, who has taught for 18 years, works hard to foster a spirit of teamwork in her class. A banner on one wall in her classroom reads, "We are a community of learners." Another sign says, "None of us is more able than all of us."

In one class recently, Brown told students: "I want to hear good ideas. I want to hear, 'Way to go.' I want you to think. I want to see you make eye contact."

Throughout the period, Brown ambled around the room, listening in on each group. A cacophony of voices filled the class, as students asked each other questions and came to a consensus on answers.

By the end of the 50-minute period, each youngster had stood up before the class at least once, as group representative, to give an answer.

Brown, 41, says she has found that cooperative learning works because "the focus is on the kids. It takes me off the stage and puts them onstage, where they'd like to be. They get to talk, process ideas, think out loud."

One of Brown's students, Julio Pinto, 13, explained why he likes her class. "You're not bored," he said. "You get to tell people your ideas. You're not just sitting down listening to the teacher talk."

Area schools officials say some teachers and parents, particularly those of talented and gifted students, worry that those children don't benefit sufficiently from cooperative learning.

They're concerned that, in some collaborative learning environments, smarter students end up doing all the labor in their groups, or might be held back academically by working with youngsters who are not as bright.

Proponents of the classroom strategy acknowledge that if cooperative learning isn't employed correctly, those problems might exist.

"It isn't appropriate for every situation," said Janet Funk, principal at Riverside Elementary in Alexandria. "If you do it all day long, every day, with every lesson, that might not be good for any student."

The University of Maryland's Davidson said teachers can adjust the composition of groups so that brighter students are grouped with other gifted children. Putting gifted students in groups also helps them develop sometimes stunted social skills, he said.

Students say they have been part of classes where teachers didn't use collaborative learning skillfully. "Unless there's a set goal, nothing gets done," said O'Connor, the Yorktown High senior. "Sometimes, you get off task and your group starts talking about football."

In John Strebe's algebra class one recent morning, no one was talking football. Yet Strebe, 45, a math teacher at Mount Hebron High who has used cooperative learning for about 10 years, stalked the classroom like a football coach on the sidelines.

He constantly urged students to 'get into the think mode' as they marched through one problem after another.

In Strebe's class, after each problem, each team must come to a consensus on the answer. At one point, a boy in one group had a correct answer, but his teammates rejected it. They got it wrong.

"Jonas, you gotta fight harder for your answer," Strebe said. "Will ya?'"

"Yes," Jonas said.

"Good man," Strebe said.

There were exchanges like that throughout the period. By the end of the class, Strebe had played instructor, psychologist, motivator. He did not pause once to discipline a child.

Later, Strebe said that this kind of teaching has kept him in the profession. "It's as much fun for me as it is for the kids," he said. "It's antiburnout because you're not just teaching math. You're teaching them how to be better human beings. And that's gratifying."

October 28, 1991

A Radical Prescription for Schools

Researchers See Bureaucracy as the Problem, Autonomy as Cure

KENNETH J. COOPER

Eight years ago, two Stanford political scientists set out to explore a theoretical question about public education. They wanted to know what difference it makes that public school systems are controlled by elected officials.

John E. Chubb and Terry M. Moe deliver their blunt answer in a new book published by the Brookings Institution, "Politics, Markets and America's Public Schools," which is based on an survey of 20,000 principals, teachers and students from 500 schools.

Basically, Chubb and Moe answer that politics makes no good difference in public schooling. They recommend a radical solution: Not only would they let any student choose any public school, but they would also let almost anyone operate a public school, ending the geographic monopolies of school districts.

The researchers concluded that public bureaucracies that control education block the formation of effective schools. They propose "creating a system that is almost entirely beyond the reach of public authority." Chubb and Moe estimate that the constraints imposed by central offices and union contracts cost a high school student the equivalent of a year of study.

Chubb, now a senior fellow at Brookings, said in an interview that school bureaucracy is "not just a problem, it's the problem. It's kind of a good news finding. If bureaucracy is the key problem, that's a problem the public policy-makers can control."

The endorsement of public school choice—which has been primarily advocated by the Bush administration and conservatives—has drawn attention partly because the research was financed mostly by Brookings, which retains a reputation for being a liberal think tank. The Education Department and private foundations also supported the study.

"We welcome converts," said Herb Berkowitz, spokesman for the conservative Heritage Foundation. He described the book as "full of all sorts of things the Heritage Foundation has been talking about for years, full of school choice, vouchers and all that good stuff." one critic of the Brookings study, California Superintendent of Public Instruction Bill Honig, challenged the conclusion that schools cannot improve without radical surgery on bureaucracy. He cited an increase in test scores, equivalent to a year of study, registered by California seniors in the last five years after improvements in curriculum and teacher training.

"Theirs is just all theory," Honig said. "We've got that gain another way. . . . There are other ways of building in incentives [to improve schools] without taking these radical steps."

Chubb and Moe found that a high degree of autonomy prevailed at effective schools, which are described in other education research as those having strong principals, high expectations of students and a clear sense of purpose. The authors also found that school autonomy was likely to be present only at public schools located in small suburbs with homogenous populations. But autonomy is found at private schools anywhere.

"Private schools aren't working because of some magic. . . . They're working because they're focusing on the client (student) and are more effectively organized," Chubb said.

Their proposed overhaul is intended to introduce into public education the market incentives that shape private schools.

States would set minimal standards for public schools—roughly analogous to the existing requirements for graduation, health and safety and teacher certification imposed on private schools. States would relinquish broad authority over other matters such as instructional hours, textbooks and tenure.

Conceivably, private schools could become public schools by signing a new charter. Other groups could organize new public schools and operate outside the control of existing districts. Each school could set its tuitions.

State and local funds would be rolled into "scholarships" approximating per pupil expenditures, except that states would reduce their contributions for students in rich districts and increase them for poor districts. State and federal funds for disadvantaged students would be added to their scholarships. Families could not supplement their children's scholarships, but an entire district could vote to raise its per pupil contribution.

Then through state-run "choice offices," students would get information on various schools and apply to them. Schools could set their own admissions criteria, "subject only to nondiscrimination requirements." The offices would send the scholarship money directly to the schools.

Chubb acknowledged the political difficulties of achieving such a system, which would crimp the power of local officials, teachers unions and state bureaucrats. But in another sense, he added, it would be easier to curb the government role in schools than to expand it.

"It doesn't require elaborate legislation. While it may seem radical, it's a fairly easy thing to do," Chubb said.

June 11, 1990

Schools in Transition: Parents and Educators Try Three New Approaches

Neighborhood Control, a University Affiliation and Parental Choice

DIEGO RIBADENEIRA

For years this city's public school system has symbolized the decay of urban education in America. By most educational indicators, the schools are in crisis. More than half the students who enter the public schools will leave without a high school diploma. Students who remain in the system consistently score near or at the bottom in standardized state tests.

Fifty-five percent of the system's 3,500 students are Hispanic. About three-quarters of the students come from families on welfare, reflecting the dire poverty that has made this tiny industrial city of 25,000 one of the poorest in the state. The city's teenage pregnancy rate is the third highest in Massachusetts.

Exacerbating this bleak picture has been a city unwilling to provide the funds needed to revive the moribund school system. The city allocates only 20 percent of its local tax levy to its five schools—three elementary schools, one combined elementary and middle school and one high school—compared to the statewide average of 54 percent.

"Education hasn't been a priority in this city for a long time," said Elizabeth McBride, a member of the Chelsea School Committee for 12 years. "The money has gone to the police, the fire department and other city workers. Nobody cares much about kids because they don't vote."

As a result said former School Committee member Bruce G. Robinson, "Chelsea has led the state in just about every category of academic failure."

Boston University has waded into this morass, taking over the running of the school system last September at the behest of Chelsea officials and promising to transform the schools by the year 2000 into a beacon of academic excellence. The program is being monitored by the state-appointed Chelsea Oversight Panel, a seven-member group appointed by Gov. Michael Dukakis, in an effort to assuage concern that

BU would operate the school without sufficient accountability. The panel is scheduled to release its first-year findings in mid-August.

The BU-Chelsea agreement, as the 10-year project is formally known, is being closely monitored by educators nationwide, who view it as one of the most dramatic and innovative attempts to overhaul a troubled urban education system.

But the bold experiment—the first time in the nation that a public school system has been operated by a private institution—has not gone as smoothly as Boston University had anticipated. Most BU officials believed—naively some say—that they would be welcomed into Chelsea as saviors.

Instead, the project's first year has been marked by controversy, including two still-pending lawsuits challenging the agreement's legality, that have polarized the university and the very constituents BU will need to mobilize if the project is to succeed. The university's greatest challenge, both supporters and opponents of the project say, is to forge stronger relationships with local leaders—the School Committee, Hispanic activists and teachers—vital to the implementation of the ambitious reforms it has outlined.

Much of the anger toward BU focuses on what critics say is the university's authoritarian and patronizing style of management. School Committee members and the teachers union complain that the university and new superintendent Diana Lam exclude them from important decisions, especially those concerning personnel.

And Hispanic leaders have blasted the university for failing to take their concerns, such as the fate of bilingual education, about the BU-Chelsea project seriously. Both the teachers union and a group of Hispanic leaders have sued to try to annul the agreement.

"BU will get nowhere in the efforts to improve schools unless it starts to do a better job of involving the community," said Massachusetts Education Commissioner Harold Raynolds Jr. "If you don't, then you alienate the people you need to have work with you the most. BU must strive to have all the parties with a vested interest in the schools, parents, Latino leaders and other community activists, committed to working together for change."

Nevertheless, even the university's harshest critics are optimistic that the problems can be overcome and that the project can spark an educational renaissance in this city of the working class and immigrants.

"Despite my criticisms, it still remains my hope that we can transform confrontation into cooperation, that we can change this relationship from one which is quite authoritarian to one where there is a true partnership and that this can be a national model for reform," said Michael Heichman, vice president of the Chelsea Teachers Union.

The drive to have BU take over the Chelsea schools picked up momentum after April 1988, when the university presented to the city a 300-page plan to overhaul the schools. The School Committee in 1987 had asked BU to study the feasibility of running its schools after a similar offer by the university to manage Boston's public schools was rejected two years earlier.

In a scathing report that followed a nine-month study of the school system, the university found "a failure to provide adequate educational leadership" and a school system in which "reasoning, critical thinking and creative thought are not central to the instruction and activities at any grade level."

Boston University and Chelsea officials signed the historic agreement in June 1989. In exchange for managing the system for 10 years, BU promised to introduce a number of innovations, including a network of family schools that would offer preschool classes for 3- and 4-year olds, nutritional services for infants and pregnant women, year-round child care and English and job-training classes for parents.

The University pledged to boost the school system's budget by $6 million over five years to $22 million, using state, federal and private funds. (This year the university raised $2.1 million, falling short of its $3 million goal.) In addition, it said it would build a new elementary school, a new high school and that it would renovate buildings in a system whose newest school was built in 1908.

Having crafted such a comprehensive blueprint, BU spent much of the first year laying the foundation. "Many of the things we did this year didn't touch parents and children per se but they are the things that needed to be done," said Peter Greer, dean of BU's school of education and leader of the Chelsea project.

Computers were installed in schools for student use and in the system's headquarters for record-keeping. Teachers took advantage of dozens of mini-sabbaticals to observe successful education programs in surrounding communities. Many teachers also are attending summer workshops.

After a year of contentious negotiations, teachers ratified a new contract that established merit pay and a school-based management plan that gives individual schools more decision-making power.

In controversial moves that drew the ire of teachers and School Committee members, Lam demoted the high school headmaster and fired five nontenured teachers. Opponents of the moves accused her of highhandedness.

At the Shurtleff Elementary School, fifth-graders read to first-graders under a new peer tutoring program. Bilingual students and regular education students were integrated in an effort to ease the mainstreaming of non-English speaking students into the regular education program. (English is a second language for almost half the system's students.) And an interegenerational literacy program was begun at the Williams School with 41 adults, mostly mothers, learning how to read to their children.

Boston University plans to increase the pace of education reform this fall.

The high school will be divided into schools within a school so students can have the stability of spending more time with the same teacher. There will be further integration of bilingual and monolingual students and a reduction in the removal of elementary and middle school children from their classrooms for remedial work in math and reading. Instead, classrooms will have two teachers, one of whom will work with remedial students.

A comprehensive health center will open at the high school to provide everything from physical examinations for all students to prenatal care for pregnant teenagers. A plan to better distribute minority children among the elementary schools goes into effect in September, a preliminary step necessary before the state can allocate funds for new school buildings.

If budget constraints permit, year-round kindergartens will be established. This part of the program is aimed at providing quality early childhood education, which educators consider the key to stemming the nation's appalling dropout rate.

The scope of the changes frightens some community activists, who fear that too much is happening too quickly, but Lam believes they are necessary to reverse a school system long in decline. "Schools here were not student-centered places where needs of children came first," Lam said. "They were regimented places held down by central administration mandates. If we don't take dramatic action then we're never going to turn around the failure rate of urban schools."

But while most Chelsea activists recognize that the system desperately needs help, some bristle at the style they claim BU has adopted.

"I'm not arguing that this system didn't need shaking up but it's the means to achieve reform that I question," said Marta Rosa, who became the first Hispanic on the School Committee when she was elected in November. Rosa based her campaign largely on her opposition to BU. Hispanics make up more than half of the students in the schools and Latino activists been decrying the system's poor performance for years.

"But BU forgets that the community has been looking for empowerment," Rosa said. "BU sees empowerment of the community as detrimental to the project and unless the community gets empowered it will not be an advocate for education and, no matter what the university does, the schools will not improve. We get told what's going to happen and if we don't like it that's too bad."

As an example, Rosa cites Lam's naming an interim high school administrator the morning after a meeting between members of the School Committee and the BU management team to try to improve relations. Lam did not tell committee members until the next day even though she was at the meeting.

But BU officials and project supporters said the reform of Chelsea's schools are doomed to failure if every decision is steeped in controversy. "We're not going to be slowed down by having to check with this group and fight with this group," Greer said.

And Robinson said, "In my estimation the naysayers are people who don't have a lot of their own creative ideas so they spend their time criticizing everything the university does."

Of the complaints by Hispanic leaders, Greer said, "I've sort of ignored them and that's infuriated them. I will continue to do that as long as they continue to make it a fight for political power."

But some familiar with the project say BU has underestimated the importance of gaining the confidence of Chelsea's Hispanic leadership. "The message BU is sending, through the way they have treated the Latino community, is 'we care about your kids, but we don't care about you,' " said Miren Uriarte, director of the Latino Research Institute at the University of Massachusetts at Boston, and a member of the state-appointed Chelsea Oversight Panel. "If parents get alienated from the system, then their children will be alienated from the system. It takes two to tango, and they have to tango with the community to make this work."

Ultimately, BU may be able to win over even its most virulent detractors if the reforms pursued begin to yield improvements in the dropout rate and in test scores, and the system begins to attract parents who otherwise would send their children to private schools or, in some cases, move out. An adequate assessment will require at least three to five years, most believe.

"For years there's been a malaise over the Chelsea School System," said Morris Siegal, a School Committee member. "And now things are changing. There is hope where before there wasn't any. We have goals toward which we are moving . . . We may disagree over how we get there but at least we're heading there. At least somebody is trying."

Diego Ribadeneira is an education writer for The Boston Globe.

August 5, 1990

Whittle's for-Profit Schools: Bold Claims and Criticism

Maverick Marketer Pushes Controversial Education Experiment with Burst of Publicity

MARY JORDAN

Wearing his custom-made earpiece and daily uniform, a navy suit and bright bow tie, Christopher Whittle settled into a Capitol Hill television studio one day last week to talk to 16 cities before lunch.

"If successful, these new schools will not be recognizable to the schools that you and I went to," Whittle told a television anchor in Knoxville, Tenn.

Two minutes later, Dallas beamed in. "The new schools will be as different from the current ones as the light bulb was to a candle," he told Texas.

Since Whittle's surprise announcement last week that he has snared Yale University President Benno C. Schmidt Jr. to head his latest brain-child, a multibillion-dollar proposal to build the first national chain of private schools, the Tennessee entrepreneur has become as hot as a Hollywood star.

Whittle says he will build 1,000 for-profit, top-flight schools and operate them for the same average cost per pupil—$5,500—as public schools. By creating a "breakthrough" school model that could be copied in all of America's 110,000 elementary and secondary schools, Whittle and others believe he may be setting in motion the most signif-icant catalyst ever to reshape U.S. schools. But following the burst of publicity surrounding the Edison Project, many wonder if Whittle can back up his bold claim that he is about to change the way U.S. schools do business.

For one thing, critics say business may be all Whittle has in mind.

"It's very hard to challenge someone who says he wants to improve the public schools," said Arnold Fege, director of government affairs for the National Parent Teachers Association. "But just look at Whittle's track record. He is not an educator; he is not serious about improving education; he is serious about marketing."

"I think the education community should be up in arms. He is exploiting the environment that says we need better schools," Fege said. "This is a huge dupe on America."

A technology maverick and a master marketer, Whittle, 44, is the first to agree he is controversial. He has made millions by placing "Channel One" television sets in 10,000 American schools and piping Nike, Burger King and other commercials through them.

Yes, he admits, he does plan to publish tests and films and other supplies that will be used in his schools; a concern many have is that he and his financial backers will use the students in their schools to make fortunes selling materials to them.

In addition to Whittle Communications, major backers of the unprecedented school experiment are: Time Warner, Philips Electronics N.V. of the Netherlands and Associated Newspapers, which owns *The Daily Mail* and other London tabloids.

Chester E. Finn Jr., a former Bush administration education adviser recently hired to join the team developing the $60 million design, calls those who criticize Whittle for injecting profiteering and advertising into schools "profoundly hypocritical."

In any classroom, Finn said, students see "Ticonderoga on the No. 2 pencil, Houghton Mifflin on the spine of their books and Rand McNally on the map."

Finn said the Edison Project board members, which include Brookings Institution senior fellow John E. Chubb, former *Newsweek* assistant managing editor Dominique Browning and Grand Central and 34th Street Partnerships president Daniel Biederman, "do not want to be associated with hucksterism." Finn said the team "would bail out fast" if it were.

But still others are uneasy with the ties to the Bush administration by Whittle and other backers of the Edison Project.

Education Secretary Lamar Alexander, a fellow Tennessean, was a business consultant of Whittle's, and Deputy Secretary David Kearns was a former member of the Time Warner board of directors. Saying they want to avoid any conflict of interest, the top two U.S. education officials have kept silent on one of the biggest undertakings in grammar and high school education.

The administration's proposed vouchers could be a boom to the Edison Project, where tuition will be around $5,500 a year. Parents would use vouchers, or taxpayer dollars, toward private school tuition, but Whittle said he is not counting on the program to make his project economically feasible.

Assistant Education Secretary Diane Ravitch called the Edison Project "a very important experiment," adding, "Any time anybody wants to create good schools, it's a good thing."

Peter D. Relic, president of the National Association of Independent Schools, a group representing 1,000 private elementary and secondary schools, also applauded the Whittle project, which is expected to cost as such as $2.5 billion for initial construction, staff and equipment at 100 sites. The first 100 elementary schools—including two or three in the Washington area—are to open by 1996.

"We need radical change in American education, not tinkering but a revolution," Relic said. "So my reaction to Whittle and Schaidt is that there is now a chance that change will come. I say, welcome into the fray."

It is still unknown what the schools will look like or how the curriculum will differ; even Whittle says he doesn't know. His design team, he said, is now "editing together" the best ideas in schools.

But Whittle said the schools would operate on a longer school year, an eight- or nine-hour school day and with the latest technology. Students could spend up to three hours daily on "electronic learning systems," from television sets to computers. Teachers are to be paid more than most teachers earn now, but there likely will be fewer of them per pupil. Parents and volunteers are expected to have a more important role in classroom instruction than now.

The effect of the proposed schools on a similar government effort to build "New American Schools" is unknown.

That venture, announced last year as part of the administration's "America 2000" education plan, had hoped to raise $200 million privately to design "break-the-mold schools." But as the deadline nears, only a quarter of the goal has been raised.

Meanwhile, Whittle says he has been deluged with investors who prefer to work outside the existing school system and who are more interested in a for-profit venture.

The interest rose dramatically when Whittle persuaded Schmidt to quit Yale and lend his credibility to the project.

"We intend to question everything about the current schools and build on a fresh slate," said Schmidt, 50, the former dean of Columbia Law School.

He and Whittle were talking nearly nonstop about their novel experiment last week, giving interviews to morning network news shows before Whittle, who was coached by Republican media guru Roger Ailes and had his own earpiece made after a loaner repeatedly fell out during "Nightline," gave interviews via satellite with 16 faraway stations.

"Warren Beatty and Arnold Schwarzenegger can sit down at 8 and not get up until 5" doing nothing but one interview after another, said Whittle, offering a glimpse of his show-business side that makes many educators cringe.

"Will what they [Whittle and his backers] do really result in qualitative changes to our schools?" asked Relic, the private school association president. "We will see."

May 31, 1992

Low Marks for Channel One

Study Casts Doubt on TV Program's Effectiveness in Schools

DAVID STREITFELD

Channel One, the innovative and controversial program from Whittle Communications that requires students to watch 10 minutes of news and two minutes of commercials a day, received a poor grade last week.

The first part of a three-year study being conducted by the Institute for Social Research at the University of Michigan found that Channel One viewers got only one more item correct on a current events test of 30 questions than their non-viewing counterparts.

That's equivalent to 3.3 percent better, which principal investigator Jerome Johnston calls "statistically significant but educationally unimportant."

"What the research suggests is that the average student in the typical school is not learning a lot from Channel One," says Johnston.

Critics of Channel One have been quick to trumpet the report's conclusions. "It takes away what Whittle would like to claim as one of its most compelling arguments: that this has a definite educational role," says Stan Soloway, co-chair of a task force seeking to remove Channel One from Stuart-Hobson middle School on Capitol Hill.

Channel One has been playing in 53 District schools since September, and will be voted on by the Prince George's County Board of Education Thursday. "The report's going to have an impact," says Suzanne Plogman, Board of Education chairman. "I can't ignore it." The board, eager for the video equipment that Whittle lends schools for the duration of the contract, is leaning toward voting yes.

Whittle spokeswoman Nancy Young concedes that "certainly there's some disappointment we didn't make as much headway as we hoped." But she's trying to look on the bright side of things. At least, she points out, "It didn't make the students stupider. There were larger improvements among the brighter ones. We didn't do as well with average students as we'd like to, but we'll do better."

In spite of the publicity generated by the study—which was paid for by Whittle but was conducted independently by the institute and

Interwest Applied Research—Young says, "I don't know of a single phone call from a school saying this isn't what we were promised. There've been no complaints."

Eleven sites around the country participated in the study, which paired a Channel One school with a non-Channel One school. The sites represent all types of locations, from a parochial school district in a large California city to an extremely rural district in Oklahoma to medium-size cities in Florida, Massachusetts and Virginia. All told there are 3,200 students involved. No comparisons were made with other broadcasts geared to students, such as CNN Newsroom.

The study moreover deals only with the news side of Channel One—especially the four minutes or so of hard news at the beginning—and not the commercials. That's the way Whittle wanted it. In his report, Johnston says that "the researchers were not in agreement with this exclusion, but they had to admit that the task of reliably estimating such effects is daunting at best." Kids, after all, see the same commercials at home, so it would be hard to measure any additional effect from those in school.

In any case, Johnston writes, "Those for whom the presence of commercialism of any form in the school is unacceptable do not need any data to guide their response to Channel One. Others who do not reject commercialism on purely philosophic grounds probably think of the issue in cost-benefit terms. Are the schools and students receiving sufficient value?"

This study, he concluded, should help the 10,000 Channel One junior high and high schools "decide if their initial judgments were appropriate."

And were they? Pressed on this point in an interview, Johnston pauses and says: "That depends on their motives. Most took it for some mix of equipment and education. On the education question, I think they have been disappointed."

During the two years the study has yet to run, Johnston hopes to answer some of the perplexing questions it has already raised—in addition to determining if the Persian Gulf War, which took place during part of the survey period last year, had any distorting effect. The war was such a compelling news event that it's possible students found Channel One added nothing to what they already knew.

One of the questions he hopes to answer: Even if students on average weren't picking things up, why did they think they were? Forty-seven percent said they felt they were learning something important either always or most of the time, while 39 percent said that was true only some of the time and 14 percent said never.

In addition, when asked if the news from Channel One was equal in value to other material they learned in school, 42 percent said yes. Another quarter found it more valuable.

Enthusiasm among teachers is also high. Sixty percent of those in the Channel One schools said they would recommend it strongly or very strongly; only 6 percent had strong reservations.

"If we really had a loser here, the teachers should be saying, 'Get it out of here.' And they're not," Johnston says. "My guess is that educators share the view that our kids don't know a lot about current events, that they think the problem ought to be solved, and if Channel One is there solving it they can go on teaching English or French or whatever."

In reality, however, there was great variation in the testing scores between schools. There were some schools where Channel One made no difference at all, while in others the viewing students did much better in the testing than the non-viewers.

The report speculates that these latter schools "figured out how to take advantage of what the news program brought into the school by devoting instructional time to current events above and beyond simply watching the broadcast."

Of course, once teachers start wrapping more classroom time around the Channel One broadcast, there will be a knotty methodological problem in determining who gets the credit for any increase in current events knowledge: the teacher or the program.

Whittle is seeking to improve its programming. But perhaps the larger lesson is that people shouldn't expect too much from Channel One in the first place, spokeswoman Young cautioned.

"I'm not sure what the average Joe who's watching NBC or CBS evening news would retain from it," she said.

"There's no way that a day and a half worth of television-watching"—which is what the hard news segment of Channel One adds up to over a school year—"is going to enormously change students' knowledge base or their attitude to news."

May 1, 1992

The News on Channel One

Communications and its Controversial Program

DAVID STREITFELD

Homeroom has started at Stuart-Hobson Middle School on Capitol Hill but first . . . a word from our sponsor. It's 9 a.m. and the television monitor perched on the wall above Alberta Clement's seventh-graders glows and comes to life. It's time for Channel One, a controversial news-and-commercials broadcast that has been a fixture in 53 District schools since September.

The pace is fast, the graphics colorful, the anchors much more likely to have suffered recent bouts of acne than Dan Rather or Peter Jennings. The 17 students in the room swivel and watch, some sitting up straight, others in the ubiquitous student sprawl. A few are taking notes.

On top of the news: brief wrap-ups on the continuing pursuit of Libya over the Pan Am bombing; a volcano eruption in Sicily; the Chicago flooding; the Caterpillar strike. Break for commercials: M&Ms, Diet Pepsi. Then a science feature on using DNA as evidence in criminal cases and a piece on new music technology, along with an Arrid deodorant spot. After 12 minutes, it's all over. Quiet settles again on the classroom.

Clement is enthusiastic about Channel One. "We're not losing any lesson time," she says, explaining that these minutes were previously used by the students to ask questions. "In fact, I'd say it's an enrichment."

Others feel quite the contrary and are trying to get Channel One removed from Stuart-Hobson. A task force of parents is looking into raising the $5,000 needed to replace the 15 monitors, satellite dish and other equipment that Whittle Communications has lent to the school so that its Channel One broadcast can be viewed every morning. Then, the parents say, the students will have the advantage of video technology without being held captive to an entrepreneur seeking to make a profit.

"I believe, and everyone on our task force agrees, that schools should be a haven from commercialism," says co-chair Stan Soloway.

"We have a law that you cannot sell or serve junk foods in schools, yet now students can go to school and see advertisements for them. There's a real contradiction here. . . . We're offering our kids up as the price for getting a few televisions."

Channel One has provoked an abundance of similar criticism in its three years of existence. The New York State Board of Regents, for instance, voted unanimously to ban Channel One, while California State Superintendent of Public Instruction Bill Honig said at a 1989 news conference that "it's a bad deal for kids, a bad deal for education, and it sets a terrible precedent." His efforts to reduce state funding to any public school that uses Channel One has kept enrollment there to a minimum.

Elsewhere, however, Whittle is doing fine—ahead of projections, the Tennessee company says. It currently is in 10,000 public or private middle and high schools, which is about a third of the U.S. total.

Besides the District, in this area Whittle says it has a contract with 74 Maryland schools, 55 of which are in Baltimore. Seven are in St. Mary's County, seven in Calvert. In Prince George's, Whittle was turned down by the Board of Education two years ago in a 5 to 4 vote.

There are no schools with Channel One in Montgomery County. Of the 246 schools with contracts in Virginia, none is in Fairfax, Prince William, Alexandria or Loudoun. Arlington has three—all parochial.

This suggests Whittle has found some of its most eager clients in the more strapped school districts. "The poorer you are, the more likely you are to sign on, because anything free looks better than nothing," says Peggy Charren, president of Action for Children's Television and a leading Whittle critic.

Last May the D.C. school board voted unanimously, with one abstention, to move forward with Channel One. The head of the board's technology committee, vice president Nate Bush (Ward 7), was its main sponsor.

"The obvious disadvantage was the two minutes of commercials," Bush says. "But we weighed that against the possible benefits." Those included the loan of the monitors by Whittle, which then could be used during the day for other educational purposes, including additional (and commercial-free) programming from Whittle or competing cable material, or the school system's own TV channel. "My understanding," Bush says, "is that some schools are making a great deal of use out of the equipment."

As for the 10 minutes of news on Channel One, Bush believes it is "an excellent program that focuses on whatever's happening in the world. Channel One ran as a pilot at Jefferson Junior High School.

Consistently, we found that it provided the first real contact the students had with current events."

During the trial period, Bush says, "we asked students what they thought about the commercials. In some instances they said they tuned out when the commercials came on. Also, they said, 'We're not seeing anything we don't see on TV each day, so what's the big deal?'" His own son, he notes, attended Jefferson. "I don't think he's been contaminated."

Yet even such a supporter as Bush notes that advertiser-driven programming in the schools is not a choice every parent will have to confront.

"It's become an issue of the haves and the have-nots, no doubt about that," he says. "Poor people in poor school districts are always forced to make decisions that affluent people in more affluent districts do not."

What the Critics Say

Channel One, its critics argue, is capitalism run amok, renting children's class time to sell such products as Snickers, Burger King, Three Musketeers and Mountain Dew in exchange for loaned technology of dubious value.

At best, these opponents assert, students are going to get a mixed message from seeing this material promoted in the classroom; at worst, the idea that junk has an official stamp of approval.

Schools, they add, are places where students are supposed to learn to be good citizens, not good consumers. "The schools are caught between a rock and a hard place. They don't have the money, and along comes this huckster with some fancy-schmancy goods. It's hard to say no," says Jill Savitt of the Center for the Study of Commercialism. "Whittle is seizing on a desperate situation."

The news part of the programming is touted by Whittle as "10 minutes of news and geography that have proven a valuable learning tool for teachers and students." Whittle sent *The Washington Post* for review a week's worth of March programs containing an AIDS series of which the company is particularly proud.

The first day featured a teenager who had been infected through sexual contact with her hemophiliac boyfriend. It was a monologue rather than an interview in the traditional sense, with truly odd camera angles that would focus in tight close-ups on different parts of her face. The fifth day also was a profile, this time of a 22-year-old man. Again, it suffered from excessive melodrama and a lack of hard information.

The middle three days featured a more straightforward presentation of the disease, with cameos and contributions from such young stars as Khalil Kain and Chubb Rock. This was excellently done, and it's hard to imagine any teenagers—particularly the urban youths at which it was aimed—not watching it and being affected. That was Channel One at its best.

AIDS, however, is a topic of special urgency. More typical five-part series over the past year were "Natural Disasters," "Teens on TV" and "The Science of Speed and Motion." This is not, Channel One opponents argue, the sort of "news" that is worth taking away class time.

A daily dose of Channel One, which the schools are contractually bound to show at least 90 percent of time, adds up to six full days of the school year. "In a district where school kids have greater needs and should be receiving more instruction for longer periods of time with greater academic rigor, that's immoral," says Arnold Fege, director of governmental relations for the National PTA.

In Detroit last month, four science teachers were caught turning off Channel One so their students could do lab work instead. "The teachers thought the priority was the curriculum of academics as opposed to the curriculum of TV," a chemistry teacher and union spokesman told the Detroit Free Press. The teachers thought wrong; they were reprimanded for violating the district's contract with Whittle.

More scholarly arguments also have been made against presenting news to youngsters in this format. Television is both a passive and a rapid-fire experience, even if you take notes and discuss it later. Learning is supposed to be less hurried and less placid. Good teachers slow down when the material gets too tough, respond to the eagerness of the class know-it-all, call on the daydreaming student to make him pay attention.

Television prevents all that. The Whittle approach to news, opponents assert, makes *USA Today* look as wordy as the *Federal Register*. This isn't news, they argue; it's the illusion of news.

"If the goal is to produce a well-informed citizenry," wrote Cassandra Tate in an opinion column in *Columbia Journalism Review*, "it could be better served by reinstituting an ancient custom: current events quizzes."

Another argument made against Channel One is the problematic nature of the toehold it establishes. Other companies are likely to imitate Whittle's lead in leasing schools something in exchange for a chance at a valuable captive audience.

"A free, shiny history book with an ad every 10 pages will mean as much to a poor school system as a TV, and maybe more," says ACT's Charren. "Or a computer company will give you free computers as long as you use their software, which just happens to be filled with ads directed to teenagers. . . . The marketplace is winning. That's what's the matter."

Putting It to a Vote

The one member of the D.C. school board who abstained from the unanimous vote last May was Erika Landberg (Ward 3). Now, she says, "since I haven't been persuaded otherwise, I think I would vote no." She felt a bit rushed. The way the issue was presented, "we couldn't defer. The opportunity with Whittle was at that time."

Board member Bush confirms that, because of a shortage of monitors, the word from Whittle was that an immediate yes vote meant the system would be up and running by September. If there was a delay in voting, on the other hand, the schedule got much more vague.

Nevertheless, Bush says, "I don't think board members felt they had an obligation to do it at that time."

In addition to the now-or-never flavor of the debate, Landberg says there was something of all-or-nothing thrown in as well. "The first contract read that we would be agreeing to put Channel One in all of our secondary schools and adult education centers," she says. "After that, the principal at Wilson raised questions. She caused the administration to go back and see if they could change a few things, and Whittle accepted it."

There were no public hearings on the issue. News traveled slowly. Since it was then summer, with kids out of school and parents concerned with other than scholarly matters, there was perhaps less immediate feedback than there would have been at other times of the year. Silence was taken for assent.

"In retrospect," says Bush, "perhaps we could have done more to bring the matter to the attention of the public, so they could be aware of what we were contemplating." He adds that "by and large, the program has been received with a great deal of enthusiasm by 80 to 90 percent of the community."

One place where it wasn't was Wilson High, the only school to opt out of the program. "We want the hardware, we want the technology, but we do not want to abide by the stipulations that would be placed on us," says principal Wilma Bonner, who made the decision based on input from faculty, her PTA and "certainly my own very serious concerns about the contract."

At Stuart-Hobson Middle School, the system was up and running before the opposition began to form. "We weren't aware that Whittle was coming," says Dan Harrison, president of the Capitol Hill Cluster PTA, which includes Stuart-Hobson. "I wasn't aware of any notices coming to me or to schools allowing parental input or discussing who, what, where, when or why."

The task force will make its recommendations next month. "No one is against educational programming," says Harrison. "The question is, do we want it at the expense of commercialization?"

An alternate source of news programming is CNN Newsroom, a daily, commercial-free and free 15-minute program that is expressly designed for schools. For general classroom material, a primary resource is Cable in the Classroom, a nonprofit organization to which 20 cable networks contribute. It offers 500 hours of commercial-free programming a month to any school that has access to cable, which either is in place or on the way for all the city's schools.

Meanwhile, in Prince George's County, Channel One is scheduled to be voted on by the board of education for a second time early next month. "Our school board is going to base its) decision on the pulse of the community," says chairman Suzanne Plogman, who says she voted against it "with very, very mixed feelings" last time.

The battle lines developed this way, Plogman says: "Those opposed felt that teenagers as well as most other people are exposed to too much TV as it is, and inundated with too much commercialism as it is, and they didn't want to see the schools used to promote it."

Whittle's supporters, meanwhile, didn't find the commercials objectionable in either theory or practice, and also felt "this was a way for the school system to acquire a lot of hardware we otherwise would never have been able to afford," Plogman says. "I think they were also impressed with the quality of the programming."

She predicts: "It's going to bring out strong reactions again, either pro or con."

Whither Whittle?

In a move that the critics view as significant, Nike has not renewed its advertising with Whittle. Partly, the sneaker company makes clear, that's because it's made no advertising commitments in the next year to anybody. But ad director Scott Bedbury concedes that the company has some particular problems with Channel One itself.

"We're not crazy about taking a direct product message at kids in that particular venue," he says. "You have to take a step back and look at it from ethical considerations." Nike is in negotiation with Whittle on ways to do something that has more innovation and less hard sell than a traditional ad.

Whittle, meanwhile, is not exactly standing still. *The New York Times* reported last fall that the company was considering the introduction of an elementary school version of Channel One. Whittle didn't exactly deny the story, saying "we're not far enough down that path yet" to discuss details. And the company, which is partly owned by Time Warner and the Dutch consumer giant Philips Electronics, has announced plans to start 200 schools of its own by 1996. Whittle Schools & Laboratories, the company says, "will be a private, for-profit company with a public agenda."

In D.C., the Channel One contract runs three years. It's been indicated to the parents at Stuart-Hobson that, if a majority decide against Channel One, the board of education will support its removal. "I think parents should have the choice," says Bush.

And what of Christopher Whittle himself? His company's promotional literature stresses the advantages of making "world news relevant to the concerns of teenagers" via television. The 44-year-old entrepreneur was once asked in an interview what he watched on TV as a child.

He laughed and said: "I was in a small town in Tennessee, where the reception wasn't very good. And frankly, when I was a kid, I worked a lot. I carried newspapers in the early morning and late afternoon, and then it was homework at night. I didn't watch much TV."

April 20, 1992

Multicultural Education 8

When School Becomes a Melting Pot

Annandale Seeks to Close Language, Education Gaps

PETER BAKER

Thien Nguyen spends his days at Annandale High School tinkering with automobile engines.

Hunched over the hood of a malfunctioning Chevy, his hands stained by motor oil, Nguyen quietly and diligently labors in the auto mechanics garage at the Fairfax County school almost all day long while teacher Earl Stinson conducts his mechanics classes for other students. Nguyen doesn't take history, math or biology.

"Here's a kid who's not going to graduate; we know he's not going to graduate," Stinson said. "So they assigned him to me for five periods a day to double up his experience and prepare him to make a living." Without the automotive training, Stinson said, "he would've been a throwaway."

The situation of students like Thien Nguyen illustrates a quiet but extraordinary transformation taking place at Annandale High.

Once known as a typically suburban, predominantly white, high school with a piledriver football team, Annandale today reflects the tremendous influx of non-English-speaking immigrants into Fairfax, the Washington area's most populous jurisdiction.

Schools in the eastern county, such as Falls Church or JEB Stuart high schools, already have felt the impact of increasingly diverse student bodies, while those closer to the central part of the county are now beginning to see the changes in store for the region: By 1998, the proportion of minority students will rise from 26 to 37 percent, primarily Asians and Hispanics, and most classrooms in the east will be less than half white, according to county projections.

At Annandale, roughly one-third of the 2,007 students are minorities and 31 percent of students have native languages other than English. Signs announce the main office, guidance center and attendance office in six languages. English as a second language classes are overflowing, growing sixfold in the last 10 years. Immigrant students speak of painful social and cultural adjustments.

And increasingly, students such as Thien Nguyen are entering the school system late in their youth, with fragmented academic backgrounds, little or no grounding in English and, especially with recent Afghan arrivals, war-torn histories—forcing educators at Annandale to address problems that barely existed five years ago.

Principal G. Raymond Watson, who takes "Polyglot" groups of students on occasional field trips to build intercultural ties, said he has exempted two or three students such as Nguyen from classroom requirements because of special circumstances.

"They're almost always kids who arrive in the country late in their educational careers," he said. "In fact, I don't know of an exception. They're highly motivated; they're not kids who are asking for anything. They just need an opportunity."

A 20-year-old native of Vietnam, Thien Nguyen arrived here in the summer of 1985, escaping the destitution of his homeland. "They are communists and they don't give you any job," he explained matter-of-factly. His family stayed briefly in Pennsylvania, but finding no school programs for foreign-born students, they moved to Northern Virginia, where they had heard about a thriving Vietnamese community.

In school, Nguyen found he could handle the classes in social studies, science, math, but English proved almost indecipherable. He said he could manage the grammar rules, but became lost when it came to vocabulary or writing a paragraph. Without the requisite four years of English, it became clear he would not be able to don a cap and gown and graduate.

Rather than let him leave school without any marketable skills, Stinson agreed to supervise Nguyen in his auto mechanics shop for most of the school day. Nguyen is good with a monkey wrench, interested in automobile engines and is a dedicated worker, Stinson said, so he is training Nguyen and will help find him a job with a local auto shop or dealership.

To Nguyen, the arrangement could serve as a springboard to Northern Virginia Community College, where he hopes to take some vocational classes and possibly more English, and gives him the satisfaction of working on something at which he excels. "If car cannot run, you try to figure out (what's wrong and) fix it," he said. "You feel like doctor." To Stinson, the situation makes lemonade out of lemons, saving an intelligent, hard-working young man from an educational system that could not help him within its normal bounds. "He's a good kid and we're going to do something with him," said Stinson, who has taught at Annandale for nine years. "We're not just going to let him get lost in the shuffle."

Still, even administrators at the school remain unsure of how to best serve Nguyen. Last week, they reduced his time in the auto shop and put him in another English as a second language class.

"Speak English is the most difficult thing I have had to learn. It still make my heart stuffy. As I speak English, I can't speak English completely. I always want to speak fast and nicely but I cannot do that. Sometimes I speak like a normal American kid, then they do not understand that what am I saying. That make me feel bad."

Annandale students speak more than 15 native languages, and at times, said first-year Spanish teacher Cheryl Moore, "it's like teaching the United Nations."

At Annandale, the booming English as a second language program is a daily melting pot for students from countries that include Vietnam, Chile, Honduras, Ethiopia, Afghanistan and Sierra Leone.

Teacher Kathy Hermann's beginning ESL class is rambunctious, and most of the students' banter comes in native tongues that make the class a virtual Tower of Babel. "I'm hearing a lot of Korean," Hermann admonished at one point recently.

ESL classes, intended to provide foreign-born students with enough tools to survive in mainstream classes, focus on English, geography and culture. At the basic level, in which students spend three of their six periods a day in ESL, teachers concentrate simply on the fundamentals. But as the students progress, program coordinator Lillian Arezina likes to have them write journals, both to practice their language skills and to help them express the trials of adjusting to a new country.

ESL classes are taught exclusively in English, as Fairfax education officials believe bilingual education is virtually impossible in a county where more than 75 native languages are spoken. Hermann said she speaks Spanish, but does not use it in class. "When you use it, others [with different native languages) feel deprived," she explained.

In their first year in ESL, students are generally seated next to those who speak the same native language for support. By the time they get to advanced ESL, that's reversed, on the theory that they should be weaned off their crutch.

"The natural way to learn a language is to learn it the way these kids learn it, even though it seems hard," Hermann said. "You've got to remember, throughout the school day, that's all they hear."

"I don't feel comfortable with Americans. I know lot of American and very close but I still don't feel comfortable with them. I just can't tell why I feel uncomfortable. It's just a random American but why should I feel this way that I never had before."

Fitting in during high school can be traumatic enough for teenagers. At Annandale today, there are the added factors of language and culture.

"The school is nice for foreign students," said Seung Han Yoo, a 17-year-old Korean who moved to the area a year ago after living in Paraguay. But friends tend to congregate according to background, he adds. "Korean students play with Korean students, ESL students with ESL students, Americans with Americans."

Sitting in the lunchroom eating pizza and burgers, wearing fashionable white sneakers and designer clothes, he and several of his fellow Korean students explain the dynamics of social life and acceptance at Annandale.

"We want to be in the part of the group," said Steve Sung, an 18-year-old who Americanized his name from Won Man Sung. "If you want to be in the group, you have to be like them. . . . We're following American style."

The longer they're here, the easier that becomes. "Those Koreans who've been here more than 10 years, they don't play with us. They don't speak Korean," said Seung Han Yoo. "They're more like Americans. They wear (clothes) like Americans. They speak like Americans."

Across the cafeteria, another group of Korean-born students idle away the lunch hour, sitting separate not only from Americans but also from those fellow Koreans who arrived here more recently.

Peter Chung, a 17-year-old senior who has been in the United States for eight years, points to a group of Korean students sitting at the next table. "See them over there? They've only been here five years," he said, by way of explanation.

"We don't know much about Korean culture because we left there early when we were kids," said Wayne Choi, 19.

"I never see them," Sunny Yoo, a 16-year-old who has lived in the United States since she was 4, said of the newer arrivals. "They're not in any of our classes . . . . They look at us weird. I guess it's kind of envy or something."

"One day I was sitting in beauty salon with my sister. This old lady came and stood beside me then as Ethiopian custom I stood up and told her to sit in my sit. The lady was so angry because she think I looked at her like weak old lady. So she start yelling at me. . . . Sometimes to do something good gets you in trouble."

Sometimes trying to do good gets teachers in trouble, too. Stumbling over cultural protocols has become an occupational hazard at Annandale these days.

Sometimes Afghan boys, for instance, are uncomfortable taking orders from female teachers or administrators, teachers said. A Vietnamese boy recently complained to an assistant principal that he did not like to be touched even in an affectionate way because that is unusual in his culture. And some female students raised in a strict Moslem tradition are uncomfortable undressing and changing into shorts for gym classes.

Arezina, who runs her ESL class like a stern but caring mother who is as likely to hug her students as scold them, likes to tell stories of culture shock that made her stop and rethink her traditional class lectures: Such as the time she "got on the case" of an Afghan teenager who smoked cigarettes, only to be told that he picked up the habit when he joined the army at age 12; or the time she preached to her class that money can't buy happiness, only to have a stubborn Vietnamese boy tell her that money had literally bought his family freedom.

"To me, geography was just something where you point at a map," she said. "These kids have made it so real. You really get to meet the world."

October 29, 1989

More Immigrant Children Face Double Disadvantage

Many Have Had Little or No Schooling

ERIN MARCUS

As a young child, Chek Sem saw a bomb explosion kill his friends in a field in Cambodia. He escaped the Khmer Rouge when he was 9, trekking through the jungle to the Thai border with his mother and sister.

But after immigrating to the United States, Sem ran into an obstacle that seemed even more insurmountable: getting his high school diploma.

The 21-year-old Silver Spring resident first walked into a classroom at age 11, illiterate in his native language and unable to speak English. Eight years later, he had finished all the course work needed for graduation, but had failed the Maryland Functional Writing Test, which Maryland requires for a diploma, five times.

"I felt kind of down on myself," Sem said. "Like, how come I didn't pass?"

Sem's struggle, educators say, is becoming an increasingly common story in U.S. schools as the number of immigrants reaches new highs and more foreign students enter the school system. More than 9 million people immigrated to the United States during the last decade, more than in any other 10-year span since 1905-1914, when 10 million people arrived, according to the Washington-based Urban Institute.

Unlike immigrants of 20 to 30 years ago, many of whom had attended school and could read, a growing number of today's immigrants received no education in their homelands because of war or poverty, some school officials said. High school teachers are seeing more students arriving who are illiterate or have only second- or third-grade educations, with few of the basic skills that are developed in the early years of elementary school.

At Montgomery Blair High School in Silver Spring, which has one of the largest English for Speakers of Other Languages (ESOL) programs in Maryland, officials said nearly a third of their 353 ESOL students arrived with "interrupted" educations, meaning they have missed at least a year of school and are below the grade level for their age. Blair ESOL director Joseph Bellino said some are enrolling in classes here with no prior schooling at all.

In the District, officials estimate that more than 80 percent of their 1,200 high school students who speak limited English are entering at least two grade levels behind their English-speaking peers.

No official estimates are available on the number of immigrant children who are arriving with "interrupted" educations nationwide or throughout the Washington area. But teachers and school officials said the problem is greatest in areas with large immigrant populations, such as Washington. The 1990 Census revealed that more than 568,000 area residents speak a foreign language at home. More than one-fifth of Montgomery County residents speak another language at home, and more than one-quarter of Arlington County residents do so, according to the census.

Some of the teenage immigrants enrolling here have missed so much school that catching up and getting their diplomas is a herculean task, teachers said. The older they are when they arrive, the less time they have to catch up, and some students never do.

"For every success story, there are two failures," Bellino said of the students who arrive with little formal education.

In addition to missed schooling, the students often are struggling to recover emotionally from the experience of war and have chaotic family lives. Others spend hours at jobs to help support their families and come to school hungry because their families can't afford food.

The problem is most acute in high schools, where the students who are behind have less time to catch up than they would in elementary or middle school. The influx of such students is placing new demands on high school ESOL programs, which traditionally have assumed that a student can read and write in a language other than English—an assumption that many of these students don't meet.

It also is placing new strains on high school ESOL teachers, who were trained to teach English to teenagers but are finding themselves responsible for some of the instruction an elementary school teacher would do.

Dropout figures have not been compiled for ESOL students with "interrupted" educations, but school officials said their dropout rate is likely to be much higher than the rate for other students. At Blair High School, for example, Bellino estimated that 15 of the approximately 200 "interrupted" education students who entered his ESOL program since 1989 have graduated, while 42 have dropped out.

The main reason students drop out, Bellino said, is "frustration . . . the school's really difficult, the family needs money, he or she is getting older and the material isn't getting any easier."

"I don't think we can reduce the dropout rate," he added. "I don't know how to reduce the frustration factor."

Even when a student is persistent and committed to graduating, getting a diploma can be extremely difficult. Chek Sem, the Cambodian immigrant, is one such example.

Determined to get a diploma so he could have something to show his relatives, Sem chose to stay in school after finishing his course requirements in order to qualify for taking the functional writing test again.

But the next time he took the test, after a summer of additional study, he failed. So he took it again—and failed.

At age 21, he took the exam for the eighth time—and finally passed.

"I came to the United States and I had to have something to show for it," he said proudly. "I had to accomplish what I got."

To help students like Sen, teachers are improvising with new techniques and materials because traditional high school ESOL books are designed for people who already have been to school. At Blair High, Bellino said, teachers have turned to elementary instruction techniques to teach basic concepts such as addition and subtraction to students who are sometimes 17 and 18 years old.

At High Point High in Beltsville, ESOL teacher Lois Nahmani said she tries to use role-playing to get students who aren't used to sitting in a classroom all day out of their seats. "For many, it's hard to sit down all day. Their attention spans are short," she said.

Teachers stressed that many of these students are intelligent and can learn quickly, despite their lack of formal schooling. But they said that teaching students with widely varying educational backgrounds in the same classroom can be difficult.

In Montgomery County, which has the most ESOL students of any school district in Maryland and in the Washington area, 13 high schools have ESOL departments that teach low-level reading and subjects such as social studies to students who speak limited English. But none of the ESOL departments teaches electives, and nine do not teach low-level math, instead dispatching the students to regular math classes.

ESOL teachers said it is important for their students to take electives and other classes with the English-speaking students so that they don't become isolated.

"They need to integrate themselves," said Nivea Berrios, a teacher at Springbrook High School in Silver Spring. "It's no good if they stay in the ESOL bubble."

But Berrios said some of her students are terrified of their electives because the U.S.-born students sometimes ridicule them and the teachers are not always used to working with them.

At Springbrook, Berrios said, one 17-year-old, a Vietnamese Amerasian who barely spoke English, avoided school for two days because he hadn't understood anything his baking teacher had said. When the teacher gave his a six-page test—in English—he refused to go to class, she said.

She said another student, a 15-year-old from El Salvador, came to her distraught after her first ceramics class. "She came to me crying and said, 'I don't understand,'" Berrios said. "Everybody laughed when she tried to talk, and she felt so embarrassed."

Even within the ESOL "bubble," school can be a tremendous struggle, Berrios and others said. The struggle is reflected in the students' performance on the state's functional tests.

In Maryland last year, 41 percent of ESOL ninth-graders who took the reading test failed, compared with 5 percent of all ninth-graders. The disparity was not as great on the math and writing tests, but even on those, the ESOL students' failure rate was nearly twice as high.

Maryland School Superintendent Nancy S. Grasmick defended the functional test requirement. "These are considered minimal standards for graduation," she said. "We think the diploma has to represent something, and what it represents is that the student has mastered that minimal level."

Some teachers, such as High Point's Nahmani, said the state should give students who pass all their courses but fail the functional tests a certificate to recognize that they survived four years of school.

"It's really important for the State of Maryland to understand that all kids are not the same," she said. "It's such a disappointment to these kids not to be able to go through the senior ritual of graduation."

Several teachers said they are concerned about the potential effect on the ESOL students of Maryland's plan to increase the course work needed for graduation.

"The more requirements they put up there, the harder it is and the more drop-outs they'll have," Bellino said.

May 24, 1992

Court Cuts Federal Desegregation Role
Schools' Anti-Bias Obligations Eased

RUTH MARCUS

The Supreme Court made it easier yesterday for public school systems to get out from under court-ordered desegregation plans, even if the schools have not been fully desegregated.

The court unanimously overturned a federal appeals court order that required school officials in suburban Atlanta to take extensive steps, possibly including busing, to respond to massive population shifts that resulted in schools that were predominantly black or overwhelmingly white.

The court, in an opinion written by Justice Anthony M. Kennedy and joined by four other justices, stressed the "duty" of federal courts "to return the operations and control of schools to local authorities." It was the second time in two years that the court has sided with a school board seeking relief from a desegregation order.

Kennedy also made clear that school segregation caused solely by changes in where people live was not a proper subject for federal court intervention. "It is beyond the authority and beyond the practical ability of the federal courts to try to counteract these kinds of continuous and massive demographic shifts," he said.

Lawyers for both sides predicted that the ruling in Freeman v. Pitts would prompt many of the several hundred school districts now operating under federal court orders to seek removal from court control.

"The very general effect is going to be greater discretion in school boards in desegregating their schools so long as they act in good faith," said Rex E. Lee, the school board's lawyer.

"I think we'll get a flood of litigation," said Christopher A. Hansen of the American Civil Liberties Union, who represented the black plaintiffs in the case. But Hansen said his major concern with the opinion was not the standards it sets out but what he described as 'a real tone of weariness' with hearing school desegregation disputes. 'It has the ring of 'Enough is enough ... We're just tired of it all,' " he said.

In Prince George's County, the only Washington-area school system operating under court order, lawyers for the school board and the NAACP, the plaintiff in the 20-year-old case, said they were studying the ruling.

The court has been divided on school desegregation cases and yesterday's case, while technically a unanimous ruling, prompted four opinions among the eight justices who participated. Justice Clarence Thomas, who was not yet confirmed when the case was argued last October, did not take part.

Justice Harry A. Blackmun, in a concurring opinion joined by Justices John Paul Stevens and Sandra Day O'Connor, agreed with the substance of yesterday's ruling but emphasized the need to scrutinize closely whether government actions contributed in some way to residential segregation.

"It is almost 38 years since this court decided *Brown v. Board of Education*," the landmark 1954 ruling outlawing "separate but equal" schools, Blackmun noted. "In those 38 years, the students in DeKalb County, Ga., never have attended a desegregated school system even for one day. The majority of 'black' students never have attended a school that was not disproportionately black."

Justice Antonin Scalia suggested that the court should go further in freeing school systems from court supervision. Justice David H. Souter, while joining the majority opinion, sounded a theme similar to Blackmun's.

The case stemmed from a lawsuit filed by black schoolchildren and their parents in DeKalb County outside Atlanta in 1968. With 73,000 students from kindergarten through 12th grade, the system is now the 32nd largest in the country.

To settle the lawsuit, school officials agreed to close formerly all-black schools and to assign students to neighborhood schools, among other changes. In the years afterward, however, some 64,000 blacks moved from the city of Atlanta into the county and the black enrollment of the schools surged, from 5.6 percent in 1969 to 47 percent in 1986.

That demographic change—with blacks moving largely into the southern half of the county and whites to the north—resulted in racial imbalance in the neighborhood schools. By 1986, half the black students in the system attended schools that were more than 90 percent black.

That year, school officials sought to be freed from federal court supervision, saying they had complied with their duties under the Constitution.

The legal question that has been at issue in the case as it made its way through the federal court system is the meaning of the high court's 1968 ruling in *Green v. New Kent County School Board,* in which the court set out six factors—student assignment, faculty, staff, transportation, extracurricular activities and facilities—to test whether a school system has been desegregated.

The district court in the DeKalb case found that the school system had achieved desegregation in student assignments for a time, and that the reemergence of racially identifiable schools was the result of demographic changes, not the actions of school officials.

As a result, it said it would no longer supervise the student assignment part of the case, while maintaining control over some other areas in which the system had fallen short.

The federal appeals court in Atlanta reversed the district court. It said that the school system had to take "affirmative steps to gain and maintain a desegregated student population"—coping with any intervening demographic changes—until it had achieved compliance with all six Green factors for three years.

Yesterday, the justices said the appeals court was wrong. "A federal court in a school desegregation case has the discretion to order an incremental or partial withdrawal of its supervision and control Kennedy said. "Returning schools to the control of local authorities at the earliest practicable date is essential to restore their true accountability in our governmental system."

Staff writer Lisa Leff contributed to this report.

April 1, 1992

Kansas City's Costly Integration Strategy

Results Mixed in $1.2 Billion School Plan

MARY JORDAN

Instructors at Central High peer through an underwater window noting divers' form as they splash into a new $5 million pool. Upstairs, the former head coach of the Soviet Olympic fencing team parries with sophomores. Down the hall, limber gymnasts aiming for gold medals tumble and train toward perfection.

Central High, once so decrepit that children could gaze through cracks in the roof at the clouds and crows overhead, is now the glittering flagship of the most ambitious inner-city school rebuilding effort ever undertaken.

In the new classrooms of Central High, built beside the old school that has since been demolished, and in the 80 other public schools here, an experiment of unprecedented scale and vast implications is unfolding. What this city accomplishes with an infusion of $1.2 billion, much of it from reluctant taxpayers around the state, may shed light on what effect money has on learning—and whether enough of it can lure white students to predominantly black schools.

"Conservatives say the '60s proved you can't solve social problems by throwing money at them, and liberals say the '60s proved you can't solve social problems without throwing enough money at them," said Arthur A. Benson II, the lawyer who brought the lawsuit that forced the massive rebuilding effort. "What we are doing here should resolve that debate."

This novel strategy for integrating and improving poor inner-city schools began in a courtroom in 1985 in a case brought on behalf of black and white schoolchildren. U.S. District Judge Russell G. Clark ruled that the state and the local school district had failed to eliminate the vestiges of Kansas City's state-decreed segregated school system, which became unconstitutional after the Supreme Court's 1954 *Brown v. Board of Education* decision. His remedy was unprecedented: Missouri and Kansas City must tear down the "literally rotted" buildings and construct the best facilities and educational programs money could buy.

White students would not be forced to enroll in the schools, Clark said. They would want to.

It is still early in the experiment, and the results are mixed. While relatively few whites have returned to city schools, officials say they have at least succeeded in stopping white flight.

Until 1969, there were more whites than blacks in the system. But now, only 25 percent of the school population is white, compared to 67 percent of the city population.

The last year there was a majority white population in the schools was also the last year voters approved new money for them. In the next 20 years, 19 consecutive school levies and bond measures were defeated. In a surprise decision in 1990, the Supreme Court upheld Clark's controversial ruling that ordered local officials to increase the property tax to pay for the desegregation plan.

"This is the largest remedy for discrimination ever attempted," said Art Rainwater, associate superintendent of the school system and former Central principal. "Since ours was one of the later (desegregation) cases, forced busing had already been tried and failed. The idea here was to desegregate the city by choice."

"If we fail," said Rainwater, who used to place nine trash cans in his office at Central High to catch rain, "it will not be because we didn't have enough money."

An outdoor amphitheater, a $250,000 planetarium, 15 new fully equipped science laboratories, 11,280 personal computers, smaller class sizes and a massive "magnet" program to transform most of the traditional schools into ones whose curriculum is built around single subjects, have cost $500 million so far. Over the next six years, another $700 million worth of improvements and changes have been approved.

The $1.2 billion price tag, equaling a $33,333 expenditure on each of the system's 36,000 students, has divided the state into two camps. Supporters say it's about time educating poor children was a priority. Critics say they don't see it making a dime's worth of difference.

The overall racial balance in the schools has not budged since the court order; it remains 75 percent minority and 25 percent white. However, unlike most other major cities, white flight has halted. And, in the past two years, as school improvement has become more visible, 1,355 white students have switched from suburban and private schools to city schools.

Because the state must pay for at least 75 percent of the rebuilding, more if the city cannot muster its remaining share, many missouri officials and residents resent the court order. Gov. John D. Ashcroft (R), who has termed it a "tragedy," fed the anger last year when he transferred $71 million from schools around the state to pay for Kansas City's desegregation plan.

"The rest of the state is mad as hell," said Michael J. Fields, Missouri's assistant attorney general. "Some districts are going bankrupt, firing English and math teachers, and then they look over here and see these Taj Mahal buildings."

But many education officials insist $1.2 billion is not too much to pay for past neglect and discrimination. The entire state, they argue, should spend more on its kids.

"How much is too much to give 36,000 kids a good education?" asked Aasin Baheyadeen, treasurer of the Kansas City School Board. "We are talking about our children. Everybody talks about how much we are spending here, but nobody talks about the monumental cost of bailing out Chrysler," he said, referring to the government's guarantee of $1.5 billion in loans for the ailing automaker more than a decade ago.

For Sean Bates, the new and improved Central High has meant a chance at a college scholarship. Until October, Bates, 16, had never been much of a success at sports. But after four months of practicing with Vladimir Nazlymov, former head coach of the Soviet Olympic fencing team, he competed in the Junior Olympics and placed fourth nationally. Nazlymov said through an interpreter that he moved here from moscow because Central had the best facilities he knew of in the United States.

"My dad is surprised I'm so into school," said Bates, who earned a 3.6 grade point average last semester. "I stay here until 6 every day."

Six years ago there was not one white student at Central, a magnet for those interested in sports and computers. Now 170 of the 1,100 students are white.

Jonathan Kozol, author of "Savage Inequalities: Children in America's Schools," which chronicles the neglect of inner-city schools, said he is hopeful the investment in Kansas City will pay off.

"Kansas City is a test for New York, Canden (N.J.), Chicago, St. Louis—all the big cities whose schools are in physical despair," said Kozol. "I'd say it's an even bet at whether they will achieve desegregation."

The prospects for success are aided not only by a city that still has a majority white population but a relatively manageable student population—36,000 public school students, compared to New York City's 970,000. The District has 80,000 students, Prince George's County enrolls 110,000, and Fairfax County has 133,000.

Kozol believes that if white parents opt for suburban or private schools over these free "superior schools," it will prove that white flight has occurred "not because of inferior schools or overcrowded classes, but because of simple bigotry."

"If spending a billion dollars in Kansas City does not win back the white middle class, then we will discover something very evil about America," he said.

But others say they are still far from convinced of these new schools' excellence.

Even Benson, the plaintiff lawyer who is a key supporter of the new schools, does not deny the poor instruction in some of them. "One-third of the teachers are incompetent and half the principals should get new jobs," he said.

When an eighth-grader was shot dead outside the nearby Central Middle School in November, it fed a widespread fear that the new schools may be fancy but not safe.

But school Superintendent Walter L. Marks says piecing back together a tattered school system does not happen overnight. "We have come far, and still have such to do," he said.

Test scores in the lower grades are improving. magnet schools such as Latin Grammar, where students wear school uniforms, and Longan Elementary French "immersion" school have won widespread praise. Now, Marks said, he is focusing on urging many teachers into early retirement, retraining others and reworking the curriculum.

Gary Orfield, a Harvard professor who recently completed a national survey on the status of desegregation in American city schools, said Kansas City has "already achieved a substantial accomplishment" by stabilizing the number of whites in its classrooms.

"They have broken the trend in most other big cities," said Orfield. But he believes it is a "pipe dream" to think Kansas City schools will ever achieve the court-ordered goal of a school system that is 40 percent white and 60 percent minority.

In the computer wing of Central recently, Christopher Williams sat honing his word-processing skills and thinking about all that has happened in Kansas City.

As he retrieved information about the nation's park system on his Hyundai screen, the senior said the new school boosted students' self-esteem. Instead of walking into a depressing building that many students described as a run-down public housing unit, Williams said the clean classrooms "make you feel like you are doing something worthwhile."

But Williams, who is black, said many black students feel the new computers and teachers and class trips were not really for them. "They feel these schools were not made for blacks," said Williams, 18. "They were made to get white students in here."

Erin Vancleave is one of those who arrived at Central this year from a suburban school. Because of her interest in volleyball and diving, she wanted to attend Central, the magnet for those interested in pursuing Olympic sports or computers.

But as Vancleave, 15, ate lunch in a crowded cafeteria at one of the two tables where most of the white students in the room sat, she said her old school was much more demanding. "I learned a lot more last year," she said.

As Alan Lollis, 14, a black freshman sat beside her, he had still another view on the plan that has affected thousands of lives. His new school, he said, was the best thing that has happened to him. He never swam in a pool before he started taking lessons this year; now he swims more than two hours every day, even coming to school on weekends.

"It makes me feel like I can do something," Lollis said. Before hurrying off to computer class, he said white students stuck mostly to themselves and many black students gave him a hard time for hanging out with white kids. But the remarks did not bother him too much. He said: 'I think it's good to have all kinds of people together.' "

"We have to succeed," said school spokeswoman Laurie Spoon, a school activist in Florida who recently moved here to aid in the plan. "If Kansas City does, there is hope for urban city schools."

April 11, 1992

9 Education of Students with Special Needs

Mainstreaming Disabled Students
Move in Loudoun Schools Generates Debate

ROBERT O'HARROW JR.

For eight years, Cheryl Farris depended on a special Loudoun County public school with a nurse and a separate staff to teach and care for her 11-year-old daughter, Caitlin, a quadriplegic who suffers seizures.

The school was like a second home for the profoundly disabled girl, Farris said, and a bastion of support for her family.

But this year, in an effort to place students with disabilities in regular schools, Loudoun sent Caitlin to Catoctin Elementary, which has no full-time nurse. Now when Caitlin has serious seizures, Farris gets called in to administer the child's special medication.

"The first thing I say is, 'Please don't let it be Caitie,' " Farris said of the emergency phone calls she has received this school year. "Then I say, 'I'll be right there.' "

The phone calls are a result of Loudoun's effort to place every student with disabilities, no matter how severe, in a regular school. Loudoun is the first school system in the Washington area to make the complete change.

The approach mirrors a nationwide philosophical and legal shift in the way disabled children are educated.

But as the movement takes root in Loudoun and elsewhere, educators and parents continue an emotional debate about whether it is best for children who sometimes cannot move or eat without help.

Some advocates say even severely disabled children have a basic right to attend regular schools. Others say integrating them with normal students often makes no sense. The debate focuses on a minority of students, probably fewer than 2,500 in the Washington area, who, as recently as 20 years ago, might never have attended public schools.

"The jury is still out on this," said Elaine Joyce, director of the Association for Retarded Citizens of Northern Virginia. "There is not definitive research that says every child is definitely going to benefit."

182

After using federal aid to set up model programs in the last four years, Virginia's Department of Education is beginning a statewide program to encourage all 138 school systems to adopt the approach.

In Maryland, the state Department of Education is expected to release a report this week recommending that integration efforts be expanded across the state, and offering a broad plan to do it.

Area school systems have been moving in the direction of integration for years. In Fairfax County, only about 200 disabled students attend two special centers, about half the number in the centers five years ago, said Clay Sande, the director of special education.

The numbers are similar in Montgomery County, where about 150 students with severe disabilities attend special schools. About 10 years ago there were more than 300 students in special schools.

A "Movement of Inclusion"

Supporters of placing moderately retarded or profoundly disabled students in regular schools say it is unfair to keep disabled students apart from other children, who need to learn how to deal with people who are different.

Some advocates also say disabled students don't get a fair chance to learn the social skills essential to survival after they leave school. They call the integration approach, now well-established in some other states, a "movement of inclusion."

The movement dates to before 1975, when a federal law was passed mandating that disabled children receive free appropriate education in the least restrictive environment possible. The act was amended last year and renamed the Individuals with Disabilities Education Act.

"Every student should have a sense of belonging," said Mary Kearney, Loudoun's director of special education. "Schools are for all students." Cheryl Bennett, of Sterling, said a regular school is clearly the best thing for her daughter Elizabeth, who is moderately retarded.

Elizabeth, 10, can't do mathematics problems, and she sometimes demands more attention from her fourth-grade teacher than other students. But she is learning to take care of herself and behave.

"She's happier than she has ever been," Bennett said. "She's happy to go. She does well when she gets there."

But for all the apparent good news, James Kauffman, a professor at the University of Virginia, said advocates of integration are not weighing all the implications.

Kauffman and others say there are unanswered questions about whether all students with disabilities can learn what they need in regular schools, without the attention they typically get in special facilities.

Regular classroom teachers occasionally balk at having to accept students who are mentally retarded or have multiple disabilities, while some special education staff members are reluctant to give up responsibility for their students.

Kauffman, a professor of special education, said he suspects that some of the fiercest advocates of integration are motivated by ideology.

"I would question whether we have in this society now kinder, gentler schools," Kauffman said. "At root is the view that social programs don't work, and that self-reliance is healthy and cost-effective."

Farris, some parents and other academics agree with Kauffman. Farris sharply criticized Loudoun administrators this month for moving Caitlin, who suffers from cerebral palsy and cannot speak, without fully preparing her family or Caitlin's new school for the change.

Caitlin doesn't have the same facilities, such as swing sets outfitted for wheelchairs, or the same medical support she had at the Douglas Community School in Leesburg, Farris said.

Parents' Concerns

"There are just some children integration doesn't work for," Farris said.

Loudoun officials said they are reviewing the situation and the new rules.

In Prince William County, parents of about 125 students successfully opposed an effort to close the special Ann Ludwig and New Dominion schools last year. They said their severely disabled children should not be forced to move, and accused the system of trying to close the school for budget reasons.

"You can't just say a blanket thing is good for all children," said Nancy Bleggi, of Woodbridge, whose 8-year-old daughter attends Ann Ludwig. "If they can feed her on some days, it's an accomplishment."

Effects of Cutbacks

Budget troubles could have an impact in some districts contemplating integration, even though it is not clear it leads to a saving, specialists said.

As local governments face up to another year of fiscal trouble, special education budgets, which have skyrocketed in the last 15 years, will come under close scrutiny, said Julie Jones, a George Mason University professor and regional director of a federally funded integration program in Virginia.

Federal special education aid to Virginia, for example, rose from $4.6 million in 1977 to $26.1 million in 1987, according to the most recent figures. Most of that money goes to students with mild disabilities, but students with more severe disabilities cost more to educate.

Most educators say money is not a motivation for the changes. But privately, they say they may save some money by closing special schools, if only in salaries for administrators or for transportation costs, Jones said. She welcomes the logic if it means attracting more school systems to the idea of integration.

"I think the driving force . . . will be the cost savings, the potential cost savings," she said. "That is the foot in the door into the school systems."

Prince William County estimated it could save $400,000 by closing two special schools where the cost of educating a student averages $7,553, about $2,000 more than the average per-pupil costs for the county.

But Superintendent Edward L. Kelly said the county was not trying to save money, but instead was trying to do what the law requires and what students need.

November 9, 1991

Gifted, Talented and Under Siege

LISA LEFF

Pity the poor parents of the Washington area's academically precocious. After years of fighting to ensure that local school systems recognize their children's educational needs with special programs for the "gifted and talented," they now find their cause threatened by budget cutbacks and education reformers who want to wipe out classroom practices that separate students on the basis of perceived ability.

Gifted and talented education has in the past been subjected to periodic charges of exclusivity and inequity; advocates across the Washington area say the 1991-92 school year has once again found them on the defensive. Reductions in school spending brought on by the recession have caused administrators in Fairfax and Montgomery counties—home to two of the most highly regarded gifted programs—to target for elimination the roving teachers who work part-time with some, though not all, exceptionally bright students.

In addition, a nationwide movement away from "ability grouping," the tradition of assigning quick learners to separate, accelerated classes or clustering students with similar aptitudes together within a regular class, also may be working against the gifted, parents and some school officials say. In Prince George's County, for example, talented seventh and eighth graders not enrolled in magnet schools are supposed to be grouped with other highly able students for English and social studies. But some middle schools have quietly suspended the practice in the belief that making distinctions based on ability has led to the tracking of slower students into dead-end courses, said David L. Saith, the school system's supervisor of gifted education.

"It is an extremely difficult time for gifted children right now. It is a time when the label of elitism is even more inappropriately applied to them," said Sydna K. Gong, president of the Northern Virginia Council for Gifted and Talented Education. "I see major cuts in staff and to me that threatens the program . . . And when a teacher is faced with a totally heterogeneous range of children, the temptation is to teach the middle."

Advocates like Gong say the setbacks at the local level are particularly ironic since gifted education is an area in which the federal government—prompted by concerns that Americans are losing their ability to compete in an increasingly technical world—has shown increased interest.

In 1988, Congress established a National Research Center on Gifted and Talented Education, based at the University of Connecticut. This year the U.S. government will spend $9.7 million to operate the research center and to fund demonstration projects at selected schools and universities. The support is a major departure from the early 1980s, when the U.S. Department of Education eliminated its office overseeing programs for the gifted.

While gifted education has historically enjoyed strong support in the Washington area—every school system has some kind of program—the commitment to it has tended to be somewhat uneven among local jurisdictions, said Peter D. Rosenstein, executive director of the National Association for Gifted Children, which is based in the District.

A child attending school in Virginia, for instance, lives in a state that spends $19 million a year on special educational programs for its brightest children, while Maryland devotes $1.3 million to the same purpose. In Fairfax County, the budget for "gifted and talented" services is $3 million, or nearly $143 for each of the 21,000 students who have been identified for the program. Anne Arundel County, meanwhile, is spending $630,000, or $95 each, for its 6,665 gifted students.

Since 1986, Virginia has been one of 26 states that requires its school systems to meet set guidelines for providing gifted education services, a mandate aimed at eliminating some of the wide variations in such services at the local level. The guidelines require school systems in the state to screen students for signs of giftedness beginning in kindergarten, to operate special programs for gifted students in grades K-12, to train teachers to provide distinct lessons for the gifted students in their classrooms, and to establish citizen advisory committees that monitor services for the gifted. Proponents of gifted education in maryland, which does not have a similar state mandate, say they are eager to obtain one because they think such programs have fared better in Virginia. The District also requires its schools to provide special services for students who have been identified as gifted.

"Having a mandate is the only way to go if you want to assure that when there is a program in place it will stay there," said Betty Stauffer, president of the Maryland Council for Gifted and Talented Children, a group lobbying the state Department of Education for such an order. "Right now it is considered a frill and frills can always be cut."

Despite variations, there are certain elements the programs share in common. Across the area, the most widely used method involves grouping academically able elementary school students, who have been identified as such by intelligence test scores and recommendations from teachers and parents, to work together within a regular class. In some school systems, most notably Prince George's, Montgomery and Fairfax, such students are also pulled out of their regular classes one or more times each week to work with a specially trained teacher on exercises to promote creativity and critical thinking.

In Fairfax, for example, elementary school students attending a neighborhood school instead of one of the county's special centers for gifted students spend 1 1/2 hours each week working with a resource teacher. If they are in grades 4-6, they might spend that time discussing different aspects of museums—the different types, what makes a successful exhibit, the strategies curators use to pull viewers in, said Virginia Mahlke, coordinator of gifted and talented programs. To complete the unit, the teacher might ask the students to create a photography exhibit at their school and take a field trip to a museum, Mahlke said.

In middle schools, the effort usually shifts to providing separate, faster-paced classes in selected subjects for students who have been identified as gifted or who have shown unusual aptitude in a particular discipline. In Fairfax, these students receive special instruction in either English and science or English and social studies. Howard County offers "talent pool" classes in language, math and social studies at its middle schools. In Arlington, gifted students are grouped together for English and math and attend a special gifted center once every two weeks.

Some school systems have taken the extra step of providing full-day centers that serve only gifted students and have their own advanced curricula. Fairfax has 22 gifted centers for students in grades 3-8 who must score 140 or above on IQ tests given at the end of second grade. Prince George's operates 10 talented and gifted magnet schools that are open to any elementary and middle school students who have scored at the two highest levels on cognitive ability tests or have been nominated by their teachers. But admission to the magnets is also based on a student's race because the schools were established to promote integration.

Montgomery County has four centers for "highly gifted" fourth, fifth and sixth graders who are selected on the basis of standardized test scores, recommendations from local school gifted and talented committees, and performance on a series of "thinking" activities. While such full-time gifted programs are popular with parents, they are less enthusiastically embraced by many educators, who regard then as private schools operated at taxpayer expense and an unjustified attempt to prevent upper-income parents from pulling their children out of public schools.

A study of Fairfax County's gifted program completed last year by the consulting firm of former D.C. Superintendent Floretta McKenzie found that the center programs were "widely and severely criticized by educators throughout the county" who felt the programs were "exclusionary" and "a socially acceptable form of tracking." The educators interviewed for the study also feared that upper-income parents who were eager to have their children admitted to one of the centers manipulated entrance criteria by paying for private IQ testing.

Increasingly, area school systems are answering such charges by expanding the pool of students to whom special gifted services are provided. Six years ago—influenced by the ideas of Joseph Renzulli of the University of Connecticut—Howard County revamped its program so students were no longer identified as "gifted" but as demonstrating "gifted behaviors," a definition that brought in students who excelled in areas such as leadership, art and music instead of only mathematics and language, said Robert Glascock, the county's assistant supervisor of gifted and talented education.

With that new definition, the school system appointed a resource teacher at each elementary and middle school to work with students on research and training projects geared to the students' unusual abilities and interests. Today, 21 percent of the county's elementary school population participates in the program to some extent. Nationwide, most school systems provide special gifted services to between seven and 12 percent of their students.

Rick Frankle, the gifted and talented resource teacher at Howard's Harper's Choice Middle School, cites examples of the kind of "enrichment" experiences he has set up with his students, who are excused from classes in which they excel to work on their projects. One group of students last year wanted to put together a 15-minute daily news program for the school. As part of their research, they interviewed professional journalists and television producers and hired other students to serve as correspondents. Concerned that their program look professional, they also met with a cabinet maker to learn how to build an anchor's desk. This year, one student is working on a novel, while another is transcribing onto a computer a piano composition written by his great-grandfather.

With the aid of a federal research grant, Montgomery County's Montgomery Knolls Elementary School has embarked on a similar quest to increase the number of children it classifies as gifted with a particular eye toward reaching foreign-born and economically disadvantaged students who have been underrepresented in the ranks of the gifted. The school's program for students in grades K-2 is based on the idea that "every child has strengths" teachers must identify and play to, said Deborah Leibowitz, the program's director.

During one recent science lesson, this philosophy was put into practice when a first grade teacher set up different work stations geared toward different academic abilities. Artistic students drew pictures of butterflies, while students who liked building objects made caterpillars out of egg cartons. The pupils with good language skills, meanwhile, wrote labels for charts and conducted research out of books, Leibowitz said.

Joseph Renzulli, who directs the national research center on gifted education at the University of Connecticut and who was the architect of the model that forms the basis of Howard County's program, said that more school districts are adopting his idea that "giftedness is something to be developed" in a much larger range of children rather than a static state of being that is limited to an elite few because it puts them "on politically safer ground."

With so much flux in the field, what is a parent to do?

Caroline Tomlinson, president of the Virginia Association for the Education of the Gifted, an advocacy group of parents and professional educators, suggests that parents who think their children may have unusual academic abilities, but are confused about the quality of their local school program, make a point of talking to the principal and observing several classes.

April 5, 1992

Mixed Grouping Puts an English Class on the Right Track

D'VERA COHN

Pencils and hopes in hand, the two dozen Fairfax County eighth-graders nervously awaited their spelling test. "Thirty-word people, are you ready?" teacher Alice Sontag asked.

A third of her students bent over their desks and began to write as Sontag called out the first word on the examination—"monastery"—followed by nine more.

"Twenty-word people?" Most of the other students went to work as Sontag read out the next 10 words. "Ten-word people?" The final few started up. Sontag slowly recited the final 10 words, ending in "unison."

Unlike many American classrooms, this one at Carl Sandburg Intermediate School in the Mount Vernon area of Fairfax County is not filled with students of similar academic ability. Reading levels vary from third grade to high school. And students in the class decide in advance how many words they want to be tested on: 10, 20 or 30. The staggered spelling test is designed to offer something for everyone.

Until last year, students in English classes at Sandburg were grouped by ability, a standard practice in public education in this country. But this approach, known as tracking, is increasingly under attack. And Fairfax is a particularly appropriate laboratory to illustrate why.

If there is anywhere schools should be able to overcome the burdens of poverty, race and broken families—factors that educators say predispose children to fail—it is in this affluent county, which provides innovative programs, well-kept buildings stocked with modern equipment, and the time to spend on instruction rather than coping with life's gritty realities.

Yet studies indicate that being a poor, underachieving child in an affluent, high-achieving environment can reinforce feelings of failure. And that problem can be exacerbated by tracking. Many specialists believe that a child grouped with only children of similar ability is less likely to show improved academic performance.

"You look around and say, 'Everyone in here is stupid, so I must be stupid and that's the way I'm going to act,' " said Howard Johnston, a

191

professor of education at the University of Cincinnati and a leading researcher on middle-school tracking.

"You're talking about kids identified in elementary school as blue, orange and yellow birds, and they fall into that mold and they want to break out of it," said Carol Robinson, an assistant principal at Sandburg.

Changing demographics give new urgency to the issue of reaching underachievers in Fairfax County. A decade ago, one in 11 county students was a minority; now, one in five is. Disproportionately, those minorities are likely to be poor; even in this comfortable county there are trailer parks and dingy apartments.

In Fairfax, as in communities across the country, the job of educator is being altered dramatically by social and economic trends. Nationally, the percentage of children in poverty is increasing; immigration is bringing in more students who don't speak English; teen-age pregnancy rates mean more children entering school who have been raised in less-than-ideal circumstances.

These and other factors point to more school failure at the same time the number of school-age children is declining. The implications are clear: Schools must reduce their failure rate to produce a competent work force for the next century. But the job is increasingly difficult.

Research by University of Wisconsin political science Prof. Kenneth J. Meier and associates, based on county figures, indicates that blacks students in Fairfax were only one-third as likely as white students to be assigned to a class for the gifted in 1984 and 140 percent more likely to be suspended than other students.

The county's research, first compiled four years ago, showed that minority students generally get lower grades, are enrolled in fewer honors classes, are less likely to graduate from high school and are more likely to be disciplined by school officials than their white counterparts.

Although minority children are disproportionately likely to be poor, the findings applied to all income levels. Fairfax officials came to the uncomfortable realization that the definition of a child at risk in the suburbs included more than the children of poor or unstable families.

"The black child is at risk no matter what the socioeconomic group," said Eretha Williams, a Sandburg teacher.

At Sandburg, a drop in scores on standardized tests led administrators and teachers to some hard thinking about the problems of underachieving students.

"We were alarmed that our reading scores last year were so low," English Department chairman Ebba Jo Spettel said.

Spettel and other school officials had considerable leeway in discussing what to do because the 180 public schools in Fairfax County are allowed substantial independence in devising curriculum. The idea for mixed grouping in English classes came from a county school audit team that visited Sandburg last year and recommended that it be tried. Workshops and meetings were held every week from December to June to trade ideas and hear from specialists.

"I was very apprehensive," said English teacher Carolyn Larkin. "I was used to teaching honors, average and basic classes. I didn't know where to start. But it's just organization. I like it. Kids work better together. I have fewer discipline problems."

Sandburg's program to bolster the self-esteem and academic achievement of its underperforming students has several components. Mathematics classes, which still are tracked, employ cooperative learning in which students team up to solve problems together. Evening meetings are held for parents of students in trouble. The guidance department has organized groups to boost the self-image of potential student leaders and minority underachievers, resolve conflicts among some students who were fighting among themselves, and promote cultural awareness among minority students.

But at the heart of Sandburg's effort was replacing most tracked English classes with a system of random placement. For the student who is not at the top of the class, researchers say, the mixed group offers encouragement to succeed, models to emulate and the self-respect that comes from being treated as a potential learner rather than as a behavior problem.

Sandburg, the product of the merger of two very different intermediate schools three years ago, remains mainly a white, middle-class school. It draws some of its 1,000 students from neighborhoods of $300,000 houses near the Potomac River, where children do their homework on family computers. Others come from blocks of three- and four-bedroom brick colonials, where many of their parents go to work each day for the federal bureaucracy or Fort Belvoir, a nearby Army base.

For some students, the ride down the school's long tree-lined driveway each morning offers a jarring contrast to their homes in cheap motel rooms or low-rent apartments where there may be no quiet place to study. A third of Sandburg's students move in or out of the school district each year.

The students range in weight from 59 to 238 pounds, in age from 11 to 15 and in social outlook from childhood to prematurely adult. "Some of them bring dolls to school," one teacher said, "and others have their own babies."

Teachers tell of the mother who hired a babysitter to keep her daughter away from fights and drug dealers. Some teachers say they have taken children home with them or given them clothing. They also speak proudly of one honor-roll student whose family lived in a car for several weeks.

The decision to merge the high, middle and low-track classes was controversial with Sandburg's mainly white, middle-class parents, many of whom feared their children would be cheated by the grouping. In many suburban schools, it is those parents who dominate the Parent-Teachers Association, volunteer in the classrooms and call the shots.

When meetings were held to explain the new approach, "the community went a little bonkers," said Julie Casaletto, a Sandburg parent who is the PTA's liaison with the English Department. "They said they wanted their kids with kids they'd always known. . . . There were a lot of people concerned about it."

Now, as the school year nears an end, students and teachers are enthusiastic about how things have gone.

Seventh-grader Mike Domingo, who wants to be an airline pilot and describes himself as a below-average student, likes the mixed English class he is in. "Sometimes I just don't get things," he said, "so I can ask another student."

To organize classrooms for students with different needs, students have been given more choices in how and what they learn, with the result that they take more responsibility, overcoming the traditional passivity of the low-level learner.

In Judy Seward's class, students set their own reading and writing goals. "A lot of kids have gravitated toward much more difficult books than I would have predicted, or that I would have picked," she said.

In Jon Gray's class, students choose their own reading from anything the library has to offer. most classes include plenty of work in small student groups with teacher supervision rather than teacher preaching from the front of the room.

And what the education students get is more sophisticated. This year, all eighth-graders studied a unit on Shakespeare. In the past, Spettel said, "we wouldn't have bothered" for the less advanced students. "The curriculum is higher. That's a very democratic thing."

One lesson Spettel taught she previously used only in her gifted classes: assigning students to compare critics' views of "The Taming of the Shrew."

Tony Jennings, who describes himself as a "medium student" in one of Spettel's eighth-grade classes, grinned in delight when he remembered that lesson. "Kate was a trip," he said.

Sandburg does not expect overnight miracles, but there were a few good signs by midyear. Fewer students got Ds and Fs in their English classes, and teachers uniformly said that classes were better behaved.

"I like that mixture," said Charline Barnes. "It keeps them from being snobbish, like they know it all."

But all has not been smooth. In one of Spettel's classes this year, most of the girls got As and Bs in the first semester, and most of the boys got Ds and Fs. The girls complained the boys weren't pulling their weight in class. Spettel called a meeting with the boys' parents and promised to send home weekly reports on their progress if the parents helped push for higher achievement.

For minority students, isolation is a problem that can't be solved by changing the curriculum. At Sandburg as at other schools, true integration has yet to be realized; students do much of their socializing along racial and socioeconomic lines.

And for black students there are few black teachers to serve as role models or with whom they can relate more easily. Of the school's 73 teachers, only 10 are minorities, and none of its top administrators is.

After studying federal data from 170 school systems with enrollments above 15,000 students and at least 1 percent minority, Meier concluded that there is a direct relationship between the number of minority employees in a school district and the achievement of its minority students. The higher the one, the higher the other.

"Black teachers respond to black students differently," Meier said. "They're more likely to give them positive feedback. There's an incredible amount of self-fulfilling prophecy in education. . . . The second factor is that they act as role models. Students see successful individuals and they have individuals they can pattern themselves after."

Williams and Barnes, black Sandburg teachers who always seem to be trailed by a coterie of admiring black students, wish there were more.

Williams said her daughter, a Sandburg eighth-grade honors student, has had only three black teachers since preschool, two of whom Williams specifically requested. Her fourth-grade son, the only black child in his gifted class, has had only one black teacher.

Being a minority child in a mainly white suburb "is a very lonely experience," Williams said. She tries to compensate for her children by joining black social groups and attending a black church.

"I want my child to know equality," said Williams, who attended mainly black schools when she was growing up. "Still, I want them to maintain touch with black children."

The practice of ability grouping was a form of class and economic segregation that arose in response not to blacks but immigrants from southern and eastern Europe who came to this country at the turn of the century. Out of "misguided social Darwinism," writes Rand Corp. researcher Jeannie Oakes, school officials shunted these students into a new, less demanding vocational curriculum, while continuing to enroll the upper classes in college preparatory courses.

In many schools, tracking remains a popular practice because many educators believe it works and because the most powerful group of teachers in schools—the veterans—have the clout to get themselves assigned to the more desirable advanced classes, according to some researchers.

But the conclusion of recent education research is that tracking is not justified under most circumstances, especially at younger ages or where students are learning basically the same material, as is true in many English classes.

"There's a great consensus that there are no benefits, and there is a general belief that tracking is hostile to low achievers," said Robert Slavin of the Center for Research on Elementary and Middle Schools at Johns Hopkins University. "There's certainly evidence that teachers have low expectations of students in low-ability groups."

The quickest students do not get anything more out of the high-track classes, according to research, because teachers use the same instructional techniques with honors and mixed-group classes.

But studies have found that teachers are markedly less demanding of their low-track classes; they spend less time on direct instruction and more time keeping order. Students are taught lower-level skills, such as memorization, rather than the higher-level thinking they need to make decisions. Peer pressure—so important to middle-school students teetering between childhood and adulthood—ensures that students in a low-track class do not try too hard. The cost to a child's self-esteem of being put in a low track is devastating; he meets his teacher's low expectations.

A sixth period science class at Sandburg, which still operates on a tracking system, illustrates some of the effects of separating low achievers from their peers. These students have among the school's lowest reading test scores. Some have flunked out of other science classes. Of the 14 students in class on a recent day, nine were minorities in a school that is more than half white. The class is so difficult to manage that it requires two teachers.

As teacher Jim Davis begins to explain an assignment, one boy shouts to another, "Jamie, can I borrow a piece of paper?" Several others carry on conversations without lowering their voices. Even accounting for the usual restlessness of adolescence, this class seems constantly in motion: Students fidget, wave their arms, slide from one seat to another.

The class is "very difficult" to teach, said Davis, a respected veteran teacher who is chairman of the school's Science Department.

Davis' experience is no longer typical. Nor is the experience Gray had last year with students in his low-level English class, who he says were acutely aware of their place in the school hierarchy. "Invariably it would come up," Gray said. "Someone would say, 'Are we the dumbie class?'

"Face it," Gray said. "If you're trying to raise achievement, the first thing is self-concept."

Now Gray is one of a number of teachers who say they have raised their expectations of what their students can do. "You see the best of everybody," Gray said. "Anybody who says you're going to water down your curriculum, that's incorrect."

In a series of reports running throughout the current school year, The Washington Post is examining the challenges posed to public schools in this country by the growing number of "children at risk."

These students are poor, non-English-speaking, born to teen-aged mothers or into unstable families or members of ethnic groups associated with lower academic achievement. Such circumstances predispose students to failure in school and society—by dropping out, becoming pregnant at an early age, becoming involved in crime, using drugs or becoming chronically unemployed.

The number of students at risk is increasing for several reasons: The proportion of children in poverty has risen from 15 percent to 20 percent since 1970; birth rates among poor and minority families are higher than those among middle-class whites; immigration is up, and divorce rates will put 60 percent of today's 3-year-olds in single-parent houses before they turn 18.

At the same time, the school-age population has declined, from 53 million in 1970 to 45 million in 1968.

The demographic trends have serious implications for society, especially as students move into the work force and the baby-boom generation ages. As high-school graduates drop in number, employers will have to choose from among fewer applicants, and will not have the luxury of bypassing those who are least prepared.

May 1, 1988

Fast-Track Trap—How "Ability Grouping" Hurts Our Schools, Kids and Families

Separating "Gifted and Talented" Students from Others Is Divisive in More Ways Than One

PATRICK WELSH

When the school year at George Mason Elementary School in Alexandria started two weeks ago, 15 white children due to enter the fourth grade were absent. Their parents had pulled them out, convinced that George Mason's mix of well-off white kids from the neighborhood and low-income black children bused in from housing projects was no longer working. Some of these parents had been active supporters of the public schools for more than a decade as their older kids passed through and gained acceptance at the nation's most competitive colleges.

"We became victims of a political philosophy that wants kids in the same classroom regardless of motivation, ability, interest or self-control," says Carol La Sasso, who took her 9-year-old daughter out of the school. A professor of education at Gallaudet University, La Sasso—along with other parents—had had several meetings with school principal Felicia Lanham Tarason. The parents had described almost constant disruptions by unruly students in the classroom (one teacher recently complained to me "I'm not a teacher, I'm a cop"), the virtual abandonment of instruction in science and social studies (because, a teacher explained, half the students could not read the tests) and the practice of having all students proceed at the same pace through textbooks irrespective of preparation and ability.

"Essentially, we were being asked to accept a watered-down curriculum and double standards of discipline for the sake of social engineering," says La Sasso. "Racial politics is killing us," says a George Mason teacher.

The ugly situation at George Mason highlights what is becoming one of the explosive questions in education: How can schools with increasingly diverse student bodies assure parents that there will be learning and discipline in their classrooms without segregating children into "ability" groups that often limit their development?

198

The struggle plays out in various ways in local systems. In the District of Columbia, most whites and many middle-class blacks have tried to sidestep the issue by sending their kids to private schools. "What you pay for in a private school is not the teaching, but the clientele. You don't have to worry about the underclass messing things up for your kid," says one mother who has tried both public and private education.

But most educators see disaster for public education in the flight of middle-class families. "Schools desperately need the middle class," says a D.C. school administrator. "Their advocacy for their own kids expands programs for others. That's how the successful Capitol Hill Cluster schools came about. The genius of John Murphy (the Prince George's County superintendent) is that he's convinced middle-class parents that their kids can receive as good an education in Prince George's magnet schools as in private schools. It's romantic hogwash to talk about a school system made up of poor kids and dedicated teachers. You need the pushy middle-class parents to make things happen." What the "pushy parents" often want—and get—is their own private school at taxpayers' expense. Those schools-within-a-school usually operate under the trade name of "Gifted and Talented programs." In Fairfax County, for example, students who get into GT programs, or into the Thomas Jefferson School for Science and Technology, can get an education few private schools can match. This accommodation to middle-class concerns has, however, given rise to a whole new set of destructive pressures.

In prosperous Fairfax, parental anxiety focuses not on the fear that their children will be bumping elbows with the underclass, but that they will be cast into the netherworld of the ungifted and untalented.

The winnowing starts early. In third grade, kids whose IQs test at 140 or more can leave their regular schools for a "Gifted Center," where they will be grouped with geniuses-in-the-making from other elementary schools. Most Fairfax parents view getting their 9-year-olds into "the center" as an enormous merit badge. "If kids don't get in the first time, many parents have them privately tested. It's like paying for an IQ score," says a Fairfax high school guidance counselor.

"Parents feel that they are limiting their kids' futures unless they get in the gifted program. Once a kid gets the label, everyone feels better," says Fairfax family therapist Jerald Newberry. But more than future employability is thought to be at stake. One mother worried to Alexandria Superintendent Paul Masem that her son would miss the neighborhood "social cut-off" if he was barred from the gifted program. He'd be "off the birthday-party lists," she mourned.

Those kids who score "only" 130-139 also get the label "gifted" but stay in their own schools with the "non-gifted." Although they get the label and are grouped together for most of their classes, "going to the center" has the real status. "The center kids are the terminally gifted," chuckles one counselor.

Failing the imprimatur of a "gifted" label, much less induction into the hallowed "center," middle-class Fairfax parents often ship their children off to private school. "The first line of white flight is kids who were left back with the 'average' students," says Masem. One Northern Virginia private-school administrator conceded that the bulk of his students were escapees from the "average" tracks in the public schools.

"It's not acceptable for a child to be average in Fairfax," a teacher remarked. "They're constantly comparing kids—who's on the best soccer or swim team, who's in gifted and talented." But the obsession with labeling one's kids as exceptional extends throughout the Washington area. A full 10 seconds after I met him, one Alexandria parent told me that his child was "Phase 4 all the way." (Phase 4 is the honors track.) Those cursed with average children may take refuge in other labels. "Learning Disabled" is a current favorite for the less-than-spectacular. Never mind how such a term may affect a child whose talents are still unfolding; apparently it assuages parental anxiety to feel that a child is afflicted with an identifiable syndrome, not suffering from a simple case of averageness. "The label creates an altered person and relieves the parents of the stigma of having passed on mediocre genes," says Newberry.

An Old Town Alexandria parent who had two kids in the gifted program put things in perspective: "Tracking at the elementary level is invidious. Kids are given a gifted label on the basis of social status and the level of conversation at the dinner table. The problem is that middle-class parents are at their most hysterical in those early years. I remember all these Old Town mothers talking about their 'brilliant boys.' They thought their kids deserved special attention at anyone's expense."

Several elementary school teachers whose classes are fought for by white parents told me that they are fed up with the "gifted" labeling. "It's an attempt by snobby white parents to separate their kids from the black kids," said one teacher. "Most of the white kids who get the label are not gifted at all. Many of the black kids are just as smart but haven't had the exposure."

The anxiety gifted programs cause for parents is inconsequential compared to the psychological effect tracking programs can have on the kids who don't get the "gifted and talented" label. As the late *Washington Post* editorialist Alan Barth often observed, there is hardly any kid who isn't bright enough to understand that he isn't considered very bright.

A white Fairfax guidance counselor said that her son's friends would ask him why he wasn't in the gifted program when he got such good grades. "I explained to him a hundred different ways that it didn't make any difference," she says. "But in his mind it still came out that he wasn't as good as his friends in the program." For minority students the implied label of "ungifted" is especially pernicious. T.C. Williams graduate Karen Carrington has bitter memories of the days in fourth grade when her "gifted" peers would be pulled out of class. "They got to do the interesting things that would stimulate any kid to learn. They had the plays, the fun projects; they cooked Chinese food. The rest of us would sit in the classroom and do 50 of the same problems over and over again. That would make anyone feel inferior. But when you're black and almost all the 'gifted' kids who are pulled out are white, it makes you feel even worse," says Carrington, who overcame those feelings to become a top student at Northwestern University.

Students in the gifted programs not only get the advantage of heightened self-esteem—deserved or not—but tangible resources from the system as well. In Fairfax county "the GT kids get more field trips, and special events and speakers, because there is more funding," says the Fairfax counselor. They also tend to get the better teachers. Meanwhile, the average or weak students get what Paul Masem calls the "ditto curriculum"—a constant diet of fill-in-the-blank worksheets to keep then quiet.

GT tracking also feeds the natural inflexibility of school bureaucracies. "Parents have to ride herd on the schools," says Frank Matthews, publisher of *Black Issues in Higher Education*. "I haven't been able to figure out why they are so resistant to putting kids into those programs and challenging them. You have to keep fighting to get your kids into a decent curriculum, or else they'll get shuffled off into these huge cattle-call courses where no one is challenged." Matthews, a professor at George Mason University, had to argue with school officials to get his math-talented son into appropriately demanding classes.

Black and Latino parents are often least willing or able to put needed pressure on overly rigid school bureaucracies. When Matthews asked a counselor about the push from Fairfax's central office to get minorities into challenging courses, the counselor replied that the initiative is only at the superintendent's level. "We don't feel any pressure at the school level," the counselor told him.

University of Virginia sophomore Phalana Tiller recalls that when she was in eighth grade at George Washington Junior High School, her teachers wanted to move her up to advanced science and math. "My counselor tried to hold me back. I was told that 'black kids usually don't do well in those courses.' My mom had to come in and put up a fight to get me moved up. You hear all this stuff about honors courses being so intimidating but when I got in I enjoyed them and did well. They were so different from the boring lower-level courses," says Tiller.

"I've seen brilliant kids excluded from classes where they would have excelled because they came out one point under the magic cutoff score," says Davi Walders, who has taught in both Fairfax and Montgomery counties. "Administrators go around rending their garments and saying, 'We want black kids in the GT program but we can't find many with 140 IQs.' There are all kinds of talented black (and white) kids whose abilities are not measured by those scores."

Some black educators see the tracking system as a deliberate attempt to counter legal gains won by the civil-rights movement. Howard University professor Richard Wright feels that "the whole gifted and talented movement is a political response to desegregation, an attempt to exclude certain individuals from the political elite. The schools are supposed to be the great equalizers. What is happening is that all the energy is going to the privileged." Whether the result is intentional or not, there is growing criticism from black parents and educators that attempts to deal with the special needs of minorities are not working. This week, for example, a prominent Yale psychologist issued a report concluding that Montgomery County's magnet schools were leading to more, not less, segregation. The report echoed similar recent criticisms of Prince George's County, where disproportionately high rates of disciplinary actions among black male students are also an issue. But whatever the merits of those charges, the alternatives—eliminating advanced programs for more able or ambitious students or ignoring real disciplinary problems—are not the answer.

"The pendulum is swinging toward mixing all kids together," says Bob McDonough, a College Board official. "But when they realize that doesn't do squat for bright kids, it will swing back again. When minorities complain about anything, liberal educators jump on the bandwagon. [But] if you bore bright kids by mixing them with weak students, they aren't going to respond by taking over your class and instructing other kids. They become problems, and tune out."

Still there are alternatives to either extreme. "Schools really ought to concentrate on getting good teachers for everyone," says Jim Dawes, a truly gifted former student of mine. "Right now the kids in the top tracks get the best teachers. But that is not the fault of tracking. It's the fault of school administrators who hired the real losers and won't get rid of them."

Another is to recognize that more flexible grouping can be both workable and rewarding for all levels of students—but only if the will, and the resources, are there to make it work.

I saw one great model in action this past week. At Alexandria's Cora Kelly magnet school, 40 third-graders of the same racial and socioeconomic mix that disintegrated the third grade at George Mason last year, worked quietly in groups of three or four. Some were doing material way above their grade level; others were trying to catch up. The atmosphere was serious, yet it was obvious these kids were both learning and enjoying themselves. The magnet school has the funds, the space, hand-picked teachers, an experienced principal and parents who made a conscious decision to put their kids in that environment. Perhaps most important—it had careful planning.

So we can't reform the tracking system overnight. But we can make one sure start: eliminate the labels. Peggy O'Brien, head of education at the Folger Shakespeare Library, makes the point another way. People, she says, often call her at the Folger to inquire about programs or speaking engagements and introduce themselves by saying: "I'm so-and-so and I teach the gifted and talented." O'Brien says she always responds that she thinks every kid is gifted and talented. "These people treat Shakespeare as if you have to be very bright and very white to even begin to comprehend him," O'Brien notes. "They forget that the crowd in the Globe Theater watching Hamlet in 1603 was not the 'gifted and talented'; it was everyone."

Patrick Welsh teaches English at T.C. Williams High School in Alexandria.

September 16, 1990

Classrooms of Their Own

Are Single-Sex Schools Better for Girls?

ALICE DIGILIO

When Anita Pampusch, chairman of the Women's College Coalition, goes on the rubber chicken circuit to tout the advantages of single-sex education for young women, she usually gets one of two reactions depending on her audience. Females nod their heads in agreement as she speaks, while men ask if she isn't promoting something "unnatural."

"The world is coed, after all," concedes Pampusch, president of the College of St. Catherine's, in St. Paul. "But when I explain the purpose of all-female education is to develop self-confidence everyone seems to understand."

The 71-college coalition has collected a wealth of statistics demonstrating the success of women educated at single-sex colleges as compared with their sisters at coed institutions. The coalition's studies show that a higher proportion of the former become scientists, mathematicians and economists. Although women's colleges account for only 5 percent of female college graduates, one third of the women board members of the nation's top 1,000 companies are women's college graduates. Of the 27 female members of Congress, 44 percent received their degrees from women's colleges.

There is also current research that shows early academic success among girls educated in single-sex secondary schools. But all these exercises may seem like California condor studies cataloguing the glories of a bird as it faces extinction.

Women's colleges in this country now number 94. Twenty years ago there were 228. A similar decline has occurred in the numbers of girls' secondary schools. Of the 870 members of the National Association of Independent Schools, only 109 educate only females. In 1963, 166 of 682 members were girls' schools.

Some formerly single-sex schools have chosen to accept the opposite sex, as Lawrenceville and Deerfield—in New Jersey and Massachusetts, respectively—have decided to do. When boys' schools go coeducational, girls' schools that operate in the same market or same geographical area tend to suffer enrollment declines. Such are the fears locally of St. Agnes School for Girls, a day school in Alexandria near St.

Stephen's, a formerly all-boys school that has elected to accept girls. Both are Episcopal schools, and St. Stephen's is now engaged in a dispute with the Diocese of Virginia, which would like the two schools to merge under a single board of directors.

Single-sex secondary education is almost non-existent in public education, whereas 30 years ago several girls' academic high schools flourished in major cities. In 1972 Girls' Latin School in Boston changed its name and opened its doors to males when Boston Latin, a boys' school, also began accepting members of the opposite sex. Girls High School, in Philadelphia, is one of the few public high schools exclusively for girls left in the country. It remains, according to William Thompson, a spokesman for the Philadelphia Board of Education, "as an ongoing effort to meet the special needs of female students." Admission to the school is based on a competitive examination, and the number of applications to the school have risen steadily over the past three years.

The ranks of all-male schools and colleges have been shrinking faster than those for females. There are only 96 boys' schools in the NAIS. There are only three all-male colleges left in the country.

But studies show the availability of single-sex education is more crucial for females than it is for males, at least at the secondary level.

Valerie E. Lee, a researcher from the University of Michigan, and Anthony S. Bryk, of the University of Chicago, completed a study of about 2,500 students—half of them girls—in 75 Catholic high schools, both single-sex and coeducational. The study showed that girls from the single-sex high schools were more likely to enjoy math, do more homework, have higher test scores in vocabulary, reading, math and science, as well as more ambition.

The gains of boys attending single-sex schools were statistically insignificant compared with boys in coed schools.

Followup research focusing on the same 2,500 students once they went to college showed that the gains girls made in their single-sex schools continued, even though most of them chose coed colleges. The alumnae of girls' high schools went to more selective colleges; they were more interested in politics, reported being more satisfied with their college experiences and were more apt to apply to graduate schools and choose non-traditional careers, according to Lee.

The followup study, completed this spring is awaiting publication, and now Lee is involved in another project, funded by the Klingenstein Foundation in New York and examining how girls fare in both coed and single-sex independent schools.

"Girls schools are closing right and left. The Klingenstein Foundation thought we should know if they performed a useful function," Lee said.

Advocates of all-female education say that the results of Lee's studies are not surprising. They attribute female success in an all-girls' academic environment to the role models such schools provide, plus the attention young women get from teachers. The result is their greater self-confidence.

In a coed environment, males play lord of the manor—dominating class discussions and the slates for most campus organizations. They are also, the same studies show, heads of most academic departments.

The Association of American Colleges' project on the status and education of women has documented much of this disparity in a report called "The Chilly Classroom Climate for Women."

"In coed classes women get less eye contact from professors, they get more interruptions, and when women speak out in class, they are most likely to get a bland response, an uh-huh," said Bernice Sandler, the project's executive director. "Men get the lion's share of attention. That simply doesn't happen in a women's college."

According to research done by David and Myra Sadker at American University, the pattern begins long before males and females reach college.

"At all levels in coed classes, from elementary school through college, teachers—both male and female—give male students more attention. And that is good for your self-esteem," said Myra Sadker.

Even negative attention, like discipline, can give a positive message.

"It says, 'You're important enough to invest effort in,' " said Sadker. "One reason teachers give boys more attention is they are more aggressive in grabbing it."

The result is that boys end up not only feeling more important than girls but learning more as well.

"Education is not a spectator sport," said Sadker. Although when they enter school, girls are somewhat ahead of boys, they leave high school and college with scores consistently behind those of boys, partially because, the Sadkers believe, girls have simply not had the same degree of interaction with their teachers that boys have.

Myra Sadker considers the disappearance of all-girls schools and colleges, where females do not suffer these kinds of classroom biases, a "tragedy." But she and her husband believe that most of the teachers do not intentionally give preferential treatment to males and that with training they can mend their ways. The Sadkers have given many workshops at colleges and at several independent secondary schools.

Those who support all-female schools and colleges (where proportionately more faculty and administrators are women and where all campus offices are held by females), also cite the presence of female role models as an important issue.

"Women play a more active role at a women's college. At some coed colleges, it would be possible as a woman never to have a female professor. Yet, the head of the math department at a woman's college will very likely be a woman," said Sandler, who is careful to say that the association is "sympathetic to all-women's colleges" but does not promote them as the Women's College Coalition does.

Kelly Cramer's experience at Smith College is typical of what many researchers say women gain at all-female schools.

"At Smith there was never a question of not doing something because you were a woman. That just wasn't an issue," said Kelly Cramer, of Alexandria, an '89 graduate.

Cramer also credits the college with helping her concentrate more on education.

"I think if I'd gone to the University of Virginia or another coed school, I would have concentrated much more on partying," said Cramer. "At Smith I really got concerned about my education."

"The women at Smith were competitive—not in a cutthroat way, but competitive with themselves . . . They had big plans," said Cramer, who says she wants to go to law school.

Cramer went from finding it difficult to adjust to an all-female atmosphere after coeducational T.C. Williams High School to "loving Smith." And her experience is typical, according to Sandler.

"One thing we've often heard is that a lot of women go to a women's college in spite of the fact," Sandler said. "They stay there because it is."

Alice Digilio covers education for the Prince William County Bureau of
The Washington Post.

August 6, 1989

Wide Gender Gap Found in Schools
Girls Said to Face Bias in Tests,
Textbooks and Teaching Methods

MARY JORDAN

The most comprehensive report to assess the gender gap in American schools found widespread bias against girls in tests, textbooks and teaching practices—findings that set off an immediate controversy among educators.

"The bias that exists in how girls are taught is no longer blatant, but they experience it on a daily basis," said Sharon Schuster, president of the American Association of University Women (AAUW), which commissioned the report.

The Education Department, which last month proposed eliminating the only federal program aimed at promoting educational equity for girls, said the new report lacked perspective and hard data and maintained yesterday that gender-equity programs were no longer needed.

"You have to look at the larger context, at all the great strides women have made," said Diane S. Ravitch, assistant secretary for educational research and improvement at the Education Department. "This is a period of history in which there have been the most dramatic strides for women."

Ravitch cited statistics showing the percentage of female high school graduates enrolling in college is now larger than males and that the number of women who become lawyers, doctors and other professionals is rapidly increasing.

In 1970, 5 million college students were male and 3.5 million were female, a vastly different composition than in 1989, when 7.3 million were female and 6.5 million male. Likewise, Ravitch noted that only 8 percent of medical degrees were awarded to women in 1970, but 33 percent went to women in 1989.

"But quantity does not make quality," countered Mary Lou Leipheimer, co-chair of the National Coalition of Girls' Schools, who endorses the AAUW report, which is to be released today.

Leipheimer, who runs the Foxcroft School for girls in Middleburg, recited the other side of the statistical battleground: lagging pay for women compared with men, and underrepresentation of women in leadership roles in education. Women earn 69 cents on the dollar compared with equally educated men, according to a Labor Department analysis. And, while the overwhelming number of public elementary and high school teachers are women, more than 95 percent of the nation's school superintendents are men and 72 percent of its principals are men.

However, much of what the report 'How Schools Shortchange Girls' focuses on is more difficult to quantify: little encouragement for girls to pursue math and science, few female role models in textbooks, and subtle teacher practices, such as calling on boys more often or gearing school and play activities more to the males.

The report by the Wellesley College Center for Research on Women is largely a compilation of existing studies by well-known researchers at Harvard, American and other universities and is believed to be the most thorough documentation of the gender gap in American schools.

Research by Myra and David Sadker, professors at American University, shows that boys in elementary and middle school called out answers eight times more often than girls. When boys called out, teachers listened. But when girls called out, they were told to "raise your hand if you want to speak."

Even when boys did not answer, teachers were more likely to encourage them to give an answer or an opinion than they were to encourage girls, the researchers found.

The study, noting the disparity between males and females in standardized math and science tests, said teachers often steered more boys than girls to those fields.

From 1978 to 1988, female scores on the SAT increased by 11 points while male scores increased by four points. However, males still outscored females 498 to 455.

In science, the gap is wider, and some studies indicate it might be increasing. On the 1988 SAT achievement test in physics, males averaged a 611 score out of 800, 56 points higher than females' average score of 555.

The scores are noteworthy because girls often received better grades than boys, leading some researchers to suggest bias in the tests, which often determine college admittance and scholarships.

Several studies have suggested that teachers encourage male students to work with laboratory equipment, especially in the more complex sciences. For instance, one study found that 51 percent of boys in the third grade had used a microscope, compared with 37 percent of girls. In 11th grade, an electricity meter had been used by 49 percent of males but by only 17 percent of females.

The study also shows that vocational education programs are often geared to males despite the fact that 45 percent of the work force is female. It also showed that since the early 1970s, the participation of girls in interscholastic athletics has increased dramatically, but that boys still participate in them at twice the rate.

The report, timed to be released at the AAUW National Education Summit on Girls, is drawing the attention of many of the most influential education groups in the nation, including the head of the largest teachers union.

The report says some progress has been made since the enactment of Title IX, the landmark 1972 legislation banning sex discrimination in federally funded education programs. Yet, it says stereotypical images still appear in textbooks, the overwhelming number of authors and role models studied in class are male, and problems confronting women, including sexism, the higher rate of suicide among women, and eating disorders are often all but ignored in the curriculum.

"I think you can look at any situation and see the progress or see the way we have to go," said Susan McGee Bailey, director of the Wellesley research center. "But I think it's dangerous to say that because one-third of our medical students are now women" the struggle for gender equality is over. "There is a great deal more to be done."

February 12, 1992

For Boys Only

WILLIAM RASPBERRY

Three all-male academies were to have opened in Detroit yesterday. They didn't. The schools, a desperate attempt to help the city's most troubled population group—black boys—have strong community support.

But they were opposed by the American Civil Liberties Union and the NOW Legal Defense Fund, whose lawyers argued in U.S. District Court that for the school board to establish special academies for boys is a denial of equal educational opportunity for girls.

Judge George Woods apparently bought the argument. Helping boys may be great, he said, but excluding girls violates state and federal law. The hope now is for a compromise that will create a hundred or so openings for girls who want to attend the schools.

I'm all for compromise, if that will help the new schools get started. But it seems to me that both Judge Woods and "Nancy Doe" (the anonymous mother of three public school daughters on whose behalf the ACLU and the NOW Legal Defense Fund brought suit) miss the point of what the Detroit school board is trying to accomplish.

Black boys in Detroit—and in cities across the country—are falling victim to academic failure, joblessness, crime and death. The No. 1 cause of death among young black men is young black men themselves. And increasingly their violence is spilling over to embrace the innocent. Black males are an endangered, and endangering, species.

The reasons why are not entirely clear, but they certainly include a notion of manhood that eschews academic achievement in favor of brute power and defiance.

Detroit's school authorities hoped the academies (open to boys of all races but aimed at blacks) would help to counter the deadly trend. The new schools were to place special emphasis on personal discipline, civic responsibility and high academic standards, using a curriculum with a heavy emphasis on African and African-American history.

Could such an approach help undo what is happening to black boys in America's inner cities? I don't know. I do know that an experiment at a Florida elementary school that used male teachers for boys-only classes produced exemplary results in academic achievement, school citizenship and discipline—until it was shut down as a violation of Title IX.

Something similar could happen in Detroit if people there miss the point of the experiment.

The plaintiff in the court suit seems to have missed it. The application process and indeed the very name "Male Academy" make clear the discriminatory intent, she told the court. But if Detroit's black boys are in as much trouble as I think they are in—and if an all-male environment is a reasonable approach for dealing with that trouble—Nancy Doe's suit founders on the shoals of illogic. It says: Have your male academies; just make sure they're co-ed.

The ACLU and the NOW LDF seem to see the academies as just another example of male privilege in a world in which women already are victimized by male advantage. It's as though they have grown so used to seeing male-only arrangements as subterfuges for antifemale discrimination that they cannot see even the theoretical possibility of helping boys without hurting girls.

Judge Woods seems to see the academy idea as a reproach to females. "There is no evidence the school system is failing males because girls attend school with them," he said. "Girls fail too."

Well, of course they do. But no one in his right mind can doubt that, in the special case of America's inner cities, boys fail more; or that their failure has consequences that include not just their own endangerment but the imperilment of their entire communities.

Given America's history of race and sex discrimination, it's well to be on the alert for new forms of bias. But it's also well not to become so tunnel-visioned about the possibility of favoritism that we forget common sense. Think of a sick child whose disease, left untreated, could destroy the whole family. Now ask yourself how much patience you'd have with a sibling who complained: "Mommy, Junior's getting more medicine than I am, and it's not fair!"

August 28, 1991

Religion in Schools 10

High Court Bans Graduation Prayer at Public Schools

RUTH MARCUS

A bitterly divided Supreme Court yesterday prohibited officially sponsored prayers at public school graduations, declaring that they coerce youngsters into participating in religious exercises in violation of the Constitution.

Justice Anthony M. Kennedy, writing for the 5 to 4 majority, said that even non-sectarian benedictions and invocations—a staple at graduation ceremonies in public school systems nationwide—violate the First Amendment bar against government establishment of religion.

It was the court's first major school prayer ruling since 1985, when it struck down an Alabama law allowing a "moment of silence" in the schools. It also surprised many observers, who thought that a court so dramatically reconstituted by Presidents Reagan and Bush might go the other way, breaking with its historically strict view on this church-state issue.

Two Reagan appointees, Kennedy and Sandra Day O'Connor, were joined in the majority opinion by Bush's first Supreme Court nominee, David H. Souter, and by Justices Harry A. Blackmun and John Paul Stevens.

In a written statement, Bush said he was "very disappointed" by the ruling. "I believe that the court has unnecessarily cast away the venerable and proper American tradition of non-sectarian prayer at public celebrations."

Kennedy said that although attendance at commencement and participation in the prayers may be voluntary, the real-world effect is to force impressionable students into participating in a religious activity.

"The Constitution forbids the state to exact religious conformity from a student as the price of attending her own high school graduation," Kennedy wrote. "This is the calculus the Constitution commands."

Justice Antonin Scalia, in a particularly acerbic dissent joined by Chief Justice William H. Rehnquist and Justices Byron R. White and Clarence Thomas, assailed the majority for a ruling "as senseless in policy as it is unsupported in law."

A somber-sounding Scalia underscored his unhappiness by announcing his dissent from the bench, a tool the justices reserve to signal extreme disagreement. Reading aloud the actual prayer at issue, Scalia said it was "sad that a prayer of this sort is sought to be abolished." In his written dissent, Scalia said the decision "lays waste a tradition that is as old as public-school graduation ceremonies themselves, and that is a component of an even more longstanding American tradition of non-sectarian prayer to God at public celebrations generally."

The nondenominational benediction and invocation at issue in this case, he said, "are so characteristically American they could have come from the pen of George Washington or Abraham Lincoln himself."

The ruling was applauded by civil liberties groups and some religious organizations that had been braced for a major rewriting of the court's test on separation of church and state cases, which they feared would drastically lower the wall of separation between government and religion.

"It's terrific," said Steven Shapiro of the American Civil Liberties Union, which represented the Rhode Island family that challenged the commencement prayer.

"It should end any lingering debate about prayer in school, which a majority of the court has clearly and strongly held once again is unconstitutional," Shapiro said. "Given this court and given its drift in religion cases this is really an important restatement of core principles about the importance of separation between church and state." Conservative groups and other religious organizations that thought they could count on a win from the solidified conservative majority on the high court expressed feelings of anger and betrayal yesterday.

Charles J. Cooper, the lawyer for the Providence, R.I. school board defending the prayer, said the ruling was "extremely disappointing," adding, "I would even presume to speak for the great majority of the American people. A tradition over a century and a half old in its duration and extremely widespread throughout the country will come to a halt because the Supreme Court has discovered that our founding fathers prohibited that tradition."

"This is constitutional psycho-babble at its worst," said Thomas L. Jipping of the Free Congress Foundation.

"Of the five new justices added to the court by Presidents Reagan and Bush, three joined in today's travesty," said Family Research Council President Gary Bauer. "At that rate, one has to wonder why liberal interest groups bother fighting Republican nominees to the court. Why not just support them and watch them 'grow'?"

Solicitor General Kenneth W. Starr, who on behalf of the administration had urged the court to allow the prayer, said he was "disappointed" and "surprised" by the court's "willingness to strike down a well-settled traditional and historical practice."

However, Starr said he did not interpret the opinion as placing an absolute barrier to prayer at school graduation ceremonies, suggesting that student-initiated prayers, unsupervised by school officials, might be permissible.

The court is expected to complete its term in the next few days. Six cases remain, including the Pennsylvania abortion case and a closely watched college desegregation case from Mississippi. The justices are scheduled to issue opinions Friday and spokeswoman Toni House said there are "strong indications" the court will sit Monday as well.

Church-state relations are an area of the law in which the court has been closely divided in recent years. A majority of the justices, including Kennedy and O'Connor, had expressed unhappiness with the test the court had used since 1971 to judge when government involvement with religion ran afoul of the Constitution.

Many observers had anticipated that the high court, prodded by the Bush administration and others, might use yesterday's case, *Lee v. Weisman,* to make a major change in the law. Instead, led by Kennedy, the court explicitly rebuffed the invitation to do so.

The case involved a challenge to the Providence, R.I., public schools' practice of having a clergyman deliver an invocation and benediction at junior high and high school graduation ceremonies.

At the June 1989 graduation from Nathan Bishop Middle School, Rabbi Leslie Gutterman delivered a non-sectarian invocation and benediction that referred to God. Daniel Weisman, whose daughter Deborah was among the graduates, filed a lawsuit in federal court, contending that the inclusion of the prayers violated the First Amendment. At an elder daughter's graduation, the Weismans, who are Jewish, had heard a minister invoke Jesus Christ in his prayer.

The lower federal courts agreed with the Weismans, saying that the prayer violated the existing three-part test the courts have used to judge separation of church and state cases.

That test, known as the Lemon test after the court's 1971 ruling in *Lemon v. Kurtzman,* states that to comply with the First Amendment, a challenged practice must have a secular purpose, a primary effect that neither advances nor inhibits religion, and not foster "excessive government entanglement with religion."

The Bush administration, entering the case on the side of the Providence school board, urged the court to get rid of the test, which has resulted in numerous rulings barring various religious activities. The administration said it was unworkable and should be replaced with a more lenient standard: allowing "civic acknowledgments of religion in public life . . . as long as they neither threaten the establishment of an official religion nor coerce participation in religious activities."

Kennedy, who has suggested such a coercion test, said the prayer at issue went too far under that or any other test. "It is beyond dispute that, at a minimum, the government may not coerce anyone to support or participate in religion or its exercise . . ." he said.

"The undeniable fact is that the school district's supervision and control of a high school graduation ceremony places public pressure, as well as peer pressure, on attending students to stand as a group or, at least, maintain respectful silence during the invocation and benediction," he said. "This pressure, though subtle and indirect, can be as real as any overt compulsion."

Scalia derided this approach as "the court's psycho-journey" and "psychology practiced by amateurs" and said the court was treating religion as "some purely personal avocation that can be indulged in entirely in secret, like pornography, in the privacy of one's room." He said the majority was worrying too much about the Weismans' concerns and too little about the community's interest in public proclamation of its faith in God, something that Scalia said had marked American public life since Washington's first inaugural address.

The case "involves the community's celebration of one of the milestones in its young citizens' lives, and it is a bold step for this court to seek to banish from that occasion, and from thousands of similar celebrations throughout this land, the expression of gratitude to God that a majority of the community wishes to make."

The case was noteworthy because it marked the first votes by Souter and Thomas on the subject. Thomas, who stated several times at his confirmation hearings last year that he had "no quarrel" with the Lemon test, joined Scalia's effort to replace it.

Souter, in a separate concurring opinion, joined with O'Connor, who wants a standard of constitutionality that is similar to the existing one: whether the government's action endorses religion. In fact, although they joined Kennedy's opinion, the four other justices in the majority made clear that they believe government action that endorses religion, as well as government action that coerces participation in it, violates the Constitution.

Some observers who were cheered by the ruling expressed concern that Kennedy might join with the four dissenters to allow more government involvement with religion outside the school context—for example, in cases challenging official displays of creches and other Christmas symbols.

Kennedy "appeared to leave a back door open to a weaker standard, particularly outside the public school setting," said Elliot Mincberg, legal director of the liberal People for the American Way.

The benediction delivered by Rabbi Leslie Gutterman at the Nathan Bishop Middle School, Providence, R.I., graduation in June 1989:

O God, we are grateful to You for having endowed us with the capacity for learning which we have celebrated on this joyous commencement.

Happy families give thanks for seeing Your children achieve an important milestone. Send Your blessings upon the teachers and administrators who helped prepare them.

The graduates now need strength and guidance for the future; help them to understand that we are not complete with academic knowledge alone. We must each strive to fulfill what You require of us all: to do justly, to love mercy, to walk humbly.

We give thanks to You, Lord, for keeping us alive, sustaining us and allowing us to reach this special, happy occasion. Amen.

June 25, 1992

California Proposal Could Alter Teaching of Evolution Nationwide

JAY MATHEWS

Supporters of teaching evolution in public schools have sharply criticized California state school officials for changes in science teaching guidelines because they fear the effect on textbook publishers and teachers if the guidelines are approved, as expected, by the state school board this week.

The latest stage in the evolution controversy, which could have a marked impact on how biology is taught throughout the country because California buys 10 percent of the nation's textbooks and publishers tend to conform their books to the requirements of that market, has created a split between pro-evolution education forces and their erstwhile ally, state school Superintendent Bill Honig.

Honig argued that compromise language in the new guidelines will ensure board support for teaching evolution, but groups such as the National Center for Science Education and People for the American Way said the changes create an opening for more attacks on evolution by religious-oriented groups.

"Any weakening amendments are unnecessary and can only be seen as accommodation to the political pressure exerted by the religious right," said Michael Hudson, western director of People for the American Way, an anti-censorship group engaged in evolution controversies here and in Texas.

The state board of education strongly endorsed evolution education in January. Since then, it has been bombarded by letters and statements from evolution critics and has acquired four new appointees of Gov. George Deukmejian (R). It is scheduled to vote Wednesday on a new science framework to guide publishers preparing textbooks, although at least one board member said he wants to postpone the decision.

Advocates of teaching evolution say publishers have treated evolution vaguely and given credence to the creationism theory supported by religious groups. Charles Darwin's theory of evolution, which is the unifying principle underlying all modern biology, holds that human beings are descendants of more primitive species that evolved over millions of years. Creationism argues that God created mankind and all other species almost simultaneously.

The changes supported by Honig and board president Francis Laufenberg, a former school superintendent in Long Beach, Calif., would remove from the framework part of a detailed defense of evolution teaching, including a reference to the 1987 U.S. Supreme Court decision in *Edwards v. Aguillard,* which struck down a Louisiana law putting evolution and creationism on a par in science classes. In response to arguments that all scientific theories are open to review, the compromise would also remove this sentence: "There is no scientific dispute that evolution has occurred and continues to occur; this is why evolution is regarded as a scientific fact."

Honig, in an interview, said the changes would not alter the board's commitment to limit discussion of creationism to social science and literature classes. Board members had criticized an earlier draft of the science framework as too focused on a defense of evolution teaching.

"The changes do not remove all the hostility," said the Rev. Louis P. Sheldon, a Presbyterian minister helping lead the creationism forces. "It doesn't go quite far enough."

Eugenie Scott, a biological anthropologist who serves as executive director of the National Center for Science Education, said that although the changes might create doubt among some teachers about the board's commitment to evolution, she could accept them. "But what I'm worried about is that there are going to be extra changes as well," she said.

Hudson, of the People for the American Way, said the revised framework was still strong but that the revisions would suggest to publishers that the board "is very weak" politically and might not resist future criticism if textbooks emphasized evolutionary theory.

Honig called Hudson's argument "tactically wrong." Supporters of evolution teaching should celebrate the framework's strengths, he said, because acting as if the board had wavered will give the creationists "a victory for free."

November 7, 1989

Teacher Training Program to Introduce Religion Curriculum

LAURA SESSIONS STEPP

A group of national educators led by former education commissioner Ernest L. Boyer announced an ambitious program this week to train teachers to teach about religion, religious liberty and civic values in the public schools.

The First Liberty Institute, housed at George Mason University, will train social studies teachers from around the country in the use of a new curriculum designed for elementary, junior high and senior high school students.

The new lesson plans—on topics ranging from Jewish settlers in 16th-century America to Moslem government workers today—were tested last fall in 150 classrooms, including some in Anne Arundel County. Now revised, the lessons, called "Living With Our Deepest Differences," are beginning to be adopted in school districts around the country, according to Charles L. Haynes, the institute's new executive director.

The educators said Wednesday at a news conference that the curriculum is the first of its kind in the country. It was drafted with the help of the National School Boards Association, university education departments and faith communities including the American Jewish Committee, the U.S. Catholic Conference, the National Council of Churches and the National Association of Evangelicals. It also has the support of Americans United for Separation of Church and State.

The brainchild of the privately funded Williamsburg Charter Foundation, the First Liberty Institute evolved out of a concern that an increasing number of American students are ignorant of the institutions and ideals upon which the country was founded, Haynes said.

Schoolteachers feel unprepared to teach more about U.S. religious history and civics, Haynes added, even as an increasing number of school boards are telling them to do so in the name of multicultural education.

Boyer, author of the 1983 report on public schools, "A Nation at Risk," which stimulated many of the changes taking place in public education, said he believes the new program "moves us beyond the regulatory aspects of more homework and higher test scores to focus on . . . fundamental values of freedom of religion, freedom of speech and respect for diversity upon which this nation was founded."

Religion, Boyer continued, is one of those "flashpoints" in American culture that, like sex education, teachers avoid. "The failure to include the study of religion in the school curriculum has reduced the quality of the education we are providing to our children," Boyer said in prepared remarks.

First Liberty Institute, an independent, nonprofit organization funded principally by private foundations, will run on a budget of about $200,000, according to institute officials, with two full-time teacher-trainers. One of those trainers, Haynes, has led a summer program for D.C. area teachers for four years at George Mason. It was his connection to the school's Department of Education that resulted in the university's providing office space.

Haynes, a former world religion professor who has taught hundreds of teachers locally and nationwide, said several states recently ordered their school districts to incorporate instruction on religion and religious pluralism in the classroom.

One state, California, already has placed the First Liberty materials on its approved curriculum list, he said. California teachers who used the material during last year's pilot program "were quite pleased," said Diane Brooks, manager of the history/social science unit for the California State Department of Education. "The staff development that went along with it was excellent. There were some questions raised at first—was this doctrine or a more factual, historical approach? The evidence pointed to the latter."

Locally, Prince George's County as well as the Salisbury, Md., school district have shown an interest in using the curriculum, which begins at grade 5 with a discussion of the settlement of Jews in this country from 1492 to 1654. That section, like all others, ends with a parent participation exercise: Fifth-graders are asked to find out where their ancestors came from, whether their ancestors were part of a religious community and whether religious liberty played a role in their family's past.

First Liberty Institute Questionnaire for Senior High School Students

1. There should be laws against the practice of Satan worship.
   . . .. Agree . . .. Disagree . . .. Don't Know

2. Followers of the Rev. Sun Myung moon should not be allowed to print a daily newspaper in Washington, D.C.
.... Agree .... Disagree .... Don't Know

3. It should be against the law for preachers to use television shows to raise money.
.... Agree .... Disagree .... Don't Know

4. If a group is named as a threat to democracy, do you think some of its public activities should be restricted?
.... Agree .... Disagree .... Don't Know

November 3, 1990

Sex Education in Schools 11

A Tough-Talking Teacher Tells Teens About AIDS
Educator's Candor Gets Attention of Students and Critics

SHAUN SUTNER

She calls herself the Julia Child of sex education, and her trademark is a recipe for straight talk about AIDS in a city with one of the highest rates of teenage HIV infection in the country.

A roly-poly, gray-haired woman with twinkling eyes and a penchant for bright colors and slogan buttons, Jackie Sadler, head of AIDS education for the D.C. public schools, is one part stand-up comedian and one part zealot mixed with a hefty dose of confrontational style.

"I've mastered the art of masterful people harassment," she said with a laugh. "Kids get embarrassed sometimes when I talk, but then they don't walk out."

That may be because, unlike the AIDS prevention campaign launched last week by the federal agency that pays her salary, Sadler uses the word "sex" in about every other sentence. And she tells students straight out: If you're going to have sex, use a condom.

Here's how to get one. Here's how to use one. And always be sure he's got one on.

She has her share of critics among church leaders and gay-rights activists. Yet she carries on, peppering her message with wry humor and rhyming raps, short questions and funny answers, hoping to win the ears of young people who need to hear.

Still, they may not be listening.

Though only eight cases of AIDS have been diagnosed among D.C. teenagers since 1983, several hundred of the nearly 3,500 cases citywide have surfaced in people in their early twenties, people who probably were infected with the virus as teenagers.

A five-year study of about 15,000 teenagers at Children's Hospital estimates that 750 to 1,500 teenagers in the District are infected with the AIDS virus today.

In 1987, about three in every 1,000 teenagers in the study were HIV-infected. It's now about 12 to 15 in every 1,000, according to Lawrence D'Angelo, chief of adolescent medicine at Children's, who conducted the study.

That is 20 times higher than the rate among teenagers nationwide.

"Adolescent AIDS is a growing problem, especially in the cities," as are other sexually transmitted diseases, including syphilis and gonorrhea, said William Cannon, outreach coordinator for the adolescent AIDS program at Montefiore Medical Center in New York City.

The sexual activity of District teenagers explains the health concern: In 1991, more than 75 percent of 10th-graders in D.C. public schools said they were sexually active, with 65 percent of boys and 20 percent of girls acknowledging four or more partners, according to a study of D.C. teenagers by the Centers for Disease Control.

"I like to feel I'm out on the battlefield," Sadler said. "If I didn't feel optimistic, I couldn't go on, but it takes its toll. I'm just one person with a staff of four. We need more people and much more money."

Sadler's job was created in 1987, when the CDC offered to fund 16 school programs to help students understand this new public health threat, and the District's proposal landed the funds.

Her approach is simple. To reach young people, she said, you must talk their language.

So, there she was one January day, dressed in a purple paisley pantsuit, this 53-year-old woman little children call the "Button Lady," talking to 100 tittering first-graders at Takoma Elementary about safe sex and semen, with buttons on her lapel that read "Love Me, Love My Rubber" and "Touch Me, Hold Me, but Keep Me AIDS-free."

And offering up a nursery rhyme that was vintage Sadler:

"Jack and Jill went up the hill to fetch a pail of water. Jill forgot her pills. They had some fun. Now she has a son. Whoops. Upside your head!"

Seated on the sidelines was Naomi Washington, the grandmother of a first-grader, who didn't wince once. "I'm glad there's someone to tell us, so we all understand. Her way is an excellent way to get information to kids."

"We need to clone Jackie Sadler," agreed D'Angelo, of Children's Hospital. "She's honest, she's direct. And she's one of the hardest working people I've ever been around."

Maybe so, but "she's paving the way for the distribution of condoms," said the Rev. Cleveland Sparrow, pastor of Sparrow World Baptist Church in Oxon Hill. "What she's doing in essence is promoting fornication and adultery."

To which Sadler, her bifocals perched at the end of her nose, responds: "I don't think honesty is ever unorthodox, and I wouldn't tell anybody anything I wouldn't tell my own child. . . . But whether someone is sexually active or not doesn't depend on me or Rev. Sparrow. We're moving in the realm of thinking we're omnipotent if we think we can control what happens in the bedroom."

She gets even more defensive when critics in the gay community criticize her as not being frank enough about the unprotected gay sex that goes on among teenage boys.

Jim Graham, director of the Whitman-Walker AIDS clinic, said that he is a "big fan of Jackie Sadler" but that she does tend to sidestep the issue.

"I think we need to make a point of it," Graham said. "We need to come to terms with the fact that many of our teenagers are having same-sex activities. We have to have a better level of candor." In fact, the latest findings of the Children's Hospital study indicate that half of all infected teenagers in the District probably are young men who engaged in homosexual sex. The other half are girls, most of them infected by older men who are intravenous drug users.

"I talk about how the virus is transmitted, whether it's by homosexuals, bisexuals or heterosexuals," Sadler said. "But I try not to get into labels."

Her own upbringing was sheltered and middle-class in Macon, Ga. A dentist's daughter who graduated from Nashville's Fisk University at age 18, she went on to receive two master's degrees—in public health and maternal and child health.

"My goodness, girl," her father would kid her. "I made all those sacrifices to send you to school, and all you can do is get up and talk about sex."

Today she and her husband, a career Foreign Service officer, live in a comfortable home in Shepherd Park, where she also sings in a Presbyterian church choir. Their daughter, Zara, 21, whom Sadler calls "my heartstring" and "my consultant" is a pre-med student at Lincoln University in Pennsylvania.

Sadler came to her job on an extended loan from Howard University Medical Center, where she had worked for 15 years teaching people about family planning.

Her program, renewed with a $323,000 grant last year, authorizes her and her staff to coordinate AIDS-prevention education for fourth-through 12th-graders by teaching teachers, visiting classrooms and distributing educational materials.

But she is best in front of a room full of teenagers, as she was at the National Press Club preview of a PBS special on teenage sex last spring, when she had the audience howling with her safe-sex rap and candid comments on topics such as masturbation and recreational sex.

"When Ms. Sadler talks, you understand," said Faith Culbreth, a Spingarn High School senior who is among dozens of peer educators Sadler has trained.

The lessons about HIV need not be presented in dire terms, Sadler said.

"Homelessness, hunger, those are emergencies," she said. "Anything you can stop by modifying behavior is not an emergency. It's just urgent."

And the consensus is that the information is getting out there, she adds. "Among students I talk to, they say they've started to use their 'jimmy hats' [street slang for condoms]," Sadler said. "We all would like to feel that we're doing a dynamite job, but the verdict is still out."

Because ultimately young people won't change their behavior until adults change theirs, she says. As long as the reports about William Kennedy Smith and Mike Tyson are in their consciousness, teenagers will keep getting the message that promiscuous and unprotected sex is okay, Sadler said.

That's why she takes the time to talk to first-graders. The only way to change the course of this disease, Sadler said, is to instill values and talk frankly to youngsters about love and sex and caring long before they go off to high school.

And then? Well, she said, with her signature candor: Allowing condoms in a household with teenagers may not be such a terrible idea, either.

About 58,000 youths ages 12 to 19 currently live in the District.

About eight cases of AIDS in this age group have been reported since 1983.

Between 750 and 1,500 teenagers are believed to be infected with the HIV virus, according to estimates from a five-year study of about 12,000 youths ages 13 to 19 by Children's Hospital.

About half of infected teenagers in the District are girls, most infected by having sex with older, infected intravenous drug users, according to researchers involved in the Children's Hospital study.

Homosexual sex is believed to account for most HIV infections in teenage boys here, researchers said.

Since 1987, when the study was started, the rate of infection has increased from three per 1,000 to between 12 and 15 per thousand.

That rate per thousand is about 20 times higher than the U.S. rate.

The number of AIDS cases among teenagers nationwide since 1983 is 789, according to the Centers for Disease Control.

April 2, 1992

Schools Aim to Balance Sex Education

Protests Have Subsided, but Virginia Programs Continue to Draw Criticism

STEPHANIE GRIFFITH

Susan Hu plucked a letter from the crammed carton atop her desk and began reading it to the seventh-grade girls in the sex education class she teaches at Kenmore Middle School in Arlington.

"Dear Mrs. Hu," the letter said, "I like this boy, but all he wants to do is have sex."

"What do you answer her?" she asked the 12- and 13-year-old girls, some of whom had placed questions anonymously in the box.

One girl recommended that the letter's author say no to the boy. "He might be HIV positive," she said.

Another student cautioned that the writer could get pregnant. "Then he'll say he doesn't want to have anything to do with her," the girl added.

Hu didn't tell the girls, who were separated from their male classmates for the discussion, that it was wrong to have sex but agreed with her class that it would be a mistake.

"I try to be upfront and straight and not give them moral judgments," she said. "I talked about the consequences of having sex."

A year after the debut in Northern Virginia of a state-required program known as family life education, the practice by public schools of teaching consequences rather than preaching values remains a sensitive issue as school officials struggle to find the right balance in telling students about human sexuality.

Though parents skirmished with school officials to block the introduction of the courses, massive protests now have been replaced by sporadic objections.

Teachers also seem to be more confident, though some say they are not entirely comfortable with the curriculum.

"A lot of people are afraid of the worst scenario—some parent coming back and accusing you of giving students misinformation," Hu said.

In Virginia and Maryland, state law requires public schools to teach family life, a curriculum taught from kindergarten to high school that includes not only human sexuality but also such diverse topics as substance abuse and stress management. Courses vary based on the policies of local school boards.

In the District, where courses also are mandated, individual schools and teachers have broad latitude to decide how and when sex education is taught.

Just as in Northern Virginia, parental protests in the District and Maryland have subsided, but complaints can surface over program changes.

In a recent confrontation, for example, some members of a Montgomery County community advisory committee objected to a school board decision to use a sealed contraceptive display kit for ninth-graders.

Since family life classes began in the fall of 1990, most Northern Virginia schools report that fewer than 2 percent of parents have opted to remove their children. Some said they decided to keep their children in family life classes although they oppose them.

"They don't do anything constructive in the opt-out program," said Sherry Icenhower, mother of a fifth-grader at Taylor Elementary School in Arlington. Icenhower, who said she believes the sex education courses expose students to sexual concepts before they are ready to handle them, added she feared that removing her son from the class "would just make him more inquisitive" about sex.

One way to defuse some of the concern has been to include parents in homework assignments.

"The idea is to encourage parents to be aware of what we are doing in the classroom so that they can become more comfortable with it, and to help the children feel more comfortable with approaching the parent about sexual issues," Hu said.

Because some students are uneasy about raising issues among their classmates, Hu's letter box lets them ask some of their most embarrassing questions. Recently they included: How long does a sperm live when it's in a woman's body? Why does the penis get hard during intercourse? Can a woman have sex during her period?

Those questions, Hu said, "give me an idea of where they're coming from, what their concerns are, what I should try to direct some of what they're learning to."

School administrators in Arlington and elsewhere said they have bent over backward to inform parents about the family life curriculum, distributing newsletters and brochures about the classes.

But some parents still feel the communication process is flawed. Pat McWethy, parent of a second-grader in Arlington, said that although she filed a form last year to take her child out of sex education, when the school year came to an end, "my 7-year-old told me that she'd never been asked to leave."

Although many teachers endorse the content of the classes, some would prefer more flexibility. Rita Stauss, coordinator of the family life education program at Taylor, said she longs for the freedom to talk about issues that diverge from the curriculum when they come up in classroom discussion.

Under the current policy, Stauss said, "you dangle some information in front of them and then say sorry, we can't discuss that. You have to go home and ask your parents."

Stauss said she also feels hampered because according to county guidelines, sexual organs can be represented pictorially only in isolation, not on the whole body. "You see the reproductive organs out of context" Stauss said. "A lot of kids ask, 'Where is this on the body?' "

Icenhower's son, Emil Viano, 10, said he has learned a lot about the reproductive system in his fifth-grade class, although he would have preferred that a discussion about male sexual responses had been conducted by a man.

"We all wished we could ask [the teacher] questions," Emil said, "but a lot of us felt embarrassed."

February 16, 1992

New York Schools May Liberalize Condom Policy
Disputed Plan Would Allow Unlimited Distribution

LAURIE GOODSTEIN

Schools Chancellor Joseph Fernandez proposed to the Board of Education today a groundbreaking AIDS-education plan that includes making condoms available free to students in all public high schools, even without parental consent.

"We are sitting on a ticking time bomb," Fernandez told the seven board members, referring to AIDS cases among adolescents. "I think a lot of people are watching us to see what we're going to do."

If the board approves the plan despite militant opposition from church and community groups, it likely would be the nation's most sweeping AIDS-education initiative. While some schools with health clinics distribute condoms, no other school system has authorized making condoms available on an unlimited basis, school district officials here said. The board is expected to vote on or before Jan. 5.

Dr. Karen Hein of the Albert Einstein Medical Center in the Bronx told the board today that New York City "is the leader in the nation for AIDS cases among adolescents." She showed a chart documenting a leap from 10 AIDS cases in 1983 to 111 in 1988 among New York youths ages 12 to 21.

She added that those numbers are deceptively low because they account only for people who actually have AIDS, which can take five to 10 years to develop. They do not include those who have tested positive for HIV, the virus that causes AIDS, or are unaware that they carry the virus.

Some school board members bristled at the slide presentation. "There are statistics, and there are statistics," said Michael Petrides, who represents Staten Island and said he opposes the condom plan.

Only Petrides and Irene Impellizzeri, representing Brooklyn, appear firmly antagonistic toward Fernandez's proposal. Approval would end a longstanding policy not to have birth-control devices available on campus, said James Vlasto, a spokesman for Fernandez.

By far the most controversial step in the proposal would have each school select volunteers, usually one male and one female faculty or staff member, to distribute condoms on campus during school hours. These volunteers would be trained in AIDS education at school district headquarters but not be required to offer counseling along with the condoms.

"We're not going to put a student in a situation where they have to go get counseling in order to get a condom," Fernandez said today. "That takes the heart out of the plan."

The proposal also calls for updating the AIDS curriculum, mandating AIDS education from kindergarten through sixth grade and expanding the chancellor's advisory council on AIDS education to include students and AIDS patients.

The proposal by Fernandez, who is nearing completion of his first year as chancellor, has created an uproar in some quarters, making administrators nervous about implementing it.

"In certain communities where people because of religious reasons or other reasons are opposed to this, we don't want our principals to be caught between the chancellor's regulations and serious problems that might develop in the community," said Neil Lefkowitz, director of field operations for the Council of Supervisors and Administrators, the principals' union.

Joseph Zwilling, spokesman for the Roman Catholic Archdiocese of New York, said, "We don't think it is right to implicitly endorse the idea of sexual activity among our teenagers. By distributing condoms, I think that's what you're doing, or at least implying . . . that we think this behavior is okay."

Several Catholic, Jewish, Greek and Russian Orthodox and Protestant churches—the latter including some predominantly black, inner-city congregations—recently formed the Coalition of Concerned Clergy to lobby against the proposal.

Students leaving Washington Irving High School in Manhattan today had heard about the condom controversy and expressed an array of opinions about it.

"Do you know how many girls are walking in here pregnant?" asked Tamessa Lynah, 16. "If there were condoms in here, they wouldn't be, and they'd be protected from diseases too."

Her friend, Elizabeth Taylor, 17, disagreed. "If you want condoms, you should have the confidence to ask your parents for it. It's better that your parents know what you're doing than someone in school because, if you get pregnant, who is going to help you? Your parents."

Asked whether students would be comfortable asking a teacher for a condom, Frank Gifford, 16, said, "Some students would be embarrassed. You have to see that teacher every day. You don't have to see the drugstore clerk every day."

December 6, 1990

High School Clinic Case Study in Sexual Risk

In Rural Florida Town, Impact of Offering Free Condoms to Teenagers Remains Unclear

PAUL TAYLOR

Whenever his supply runs low, Elijah Hobley heads over to the cramped trailer that houses his high school's health clinic and picks up 20 condoms.

He's been making these visits since he was in the ninth grade, as have scores of his classmates. "If it wasn't for the clinic," said Hobley, a soft-spoken preacher's son who is the star senior forward on the Shanks High School basketball team, "there'd be a lot more pregnant girls in school."

Five years before the New York City Board of Education made national headlines with its recent vote to dispense condoms in high schools, this poor, mostly black rural community in Florida's panhandle took a similar step.

The clinic has been a magnet for controversy ever since. It offers a case study in how difficult it is—medically as well as politically—to reduce the high-risk sexual behavior of adolescents.

Not long after the state Department of Health and Rehabilitative Services accepted the invitation of the local school board to open a clinic at Shanks, Gov. Bob Martinez (R) ordered it off the high school campus, arguing that it sent the wrong message about teenage sexuality.

Local officials responded defiantly: They moved the trailer a mere 100 yards to a city-owned lot across the street, where it continued serving students, though fewer than when it was on campus.

Earlier this year, in one of his first acts as Martinez's successor, Gov. Lawton Chiles (D) returned the trailer to its original site. "Here's a community that sticks its neck out and wants to do the right thing, and we need to do everything we can to support it," he said.

At a time when rates of adolescent sexual activity, pregnancy, abortion, births and sexually transmitted diseases are on the rise nation-

234

wide, the boundaries of what constitutes "the right thing" are expanding. Although Shanks is one of fewer than two dozen schools around the country that dispense birth-control supplies to students, many educators believe the New York vote will give the practice a boost.

Do such programs cut down on teenage pregnancy and sexually transmitted disease, as their champions contend? Or do they promote sexual promiscuity, as critics charge? The answer here is that there is no clear evidence they do either.

Hobley's assessment of a decline in pregnancy rates is widely echoed by parents, educators and health officials here, and backed up by at least one independent study. But a second survey paints a murkier picture.

So does Hobley's own track record. Last month he came down with chlamydia, a sexually transmitted disease common among teenagers. His girlfriend is pregnant. "That was my worst mistake," he said of the baby expected this spring. "I thought my girlfriend was on the pill, so I don't always use the condoms."

Despite his lapses, Hobley is considered by health officials here to be unusually diligent—for a male—about sexual safety.

"Ninety percent of the condoms I give out are to girls," said Betsy Johnson, a registered nurse who runs the clinic, "because the boys just don't see this as their responsibility."

Shanks had the highest rate of teenage pregnancy in the state before the clinic opened, and parents here have supported the clinic from the start. More than two-thirds of parents sign the permission slips the school distributes each year that allow their sons or daughters to use the clinic's services, which run the gamut from routine health care to birth control. (By contrast, the program approved in New York City last month will dispense condoms without parental consent.)

"The subject of sex isn't talked about in most homes, because most parents aren't comfortable with it," said James Daniels, a math teacher at Shanks and father of an 11th grader. "That's why they're glad we have the clinic."

On a first visit, Johnson gives females a lesson in sexual reproduction and a pelvic exam. "I take nothing for granted," she said, "because some of the stories you hear just blow you away. I've had girls tell me Saran Wrap or Vaseline works as a contraceptive. I've had girls who tell me they can make their periods come if they eat sugar."

For some teenage girls here, pregnancy is not a time for tears. Not all pregnancies are accidents. Fewer than 10 percent of the students at Shanks go on to a four-year college; many here take motherhood, even single motherhood, to be their role in life.

"When I first moved to the county, I overheard a conversation I'll never forget," said Jerry Wynn, health administrator for Gadsden County, where Shanks is located. "There was one young woman in her early twenties with five children who was being eyed enviously by another girl, maybe 16, who had two babies. And the teenage girl said, 'Harry thinks she's so big because she has five. Well, I'm going to show her. I'm going to have more than five.' "

Likewise, for some boys, becoming a father is a rite of passage and a badge of sexual prowess. "You tell a teenage boy that if he doesn't use birth control, he'll become a father out of wedlock, it doesn't hit him," said Sylvia Bird, a nurse and community activist who founded the clinic in 1986. "If you tell him if he doesn't use birth control he'll get warts all over his penis and he might die, you'll get more of a reaction. I try to be as graphic as I can."

Rates of teenage sexual activity rose sharply around the country in the 1960s and 1970s, fell slightly in the early 1980s but increased again in the middle of the decade and in the late 1980s, at a time when information about the danger of HIV infection first found wide public dissemination. Fifty-three percent of all 15- to 19-year-old females were sexually active in 1988, up from 47 percent in 1982, according to the National Survey of Family Growth.

More than 20 percent of all AIDS victims are in their twenties; given the usually long latency period between HIV infection and the onset of symptoms, most of them probably became infected as teenagers. In addition, the incidence of syphilis, after a long-term decline, has risen by 46 percent among all adults in the past few years and by 62 percent among teenagers, pushing rates to their highest level in 40 years.

Along with these increases, there has been a rise in the teenage birthrate, which had been declining for 25 years before 1986. Just under a half-million teenage girls gave birth in 1988; 416,000 had abortions, and more than 120,000 had miscarriages or stillbirths.

Can passing out condoms reverse these trends? Shanks seemed the ideal place to find out. The year before the clinic opened in 1986, one female in every eight at the school was pregnant.

But the two studies of the clinic produced sharply different results.

Researchers at Florida State University in Tallahassee found that three years after the clinic opened, the incidence of pregnancy had been cut by more than half, from 44 in 1986 to 20 in 1989.

But a study by the Center for Population Options (CPO), a Washington-based group that researches and advocates adolescent birth control, found virtually no change in pregnancy rates. Its study relied on confidential questionnaires distributed to students, while the FSU survey was based on tallies from teachers and guidance counselors. The center's study may have undercounted pregnancies in the base year, when students may not have been as forthcoming as they were in later years, specialists said. It is also possible that the FSU study missed pregnancies aborted before school officials knew about them.

The CPO survey also looked at five other high schools around the country that have clinics that dispense birth control aids. It was unable to find changes in pregnancy rates in any of them.

"People who look to school-based clinics as a panacea to halt the rise of teenage pregnancy are bound to be disappointed," said Cheryl Hayes, director of a 1987 National Research Council study of adolescent pregnancy. "In addition to providing teenagers with the means to prevent pregnancy, you have to give them the motivation. You have to give them a sense of hope and opportunity about their lives. When that doesn't exist, teenagers have little motivation to delay."

The research does converge on one point: Condom distribution programs do not appear to promote teenage sexual activity. At Shanks, 83.4 percent of the students reported being sexually active before the clinic opened, compared to 84.6 percent last year.

The Florida Legislature last year passed a bill that will open health clinics similar to the one at Shanks in 23 other schools. Localities will decide whether their clinics dispense birth control. Few are expected to take that step, but most will offer more sex education than before.

"I'm a pro-life, conservative, Republican male legislator, and I'm not ready to put condoms in school wholesale," said state Rep. George Albright, a sponsor of the bill. "But AIDS forces you to take another look at these issues. If this is something that communities want and parents approve of, I don't think we ought to stand in their way.

March 10, 1991

12 Business-Education Partnership

Students Test Below Average
In World, U.S. Fares Poorly in Math, Science

MARY JORDAN

A new international comparison of schoolchildren shows American students performing below average in mathematics and science, a "clear warning" that even good schools are not properly preparing students for world competition, Education Secretary Lamar Alexander said yesterday.

The survey of 175,000 students worldwide, which Alexander called "the best international comparison of student abilities in 25 years," also shows American students watching more television and doing less homework than almost all of their counterparts around the world.

Alexander noted that the results show that the top 10 percent of American students "can compete with the best students in any country." However, he said, the results also show that the vast majority of American students perform below the international average.

"It means this is not just an inner-city problem or a rural poverty problem," he said. "It's a problem in the suburbs and in the middle-class families all over the country."

Education officials said the $2 million study was designed to answer criticisms of past international comparisons. It tested 9-year-olds in 14 countries and 13-year-olds in 20 countries. Notably missing from the list are Japan and Germany, which declined to participate in the survey funded by the Education Department, the National Science Foundation and the Carnegie Foundation.

The average American 13-year-old scored 55 percent out of 100 on the math test administered last March in 6,000 classrooms worldwide. By comparison, Taiwanese and Korean students scored 18 percentage points higher. In science, 13-year-olds in America fared better, scoring an average of 67 percent, 11 points below the leaders.

The brightest news for the United States were the science scores of 9-year-olds, who performed only behind Korea and Taiwan and only by

3 percentage points. The Educational Testing Service, which administered the test, said the survey suggests American students fell behind as they got older and began being tested on more complicated sciences, like chemistry.

The survey appeared to challenge some notions about what leads to academic success. Small class size, a longer school year, and more money spent on books, computers, and teachers did not make a notable difference in student achievement, according to the survey.

Korea, which along with Taiwan scored at the top, had 49 students in an average class, the largest of any country. Hungarian students scored in the top half in math and science, but go to school only 177 days, about the same as Americans and near the bottom of those surveyed. The United States is at or near the top on dollars spent per student.

The study did suggest, however, a correlation between achievement and time spent watching television, doing homework, and reading.

In the United States, 22 percent of the 13-year-olds tested in science watched at least five hours of television a day. In Korea, the top performer, 10 percent watched at least five hours a day; in Taiwan and Switzerland, also at the top, 7 percent watched that much TV.

"This suggests that within all of those countries, the more time students spend watching television, the less well they do in science," said Archie E. Lapointe, one of the study's authors.

On the average, American 13-year-olds spend, at most, an hour a week on math homework and the same on science. Chinese students spend at least four times that on math and Russians study science at home for at least four hours a week.

Previous international comparisons have been criticized for including too few countries, not accounting for curriculum differences—such as what year students in different countries learn geometry—and because only a small percentage of students attend school in some countries, effectively comparing a cross-section of American students with the elite of another country.

Iris C. Rotberg, a senior social scientist at the Rand Corp. on a leave of absence from the National Science Foundation, said she believes many of those flaws remain in the new study.

"The practicality of making comparisons across diverse societies and educational systems make it difficult to interpret the findings." She noted that "only elite schools and regions were sampled" in some countries.

"There are different curriculum emphases in different countries and the test results could reflect those," she said. "We make policy based on these findings and the findings could be misleading because of technical glitches on these tests."

In the survey of 13-year-olds, Britain, China, Portugal, Brazil and Mozambique had a low participation rate, so they were not included in the main ranking. Of the 15 countries where a large percentage of students were included, Jordan was the only country to rank below the United States in math. Ireland and Jordan were the only countries whose students had worse scores in science.

Among the countries whose students performed better than those in the United States: the former Soviet Union (Russian-speaking students in 14 republics surveyed), Italy, Israel (Hebrew-speaking schools tested only), France, Scotland and Spain.

February 6, 1992

Why Mary's Math Skills Don't Add Up

JUDY MANN

A teacher I know was trying to explain to her seventh-graders the other day how the Federal Reserve System was trying to jump-start the economy by lowering interest rates. To make the lesson more real for her students, she asked for volunteers to act out some of the roles in our ongoing economic drama.

First she asked who wanted to be a member of the Fed, then she asked for bankers, and then for builders. Only boys raised their hands. It was not until she asked who wanted to be a "teen shopper" that the girls volunteered.

Her students are in the most accelerated learning program offered to seventh-graders in Fairfax County. The best and the brightest girls cast themselves as mavens of the mall.

I was thinking about this story last week, when yet another report came out bearing bad news about how American children are being educated. In the most comprehensive international test ever given to 9- and 13-year-olds in 20 countries in math and science, our 13-year-olds scored ahead of only Ireland and Jordan. Nine-year-old American children did better in science, finishing third. But in math, they finished near he bottom.

A finding that was given less attention, however, was that in every country, the boys in both age groups performed better on average than did the girls.

That latest report card is sure to add more steam to the Bush administration's drive for educational changes. But another report, being issued today by the American Association of University Women, will try to sharpen the focus of some of the debate to what is happening to girls, whose lagging performance in math and science is rarely addressed.

The AAUW report, which was prepared by the Wellesley College Center for Research on Women, synthesizes much of the research comparing the ways in which boys and girls are educated. There is some good news: the differences between girls' and boys' achievements in math, for example, are diminishing. But girls are still much less likely than boys to take advanced math courses in high school, and they do not do as well on the most advanced math aptitude tests.

Girls who demonstrate a strong aptitude for math and sciences are less likely to pursue scientific and technical careers than are boys of similar aptitude. The irony is that if you compare girls and boys who scored the same on the non-verbal part of the Scholastic Aptitude Test, the girls end up performing better in college.

Math anxiety long has been identified as a problem that affects girls with particular force. Sheila Tobias, a pioneer in the field who coined the term, wrote in the late '70s that "feelings are, I believe, at the heart of the problem, although we are supposed to leave feelings outside of the classroom." She argues that mathematical ideas can be presented playfully and in words, not in symbols, so that learning math can be fun, instead of defeating.

Women are not the only ones affected by a system that results in intimidation, myth, misunderstanding and missed opportunities. "Observing men has shown me that some men as well as the majority of women have been denied the pleasures and the power that competence in math and science can provide," she writes.

Past studies, including one commissioned by the AAUW last year, have documented a plunge in self-esteem, beginning in the seventh and eighth grades, that affects girls markedly more than boys. Researchers now believe that this plunge in self-esteem may account for part of girls' reluctance to pursue math and science: They don't take those courses because they don't think they can do well in them.

Despite the studies, however, the problem hasn't attracted much attention at the government's top policy-making levels. Last year, for example, President Bush and his Education Department presented the nation with a set of educational goals to be met by the year 2000. None of the goals—nor the strategies for meeting them—targeted girls to bolster their weaker performance in math and science.

Yet, for a country that professes deep concern about its scientific brain drain, it would sees logical to tap into the half of the population that is clearly an underused and undervalued resource.

Educational reform will fail unless it addresses the complicated dynamics that undermine girls. Studies and tests abound that point to an unequal education. But the waste of it cones home with full force when you hear a story about how some of the best young female minds in this area are casting themselves as teen shoppers.

February 12, 1992

U.S. Graduates Seen Ill-Prepared on Workplace Thinking Skills

FRANK SWOBODA

Most high schools in America fail to prepare the majority of their graduates with the "thinking skills" needed for the modern blue-collar workplace, according to a report released yesterday by a special Labor Department commission.

Unless the situation changes, said commission chairman William Brock, the United States will have to compete in the global marketplace on the basis of the reduced wages of American workers instead of on their higher skills.

The report by the Secretary's Commission on Achieving Necessary Skills calls on the nation's public schools to revamp their curricula so that high school graduates can enter the work force without the need for additional education.

"What we have found is that we're not preparing our children for the world of work," said Brock, who is a former labor secretary and U.S. trade representative.

Seventy percent of the nation's high school graduates either don't enter or don't finish college, according to the commission. Brock said public schools have to begin focusing on the needs of these students. "They're incredibly important," he said. "They're the base of our work force."

The workplace is changing and the school systems have to adapt themselves to these changes, Brock said. In recent years, he said, "the really good companies in the United States have reorganized the workplace to take workers beyond their muscle competence." In its report, the commission said a weak mind and a strong back are no longer enough to compete in the workplace.

The commission, which spent such of the past year interviewing employers about the job skills they needed, said the new skills recommended in its report "capture what some men and women face and actually do in today's workplace."

In the next few months, the commission expects to recommend ways to test how well students are being taught the new workplace skills. In the meantime, Brock said, the performance standard for the education system can be measured in the way U.S. companies are competing in the world marketplace. Holding up the U.S. auto industry as an example, Brock said, "Toyota is eating our lunch and so is Nissan and Honda."

To help prepare high school students for the workplace of the future, the 31-member commission recommended that graduates should be proficient in what they called the "Five Competencies," or "thinking skills":

The ability to allocate resources. Entry-level workers should be able to develop work schedules, budget money and assign staff.

Development of interpersonal skills. The commission said modern workers must be able to work as team members and engage in problem solving. Workers must also be able to work directly with company clients.

The ability to assess information. Workers today are increasingly required to identify, assimilate and integrate information from a variety of sources to perform their jobs. This includes the use of computers to gather and develop information.

The ability to understand work systems. Workers in wore and more companies must not only understand their own work, they must also understand how it fits into the work around them so they can identify problems and integrate new information. This is particularly important as more and more companies employ work teams to perform tasks.

The ability to deal with new technologies in an ever-changing workplace. Again the commission noted the need that young workers be familiar with computers as well as the operation of other equipment.

None of the five competencies replace the need for proficiency in the so-called three R's—reading, writing and arithmetic. Without the basic academic skills, the thinking skills will be of little value, the commission said.

Labor Secretary Lynn Martin, in releasing the report with Brock, said, "common sense suggests this should have been done a lot sooner." But Brock reported that some of the employers interviewed for the study said that 10 years ago they could not have identified many of the needs of the workplace today.

In an open letter to parents, the commission said parents "must insist that their sons and daughters master this know-how and that their local schools teach it. Unless you do, your children are unlikely to earn a decent living. If your children cannot learn these skills by the time they leave high school, they face bleak prospects—dead-end work, interrupted only by bleak periods of unemployment with little chance to climb a career ladder."

Both Brock and Martin were careful not to point their fingers at anyone for the failures of the school systems, particularly teachers. The nation's two major teachers' unions, the National Education Association and the American Federation of Teachers, both praised the report. AFT President Albert Shanker said it provided schools "with the first concrete sense of what employers want from them."

NEA President Keith Geiger said the report recognizes "it is important to provide an education system that produces learners, not knowers. These standards reach to that. They are performance based, and they demonstrate mastery of skills rather than the accumulation of a discrete body of knowledge."

The report represents the first major follow-up by the Labor Department to a 1987 study, entitled Workforce 2000, that outlined the dramatic demographic changes occurring in the workplace.

The Workforce 2000 report, which has become the basic reference guide for government and industry, predicted that by the end of the decade, 85 percent of the net new jobs created in the United States would be filled by women and minorities. The report gave rise to the growing movement toward workplace diversity training among U.S. corporations.

July 3, 1991

Business Goes Back to the Three Rs

CINDY SKRZYCKI

Steffen Palko, a businessman in Fort Worth, Tex., didn't have to look beyond his own dining room table to understand why there's a skills gap in the American work force.

His son, Erich, was about to head off to Texas Tech University in Lubbock, but he was short on writing skills and not very proficient at expressing himself verbally.

"These are things I know you need as a businessman," Palko said. "I think he was comparable to a lot of kids coming out of school."

In response, Palko, an executive vice president of Cross Timbers Oil Co., did more than get active in the PTA. Two years ago, he landed a seat on the board of the Fort Worth Independent School District and launched an education reform program in conjunction with the city's Chamber of Commerce that may turn out to be a model for those elsewhere in the nation.

His program is called C3, which stands for cooperation among corporations, the community and classrooms. The school board voted to cooperate in the effort and consider tailoring curriculum to the findings of the commission.

Right now, 135 businesses are working on the time-consuming task of defining the basic characteristics of 1,000 real-world jobs and 5,000 tasks. Based on that information, the school board will consider necessary changes to its curriculum, facilities, staff training and equipment to see that its students are better prepared to qualify for those jobs. Palko hopes business will participate in rewriting curricula, training teachers, providing scholarships and offering jobs to smooth the way for work-bound students. Businesses also will be asked to raise money, perhaps by floating a "technology bond" to help schools buy new equipment.

"To my knowledge they have gone the furthest of any school district," said Arnold Packer, senior research fellow at the Hudson Institute. "They will pay the price of being a pioneer. Time will tell if they get arrows in their back or rewards."

Palko's idea is part of a growing effort by the federal government, a handful of states, academia and business to do systemic reviews of how well schools are preparing students for work.

Many companies already realize that "basic skills" go far beyond the three Rs and that bandaid approaches do not work. In a recent study by the American Society for Training and Development, several groups of skills, many of them conceptual, were identified as essentials: knowing how to learn; competence in reading, writing and computation; communication; adaptability; personal management; teamwork; and leadership skills.

A study by the American Management Association found that 42 percent of those tested for basic skills in the professional services field were deficient.

The problem is hitting all types of companies.

MCI Communications Corp., for example, screened six applicants for one customer service job. Then it had to teach the new employee how to express himself and perform simple calculations.

Motorola expects each of its workers to be able to participate in problem-solving teams, an ability that many students do not learn in school because such group effort often is regarded as a punishable offense—cheating.

"We have jobs but young people don't have the skills to fill those jobs. That's where the rubber hits the road," said Labor Secretary Elizabeth Dole at a recent briefing with reporters.

In fact, the rubber has hit the road so hard that Dole has convened the Secretary's Commission on Achieving Necessary Skills (SCANS), the first group to bring together business, labor, education and state officials to define what skills workers will need for the future. Those will be translated into "national competency guidelines" to be used throughout the country to help develop new curricula and training programs for school.

"All of the world of work has been transformed," said Packer, who serves as executive director of SCANS. "But the schools have not changed at all. Well, damn little."

Anyone who thinks Packer's assessment too harsh need only look at the findings of the National Center on Education and the Economy, which visited six countries to look for ways to put American blue-collar workers on a par with their international counterparts.

Crisscrossing Germany, Sweden, Denmark, Ireland, Singapore and Japan, the team of executives, union leaders, educators and government officials found fundamental differences in the way Americans do work.

"The things we saw in countries doing a good job is they had very high general education standards and virtually everyone had to meet them," said Marc Tucker, president of the center, which will release its research on June 19. At that time, the nonprofit institution will make suggestions on how to raise educational standards in the United States, how to smooth the transition from school to work, how to rescue dropouts and how to improve investment in line workers.

"Our ability to compete is going to depend on this work force," said John H. Zimmerman, MCI's senior vice president.

June 3, 1990

High Tech Just Keeps Rolling Along
Videodisc Usage Grows in Nation's Classrooms

JOHN BURGESS

Science teacher Pat Hagan paced her Gaithersburg classroom at Montgomery Village Intermediate School, firing off questions about heat transfer to 29 eighth graders, rapping a desktop here and there to get a young mind in gear. In her hand was a remote control device. By the lab table up front was a large-screen TV, with an electronic box resembling a VCR perched beneath it.

Hagan punched keys on the remote control and a still photo of an ice cream cone that was starting to melt appeared on the TV screen. "Tell me why this happens," Hagan said to the class, which was meeting before school let out for the summer.

"Right," Hagan said to a volunteer with the correct answer, "you have radiant heat coming down and starting the ice cream to melt." Later in the class, she punched more buttons and a brief film demonstrating different kinds of heat started to roll.

What Hagan and her students were using is a laser videodisc, yet another example of new technology filtering down to alter daily life in America. Already established in industrial and military training—Ford Motor Co., for instance, has used discs to train mechanics—it is now starting to show up in ordinary classrooms.

All of Montgomery County's high schools and many of its lower schools now have disc players. Several other school systems around the Washington area have also bought into the technology or served as test sites for it. Nationwide, an estimated 20,000 videodisc players are in public and private schools.

Many teachers swear by this addition to the "electronic classroom." The technology appeals in a positive, stimulating way to the learning orientation of the MTV generation, they say. "These kids are visually oriented," said Carol Muscara, a computer instruction official in the

Montgomery school system. "We've trained them that way. They've been watching Sesame Street since they were three years old."

In the right teacher's hands, fans of the technology contend, discs encourage active participation by students. They can be used intermittently during a class to spice up a discussion, unlike a film that runs 20 minutes and evokes a largely passive response. Discs allow teachers to customize a lecture or discussion, using the remote control to call up only specific portions of the disc to make the points they want to make.

But the technology is not for everyone. Cost of the players start at about $400, while the individual discs run about $500, prices that may not appeal to schools with low budgets and competing needs. Moreover, there is no guarantee that teachers will use them to anywhere near their full potential. Like the personal computer, theoretically a teaching tool of immense power, discs could remain on the sidelines of mainstream education.

In addition, some parents and teachers object to the approach itself, arguing that the video medium will deliver another blow to American children's faltering ability to read. But for now, this camp seems very much to be the minority. "It's a skyrocketing area," said Lyle Hamilton, disc advocate and manager of broadcast for the National Education Association, which represents teachers.

Twelve inches across, the discs look like overblown versions of the compact discs of home stereo systems and harness the same laser-based optical technology. In general, they yield sharper pictures than videocassette tapes.

In the early '80s, the entertainment industry pitched them to consumers, releasing films on disc only to see the medium lose out to cassettes, which could record material as well as play it. But educators like two things that disc players can do that videocassette recorders cannot: freeze a frame in a film clip crisply and indefinitely and, in a maximum of 10 seconds, search out and display any frame or clip on the disc.

More than 300 educational discs are now on the market. Some are simple re-releases of old films. Others, like the one Hagan used, function as libraries of visual information aimed at complementing textbooks and lectures. The discs are filled with film clips, still images, diagrams, animations, maps, charts and illustrations—up to 54,000 still images per side. With an index in hand, a teacher can plan a specific sequence of illustrations for a specific class.

A few large Japanese companies control the disc player market. Putting material on the discs, however, is the preserve of a diverse collection of U.S. companies, some of them small and shaky, others big— National Geographic Society and ABC News, for example. The disc "publishing" industry has sprung up largely independent of textbook companies. But now the two media are starting to be coordinated, as disc companies put out products geared for use with specific books.

Debbie Dasgupta, one of Hagan's students, said she saw the video player as "a backup for the book." It made "a lasting impression on the mind, so you can remember things a lot longer," she said. "So it's a really fun way to learn." Student Adriana Marquez was also upbeat: "It interests people more than just drawing on a blackboard."

Saira Kahn, another of Hagan's students, was skeptical, however. "It's just there. It's something you look at," she said. " . . . It's nice to have but it's not something that schools should go out of their way to buy."

Responses like Kahn's haven't been enough to stop school systems from giving the technology a lift. Texas has spent $5 million to develop discs for science instruction. But overall, discs are no shoo-in. "For something new to move in the front door, something old has to move out the back door," noted William Clark, president of Optical Data Corp. of Warren, N.J., a major producer of educational discs.

Teachers, meanwhile, continue to experiment on how best to employ them. Hagan generally has used her players manually, creating a sometimes awkward pause as she punches into her remote control device frame index numbers that bring up specific images. At times, she has used it connected to a personal computer. That way, a lesson can be mapped out in advance and striking a single key on the computer moves the player to the next frame.

Here and there students are using discs as part of complex "multimedia" systems. Sitting at computers, they merge video footage, sounds, still images, text that they write themselves, charts and computer data to produce the electronic equivalent of a term paper—a presentation on the campaign of Rep. Richard Gephardt (D-Mo.), for instance, drawing on material from an ABC News disc about the 1988 presidential race.

Some educational specialists, however, warn against going in that direction. Disc players are most likely to gain wide use if they are simple and inexpensive to use. Schools don't always have the funds for computers, it is pointed out, and teachers may feel as intimidated as the students in using them. By fits and starts, the technology continues to advance, though most schools remain without them. But, as Frank B. Withrow, team leader for the technology applications group at the U.S. Department of Education, noted: "It's more than a fad."

July 11, 1990

A Glitch in the Classroom Computer Revolution

Decade after Acquiring Technology, Area Schools Struggling with Best Ways to Use It

MOLLY SINCLAIR

Public schools in the Washington area now own tens of thousands of computers for student use, but a decade after the technology hit the classrooms, educators are still struggling to harness its potential.

Students at Montgomery County's Watkins Mill High School—one of the best-equipped schools in the area—can use computers to track the path of satellites, draw architectural plans or plug into enormous banks of information.

Instructors there praise the machines for engaging students in ways that books and blackboards cannot. But educators still can't answer this question: Does all the high-technology equipment make students smarter?

Although taxpayers, corporations and parent groups have spent millions of dollars to put computers in local schools, the machines' impact on student performance has not been measured conclusively.

Meanwhile, the high cost of the equipment inevitably leads to questions of accessibility. A recent audit of the D.C. public schools said access to computers can fluctuate greatly because some schools benefit from parent-group purchases or corporate contributions.

And even when a school has plenty of computers, their usefulness depends on how many teachers have the training—or the inclination—to use them.

The smaller and more affordable personal computers became widely available in the early 1980s, and schools came under increasing pressure from parents to produce computer-literate students.

Initially, many educators saw the computers transforming the relationship between schools and students in the same sweeping way that the new technology was transforming the relationship between banks and depositors.

The D.C. public schools have about 8,000 computers for student and teacher use. Prince George's County has about 12,000, Montgomery County about 10,000 and Fairfax County about 7,000.

The investments are substantial. The Montgomery public school system has spent about $11 million on computers since 1983. Prince George's has spent $20 million since 1984.

In the "Apples for the Students"' grocery receipt program, which began three years ago, Giant Food Inc. has provided schools with an estimated $15 million in computers, printers and software packages.

But the nationwide revolution that some expected is, at least so far, more a series of skirmishes fought on disparate battlegrounds.

School systems across the United States have "16,000 experiments going on," said C. Dianne Martin, a George Washington University associate professor who specializes in computer competence for teachers.

"Computers have worked for some kids," said Marlene Blum, president of the Fairfax County Council of PTAs. They have worked for her two sons, now adults specializing in computer science fields. "For others," she said, "it is not clear. Many people still feel computers are a neat thing to have around but not essential to kids' education."

What school systems need to do, Blum said, is agree on their goals for the computers.

At Wyngate Elementary School in Bethesda, Principal Barbara J. Leister has sought to encourage the use of computers because she sees them as a way to help children get excited about learning and perk up teacher interest.

The school had expected funding for a computer lab, but the money was cut from the budget. Teachers, with Leister supporting them, decided to pull 14 computers from different classrooms and put them together in a lab that classes could share.

Since the lab opened in November, students get one or two 45-minute classes a week in the computer lab. Previously, they were limited to occasional computer work in the classroom.

Leister said the school has been rejuvenated by the experience.

For one recent class, fifth-grade teacher Marion Finkbinder had her students working on spelling, with two students at each computer. The exercise required students to use a software program called "Spellevator."

The students chattered and giggled their way through a cartoonlike drill that featured a small, bouncing character and a series of word lists selected by the teacher.

Which of the four words on the computer screen is spelled correctly? Students use the computer keyboard to type in their answers.

The computer gives points for correct answers and records the total score for review by the teacher.

Teachers at Wyngate are trying to expand their computer skills, Finkbinder said. But so far she is the only one who knows how to put in her own spelling words.

The usefulness of computers can be reduced if the teachers are untrained, uncomfortable with technology or unwilling to integrate it into classroom studies.

C.C. Woodson Junior High, just east of the Minnesota Avenue Metro station in Northeast Washington, acquired computers through the school system and through the supermarket giveaway program. Woodson has two computer labs, but until recently no computer-trained teacher, so the students had little opportunity to use the machines.

To help Woodson use its computers more effectively, the District established a special 15-hour introductory course in December. More than 20 teachers completed it, and one is now in charge of the lab.

Student access to computers also can depend on school system decisions, such as the move to make Watkins Mill a state-of-the-art school, and on the aggressiveness of a principal, such as Leister, in getting equipment and whipping up teacher enthusiasm. It also can depend on happenstance, such as having a catalyst teacher in a school who seizes the moment and helps get needed equipment, software and training.

Some schools benefit from major commitments of money and people for the hardware and the training. Often it's from a private source.

At Thomas Jefferson Junior High, near the Washington Channel in Southwest Washington, school officials won a commitment from the Comsat corporation to install a $1.6 million computer system and train teachers to use it.

Good as that is for the students at Jefferson and some of the other schools that profit from private bounty, the singling out of certain schools raises other concerns about equitable access.

The D.C. school audit, conducted by the American Association of School Administrators, found that some schools have up to 114 units more than those provided through the school system's program.

How do they do it? "School-based initiatives, special grants and/or purchases, donations, parent-group purchases and corporate contributions," the audit said. "No evidence exists to support the premise that either student enrollment or identified student needs are primary determinants for greater computer access."

Parents might put the issue this way: Will some students be computer illiterate because their school's PTA fund-raiser couldn't sell as many cakes as did parents at the school down the road?

In a sense, Watkins Mill High School, outside Gaithersburg, is that school down the road. Built in an affluent community as a showcase for the latest technology, Watkins Mill opened three years ago with a million-dollar computer system. It has 400 computers installed in six labs, classrooms and media centers. And it has teachers with outstanding computer skills.

Social studies instructor Dick Rattan, who writes some of his own software programs, makes an ardent case for educational technology.

Using computers, he said, "forces kids to make connections with the past and the future, forces kids to make connections with different kinds of events and people, and making those connections makes them better thinkers."

He frets that the Watkins Mill equipment, now three years old, is no longer on the cutting edge.

Teachers at Eastern Intermediate School in Silver Spring, a more typical school, laugh when they hear that lament.

Gregory Black, a social studies teacher who also is a computer coordinator at the school, calls the setup "jury-rigged." Eastern is an older school, and its 100-plus computers were installed where places could be found.

One place is a lab, equipped with 28 computers, where Sharon Lundahl teaches a seventh-grade writing class.

"They are willing to write and rewrite and rewrite because revisions are so much easier with the computer," Lundahl said as she monitored the roomful of students tapping on their keyboards. She said students working on computers typically produce better papers and write more fluently.

In the long run, students like these, who have access to computers, will have a better shot in the job market, educators said.

"Kids who don't have technology won't be as well prepared to use it when they graduate," said Monnie Edmunds, a technology specialist with the Council of Chief State School Officers. "Those who have access to technology as students will be in a better position to get jobs . . . to become the leaders."

March 8, 1992

Computing Teacher Skills

KENNETH J. COOPER

Competency testing of teachers, one thrust of education reform in the 1980s, is about to enter the computer age.

The basic skills portion of the National Teacher Examinations is being revamped so that, beginning in 1992, undergraduates who plan to teach will have their reading, writing and mathematics skills tested on a personal computer, instead of by more traditional exams that use pencil and paper.

Representatives of the Educational Testing Service in Princeton, N.J., said the computerized exam will assess basic skills more accurately because there will be fewer multiple-choice questions and more complex items, such as asking the test-taker to create a graph based on the data supplied.

"With a computer, you're able to ask non-multiple choice questions," said Paul A. Ramsey, developer of the new exam. He said the computerized test can be scored immediately, even faster than multiple-choice answer sheets. Test-makers have often defended multiple-choice questions, despite their limitations, because machines can read penciled answers rapidly.

Ramsey said changes in the composition of the basic skills test, which is to be renamed, would not make it more difficult. And simple instructions from the computer will mean students need not be computer literate, he said.

The National Teacher Examinations, first given in 1940, is the battery of tests most widely used to assess teachers' abilities. In the last academic year, 330,000 candidates took at least one part of the exams, which are used in 33 states to decide who is qualified to teach in elementary and secondary schools.

The new test of "enabling skills," as the nonprofit testing service calls it, will substitute for three existing exams on preprofessional skills, communications skills and general knowledge that prospective teachers take at various stages of their careers, depending upon state laws.

Ramsey said the new exam is designed to be taken in college, either at the end of the sophomore year or the beginning of the junior year before students declare a major and begin taking education courses. That timing permits students who fail the exam to complete remedial work before they attempt to teach a class.

"If there is a question about (basic) literacy, that ought to be cleared up before a teacher candidate is admitted to a teacher education program," said Sharon Robinson, who directs the National Center for Innovation at the National Teachers Association.

Robinson praised the new exam, as did Louise Sundin, a vice president of the American Federation of Teachers and a member of a panel advising the Educational Testing Service. Sundin called it "a much broader test" that would provide a more accurate assessment of a prospective teacher's preparation.

Taking the computerized exam will also be more convenient for test-takers. Rather than taking the exams in large groups on a few dates, individual students will be able to make an appointment to take the exam, he said. Each of three sections will take an hour to complete.

"The exam does not have to be a daylong tortuous process to find out what the (student's) deficiencies are," Robinson said.

Robinson expressed some concern that students unfamiliar with computers might be at a disadvantage. She suggested the colleges give such students an opportunity to spend time in a campus computer lab getting comfortable with the machines. "I would not want anyone's first involvement with a computer to be around a high-stakes test," she said.

Sundin said computerization would send the right signal to anyone interested in teaching. "The teachers of tomorrow will have to be computer literate, and I think this will tell them that," she said.

The results of pilot testing done over the summer are being analyzed, and some questions are being reworked, Ramsey said. More pilot testing is scheduled in February.

The revisions in basic skills testing are only one set of changes in the National Teacher Examinations. Subject area tests are being rewritten and a new kind of assessment of classroom performance is being developed, with both to be introduced in 1992. They will not be computerized.

Carol Dwyer, director of the NTE projects, said the subject-area tests were being revised because of changes in state certification requirements during the 1980s. High school teachers are commonly required to pass the NTE exam in English, math, a foreign language or other subjects in order to teach them.

Dwyer said the revised tests will include a core set of items and several components that a state can use depending on its certification standards. Although teachers' mastery of academic content continues to be a public concern, Dwyer said "there isn't any intention to make it [subject-area testing] more difficult."

The classroom performance assessment, Dwyer said, will consist of a list of criteria for principals, master teachers or other evaluators to use in measuring a teacher's ability to plan instruction, deliver it, manage a classroom and evaluate student progress. Who evaluates teachers will be determined by state and local laws or collective bargaining agreements.

"They're going to better assess the ability of a person actually to teach," said David Imig, executive director of the American Association of Colleges for Teacher Education. Robinson and Sundin, representing the nation's major teacher unions, also expressed satisfaction with the classroom assessment and subject-area test.

November 18, 1990

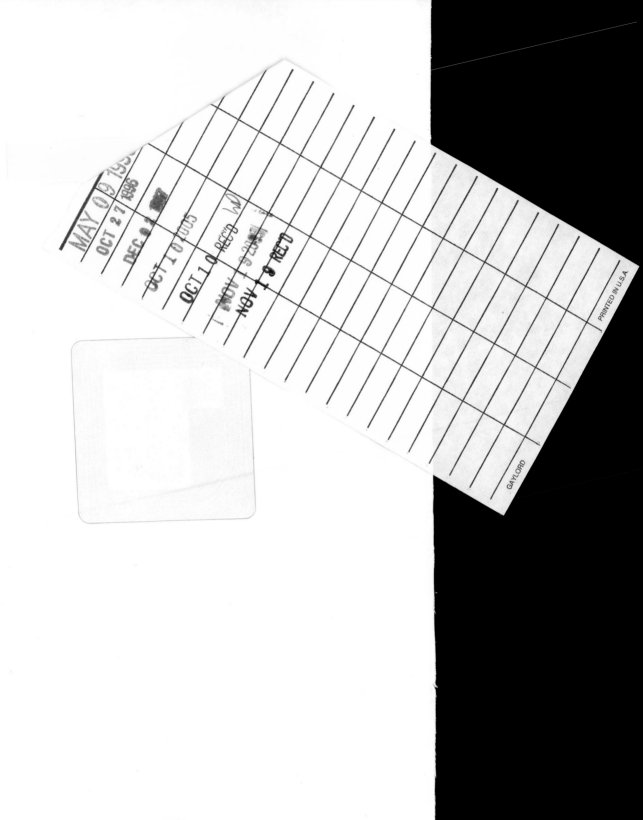